Donated to the Boise Public Library
By Jim H Reed, Deep Sea Sailor.
USS Santa Leonor  Grace Line
1950-51 South America
USS President Arthur, American
President Lines
1951 around the world going west

SHIPPING AND CULTURE

BY

OLAF T. ENGVIG

### "Leiv Eiriksson Discovers America"
They came by sea. Leif Erikson was the first named man to bring European culture to the new world.
He and his party stayed for the winter. His countrymen later developed a colony
in Newfoundland that lasted for thirty years.

Oil on canvas by Norwegian painter Christian Krogh. Photo of a reproduction at the Norwegian Club in San Francisco.
The original is exhibited in the Norwegian Maritime Museum in Oslo.

This book is dedicated to
people with vision and will to work for the exchange
and preservation of culture in international relations.

# SHIPPING and CULTURE

The Norwegian Fish Club of San Francisco 1914 - 1996

BY

## OLAF T. ENGVIG

The Fish Club
San Francisco
1996

Designed by Maggie Cox
in cooperation with Craft Press, Inc.

Computer conversion and Dingbat
by Mona Engvig and Ann Krilanovich

Paper: 100# Quintessence Dull Finish Book

Set in Palatino 11/14

Printed by Craft Press, Inc./San Francisco
Publisher's Press/Salt Lake City

First printing 1996

Front of dust jacket: *Captain Roald Amundsen's Arctic exploring sloop* Gjøa *in Golden Gate Park, 1910. This ship came to San Francisco from Norway in 1906 as the first vessel ever to sail north of the American Continent. Courtesy The Museum of the City of San Francisco.*

Front and final endpaper: *San Francisco skyline, with His Majesty King Olav V of Norway, sailing the six-meter* St. Francis VI *in San Francisco Bay, passing the Norwegian cruise liner* Royal Viking Sky, *in 1975 considered one of the world's finest cruise ships. Photo Stein Fjesme,* Adresseavisen.

Medals on title page: *The Order of the Golden Fish and The Tordenskjolds Soldater Award.*

Library of Congress Catalog Card Number: 96-71767

Copyright ©1997 by Olaf T. Engvig

No part of this book may be reproduced in any form or by electronic means including information storage and retrieval systems without permission in writing from the author, except by a reviewer who may quote brief passages in a review.

ISBN 0-9655451-0-5

Printed in the USA

# CONTENTS

*Preface*
*Introduction ... 11*

CHAPTER I
*The Fish Club Story ... 15*

CHAPTER II
*The Club, Jack's and the City ... 27*

CHAPTER III
*Panama Pacific International Exposition ... 35*

CHAPTER IV
*Golden Gate International Exposition ... 49*

CHAPTER V
*Norway House, Seamen's Home ... 63*

CHAPTER VI
*The Norwegian Seamen's Church ... 75*

CHAPTER VII
*Squaw Valley Winter Olympics 1960 ... 89*
*Prelude to the Los Angeles Olympics ... 107*

CHAPTER VIII
*GJØA, The Ship in the Park ... 109*

CHAPTER IX
*The Windjammer ... 135*

CHAPTER X
*Royal Visits ... 151*

*Epilogue ... 177*
*Notes and Sources ... 179*
*Index ... 183*

*In Memory of Christian Blom*

# Preface

*Den norske fiskeklub i San Francisco,* usually called simply the Fish Club, started in San Francisco in 1914. The purpose was to meet for a weekly luncheon of fine fish and discuss cultural relations between Norway and the USA, with a desire to encourage and help if needed. The Club was small and had the intimacy of the smaller table where everyone could participate in exchange of ideas. Most of the members were associated with the waterfront and the shipping industry.

The Fish Club made a little pamphlet for its thirtieth-year anniversary, giving a brief summary of activities until 1944. The first fifty years were remembered with a typewritten record of the Club's activities until 1964. So much happened during the next twenty years that the Fish Club felt it was time for a new review in 1984, and a supplement was added to the typescript. In 1992 the Fish Club decided to commission a formal history.

The goal of this book has been to tell about events of a community where the Fish Club belonged and in which its members participated. It includes major cultural events involving Norwegian-American relations during the twentieth century.

*Shipping and Culture* shows the impact of the Norwegian shipping establishment in the San Francisco Bay Area upon cultural matters having to do with the colony. It reviews the Club's history, highlights major events involving Club members, and uncovers new facts about the Club and what it did. It is my hope that the book will create interest and provide information also to people not affiliated with the Club itself.

I am thankful to Christian Blom and to Mr. and Mrs. Kortum for assistance during research. For help and editing I want to thank Principal Librarian David Hull of the San Francisco Maritime National Historical Park Library. I also wish to thank the entire staff of that library. I salute the Fish Club's Book Committee as well as the other members of this fine Club.

*Norway and San Francisco*
*Summer 1996*

*Olaf T. Engvig*

# Introduction

Official visitors from Norway clearly recall their encounters with the Fish Club as distinct and enjoyable. Some know the Club only by name, regretting that they missed the weekly luncheon. Whether it is referred to as "The Fish Club of San Francisco," "*Den norske fiskeklub*," "The Norwegian Fish Club" or simply the "Fish Club," this Club has long been well known among insiders, executive business people and state officials in Norway. Nevertheless, it is extremely difficult to learn anything of this body if research is conducted in the traditional way through the library.

*Riksarkivet in Oslo*—the Norwegian State Archives—has all the files of the Royal Norwegian Consulate General (RNCG) to San Francisco from 1914 until 1966. These files consist of thirty shelf meters or about ninety shelf feet of documents, including material on all formal Norwegian-American organizations and institutions in the Bay Area. In these files, nothing at all is to be found on the Fish Club. It is a subculture that needed to be recorded.

The Fish Club "case" represents an interesting challenge for the historian. It is difficult to write a history even when working with formal organizations. But here we have a matter entirely of informal networking. Where were the decisions made? Who really pulled the strings, made the significant telephone call, got enemies together, met outside the boardroom? Within the sum of available records of this Club, there exist no protocols, no boardmember names, minutes, by-laws, membership lists, books or boxes with invoices and receipts, or other informative papers.

The Fish Club is a society that never bothered about all this. It made arrangements for large ships and itineraries for the King of Norway, conducted work involving transfer of important historic items, assisted on exhibitions and in preparations for concerts and displays. It aided and assisted Olympic champions. The Club made important decisions, handled thousands of dollars at times, but owns nothing and never did. The Club's entire possessions amount to a standard-sized box, half the size of a file drawer, kept by the Rex Sole, "the Club President," filled with letters and archives, a few faded pictures, an old fishing rod and some other souvenirs, its order of merit and diplomas, and three short retrospective papers written for the Club's thirtieth, fiftieth and seventieth anniversaries.

Still, it is a body with weekly gatherings, where anyone can participate and is encouraged to become a member. The Fish Club keeps a simple, not easily noticeable, informal protocol during the weekly luncheon at Jack's. Networking and a no-name policy have always been the Club's unspoken rules. There is no secrecy involved. Everyone attending is free to speak.

Whenever a formal meeting was required to achieve a specific goal, it would be conducted within an officially existing organization, usually at one of the nearby shipping offices on California Street, following the luncheon at Jack's. All necessary work would be handled in ten minutes. It could be a real estate loan, a mortgage or another settlement, and it was always another organization acting as the Club's agent. If no suitable organization existed, the Club would create one for the occasion, registered in Sacramento. Afterward, it would either be dissolved or handed over to others. The Fish Club was only the organizer, administrator, or the midwife.

The Fish Club is an extra-legal body operating outside and in spite of all the formal organizations which dominate today's society. The unofficial, informal character of the Club has facilitated effective negotiations and the joining of forces to achieve cultural goals. Few if any other voluntary organizations have had such an impact on major cultural matters and relations between the Bay Area and Norwegian-Americans.

The Fish Club has often acted as an extended arm for the Consul and the Royal Norwegian Consulate General in San Francisco, entertaining and tending to visiting state officials, executives and other guests. It has also been a forum for ideas and new challenges, and has supported the Consulate in matters where Norway's officials could not or would not get involved. The Fish Club has always promoted and served Norwegian interests in this part of the world.

Three different characteristics have contributed to the success of this officially non-existing group: the participants' genuine interest in promoting Norwegian culture; the large number of friends and contacts who can assist; and the group's ability to raise funds, negotiate and produce results.

The Fish Club always had constituents who knew the right person, who could establish contact, communicate, understand and act accordingly.

Key participants in the Club have been shipping and business professionals, shipowners, financial and insurance men, brokers, executives of various ship services, master mariners and others from the waterfront. But the Fish Club also consists of engineers, lawyers, artists, students and many other landlubbers. Throughout its history, the Consul General and other people affiliated with the Consulate have participated, informing the Club about the latest news from Norway. In return the Consul has relied on the Fish Club to entertain visiting guests as well as for support when needed for an arrangement.

The weekly luncheon at twelve o'clock is usually held at Jack's Restaurant on Sacramento Street, which is considered one of downtown's first class restaurants. The people attending are generally middle-aged men with connections to the waterfront. Consulate and shipping people usually walk over from their offices. Occasional participants at the Club's luncheons include state officials and businessmen visiting from Norway, as well as artists and researchers. Quite often American businessmen will attend and talk about their line of work. At such times, English is spoken. Otherwise, the conversation is bilingual for everyone's convenience.

The Fish Club has always operated within the local environment of Norwegian-American organizations in the Bay Area, which are often chapters in a nationwide network of Norwegian-American organizations.

The following organizations have interacted with and played a role in the activities of the Fish Club during this century: the Norwegian Club, Sons of Norway, Daughters of Norway, Normanna Glee Club, Norwegian Singer Society, *Nordmanns-Forbundet*, Norwegian National League, some churches named below, Norweigan Seamans Mission, and the Norwegian Government Seamen's Service and Norway House Inc.

The Norwegian Club is the oldest social organization of its kind in the City. Sons of Norway was founded in the Midwest in the last century, and was an organization for the security and mutual help of its members and with Norwegian as its major language. Today it is a body of mainly second- or later generations of Norwegian-Americans who desire to maintain their Norwegian roots. The language is English

## Introduction

and Sons of Norway participates in a long range of Norwegian-American activities. This organization has different chapters in the Bay Area. *Nordmanns-Forbundet,* founded in Norway, has focused on cultural relations and participates in promoting culture and scientific achievement. Like Sons of Norway, *Nordmanns-Forbundet* encourages cultural contact, tourism, and heritage research. The Norwegian National League and the American Scandinavian Foundation are aiding organizations; the latter was established to provide financial aid to students.

Several churches for people of Norwegian descent have been founded in the Bay Area. Among these are the Trinity Lutheran Church in Oakland, the 20th Street Methodist Church in Oakland, the Norwegian Lutheran Church in San Francisco, the Scandinavian Lutheran Seamen's Mission in San Francisco, and the Norwegian Seamen's Mission in San Francisco. The Norwegian Seamen's Mission was partly established through the ladies' organization, *Tabita*, which emerged from the old Lutheran Seamen's Mission.

The Norwegian Seamen's Mission and its *Tabita*, Norway House Inc., and the Norwegian Club have—as will be seen later in this book—played a more significant part in the Fish Club's story. The founding members of the Fish Club were members of the Norwegian Club in 1914.

Key participants of the Fish Club have also been members and played important roles in other organizations. But it was first and foremost as members of the Fish Club that they found opportunities to communicate and achieve the cultural goals outlined in this book. It is, of course, important to remember that without a broad consensus from the community surrounding this organization, it would not have been possible to achieve the many accomplishments described in this book.

There are always some devoted individuals who promote cultural enterprises. For most of this century, the Fish Club and the activities around the lunch table at Jack's have been a forum for development and refinement of ideas, and the means of developing good relations between Norway and Norwegians and Americans in the Bay Area.

At times the whole group of organizations has been called upon for support and has responded readily. It is not surprising that the informal meeting place for ideas and action became the small and intimate Fish Club with their like-minded members and their many contacts and possibilities for policymaking. The Fish Club was the only body in this part of the world with both short and direct lines of communication to higher state officials in Norway, and the economic power that comes from close contacts with central members of the Norwegian Shipowners' Association, flourishing shipping lines and a network of offices all over the world. The attendee also had the great advantage of being kept updated on the actual situation around the world, especially on financial matters, as well as the advantage of the above mentioned complete openness, without record-keeping or a formal setting. More than anything, such an atmosphere gives freedom to speak and act.

And yet, if the existing material in that box kept by the Rex Sole had not been worked through while primary sources were still present to supply information to support, explain and fill in the written documents, it would have become almost impossible to reconstruct and find sense in the scattered written material. Random pieces of correspondence, schedules, itineraries, programs, personal notes and press cuttings only provide basic facts and mysterious clues for research. These old papers and the knowledge held by the participants in the special events that have occurred throughout the Club's eighty years of activity tell an amazing story. This is a book about the common goals of the Norwegian immigrants and visitors to the Bay Area, and how the Fish Club often was helpful in making things happen which were beneficial to the entire Norwegian-American community. Christian Blom stated that it was first and foremost the Fish Club that acted when other bodies couldn't, wouldn't or didn't have the ability to act.

San Francisco is host to many well-known, influential clubs. Occasionally the Fish Club has honored special guests at the Bohemian Club, the Pacific Union Club and the Burlingame Country Club, or at the Commercial Club, the Stock Exchange Club, the Merchants Exchange Club or the World Trade Club.

San Francisco also has officers' clubs. There are ethnic clubs and several fraternities for scholars, and many different sports clubs like the St. Francis Yacht Club and the Presidio Golf Club.

The latter two have played a significant part in the life of the Fish Club, as the book will show. Memberships at all of these clubs may be found among Fish Club members.

The Fish Club is in good company in the colorful city of San Francisco. People from Northern Europe definitely find the City different, a unique place that has everything you can dream of, including a little Club where a person can enjoy good company, conversation, and a big plate of delicious fish, not unlike in Norway.

CHAPTER I

# The Fish Club Story

Indeed, the Fish Club is different. Nevertheless the Club has served its purpose well and been a true cultural force since it was established in 1914, one hundred years after the Declaration of Independence in Norway. The Fish Club has not only served as a convenient excuse for a weekly luncheon, but has helped shape events of cultural importance to Norway and America. Norway's lack of interest in the San Francisco World Exposition in 1915 was one important trigger in the establishment of the Fish Club. It also appeared that a new club in San Francisco having good relations in business and the art world would further important Norwegian-American relations. People of Norwegian descent all over the United States were furious that Norway should decline participation in the 1915 Exposition. These immigrants managed to effect a rather rare event. They persuaded the Norwegian Parliament, *Stortinget*, to change its mind and say "yes" where they already had voted "no."

The Fish Club did not pull off this coup alone. It was a combination of organizations and individuals that convinced the Old Country to change its mind. Of course, any large train requires several locomotives. The Norwegian Club was one of the locomotives. The Fish Club became the new extra engine.

The founder of the Fish Club was an eccentric and outgoing gentleman named P. R. Poulsson. He had jumped ship back in the 1890's, and was an insurance broker by profession. He cherished old-fashioned club life, where men could get together and solve problems. He gathered some friends and formed a club with the goal to meet once every week, at 12 o'clock in a restaurant that served fish. The aim was to share a luncheon together, with fish from the Pacific and wine from the Californian vineyards, and to chat about current events, Norway and the future.

The Fish Club was usually attended by businessmen, shipping people, engineers and state officials. It was overseen by Rex Sole himself, the inevitable. The form was both formal and relaxed, adapted from the old club style. Participants knew the expectations and newcomers would soon find out if the form and style suited their interests. Among the club's highest traditions were contribution and discretion.

*P. R. Poulsson, founder of the Norwegian Fish Club of San Francisco, as he appeared in the early days of the century.*

15

# SHIPPING AND CULTURE

The Fish Club established itself as a place where good friends could stay as long as they liked and cherish good food, wine and company under the motto: "We resist everything except temptation."

During the first ten years of its life, the Fish Club gathered at a second floor restaurant on Pine Street, by the old California Market. The market was a traditional meeting place for city dwellers back in the good old days when prospecting and gold still had a major impact on the City's life.

*The old board with the Fish Club's emblem and the initials of the founding members has stayed with the club from the start. It is the Fish Club's oldest relic. It used to be on the wall upstairs at Jack's Restaurant on Sacramento Street.*

Of the Club's founding and the first years, little remains but the names of P. R. Poulsson, T. B. Paulson and Nicholas Gravem, and their support for the Heyerdahl Hansen mission to Norway on behalf of the Panama Pacific Exposition. Klaus Olsen of *Nordmands-Forbundet* is also mentioned. Captain Fritz Olsen, the local representative of the newly established Fred Olsen Line, is believed to have been one of the members in this period. It is likely that good friends of P. R. Poulsson and other members of the Norwegian Club participated actively in the Fish Club's life during its first years. In 1924 the Fish Club moved to the famous premises of Jack's Restaurant on Sacramento Street, and the Club has been there ever since.

After the great disaster of 1906, times changed and the old City life was not what it used to be, but still club members would often spend time beyond the ordinary lunch hour. If the subject was interesting and the problems not easily solved, the luncheon would continue. In those days a good debate on an interesting subject could be the highlight of entertainment and social contact. A good speaker would fascinate when no radio, television or other modern options were present. The fish, wine, coffee and cognac along with a devoted conversation would make the session last.

In those early days, talks and stories never seemed to end. Some more wine, and it was time for dinner. No need to move. Dinner was ordered upstairs and the good lunch party continued into the night, adjourned only when Jack's had closed and the waiters had to go home. Like other respectable French restaurants, Jack's had a hotel license in those days, for the very discreet dining with company. Upstairs, on the third floor, guests could stay the night. The Fish Club members on the second floor did not go upstairs instead of going home, at least as far as we know.

Among the steady visitors to the Club in the inter-war period, most of the names are lost. Only a few are known: P. R. Poulsson was usually accompanied by T. B. Paulson, who was not a relative. But he did have one thing in common with P. R. Poulsson: he was famous for his rhetorical ability, his good conversation and love of good food and drink. Fritz Olsen was much the same. Once, when someone complained about lack of tables to place the *pjolter*, P. R. Poulsson announced, "When a man gets too tired to hold his drink, all he has to do is to swallow it." Nicholas Gravem, Alfred Abrahamsen, J. Heyerdahl Hansen, Commissioner to the Panama Pacific Exposition, Herman Gade and his young Assistant Commissioner, Wilhelm von Munthe af Morgenstierne, who later became Ambassador to the United States, and Consul Nils Voll attended the Club in those days.

A Norwegian career consular representation was established in San Francisco in 1915 when Mr. Nils Voll was appointed Consul. The main reason for strengthening the Norwegian representation on the Pacific was the expected increase of Norwegian shipping interests in the area, a consequence of the World War and the opening of the Panama Canal.

In 1927 Consul Voll was relieved by Mr. Christopher Furst Smith, who served until 1929

# The Fish Club Story

*The persons who started the Fish Club were members of the Norwegian Club. There have been close ties between the two clubs over the years. Still today, many members of the Fish Club are also members of the Norwegian Club. Their clubhouse on Fell Street was acquired in the 1930's. Photo Olaf T. Engvig.*

when he was succeeded by Mr. Reidar Kildal. When Mr. Kildal died in 1934, Consul Sigurd Steckmest was assigned to the Consulate. The Station was upgraded to Consulate General in 1938, resuming a status that was previously effective when Consul Johnson was appointed to that post in 1866.

The Norwegian Consular Station in San Francisco was a spartan one for many years. All it could do was assist ships and sailors, help and guide people and act as legal custodians to immigrants. The Consulate had no time or money to promote cultural work, or to expand Norwegian-American relations. This situation called for assistance from private bodies like the Norwegian Club, the Fish Club and others. Eventually it was to be the Fish Club, close to the Consulate, that became the Consul's arm. The Fish Club provided access to shipping, business and maritime cultures, which provided additional venues for entertainment and assistance when cultural enterprises were at stake.

Rex Sole P. R. Poulsson was adamant about keeping close contact with the representatives of Norway. To him it was a serious matter. Whenever a new consul arrived, he would receive a formal visit from P. R. Poulsson dressed up as usual with a top hat and a white carnation in his button-hole. He would always bring a beautiful bouquet of flowers with him. He would welcome the Consul to San Francisco and formally invite the new Norwegian representative to have lunch with him at the Fish Club. Most Consuls were glad to have the help and camaraderie the Fish Club could offer.

The Fish Club took pride in actively promoting Norwegian-American relations, and shipping and cultural contact and exchange. As will be seen in later chapters, they did their job well. Little by little during the first decades, the Fish Club emerged with rituals that were all its own, including a "Chapter of Merit" that was established under "The Order of The Golden Fish," with all the pomp and circumstance P. R. Poulsson and company could cook up. It became quite a show.

To be knighted in The Order of the Golden Fish is the Club's highest reward. This honor was later supplemented with a special award called *Tordenskjolds Soldater* for long, hard and devoted work towards common goals. It was instituted in the name and remembrance of the famous Danish-Norwegian naval hero of the Great Nordic War, Admiral Tordenskjold. His common name was Peter Wessel; he was born in 1690 in Trondheim, a rebel who lived dangerously and died young. He fled to sea at age 12, made a speedy career in the King's Navy, and received command of a frigate at 22 years of age. He raided a Swedish fjord and managed to capture a large Swedish supply fleet by surprise, a major achievement in the war. He was knighted in 1715 and became admiral and chief of the Baltic fleet a year later. To fool the Swedes in Marstrand 1719, he hid his few sailors in strategic places, had them show up, be spotted, and then disappear, only to be spotted marching from somewhere else. Intimidated, the fortress surrendered without battle, as the Swedes believed they were up against a superior force.

Those few soldiers, believed to be many, gave rise to the well-known term, *Tordenskjolds Soldater*, their exploits so famous that they became Anglicized: "Ten-thousand Swedes crawled through the weeds chased by one Norwegian." Today "Tordenskjold's Soldiers" are those truly devoted and hard working persons in San Francisco who always show up, do what's needed and leave.

To be knighted by the Fish Club might be less spectacular than to receive the Nobel Peace Price in Oslo, but not by much. Rex Sole's regalia—including chain and "Golden Fish," embroidered miter, and a sword that is actually an old fishing rod—manages to be impressive without being too serious. His chancellors are the Auxiliary Rex Sole and the *Bybud* or herald, who is dressed as a Bergen city express deliveryman. They accompany the knight-elect and see to it that he arrives on time and behaves according to the ceremonial tradition, kneeling at the proper moment. The Auxiliary Rex Sole will recite the letter of merit, written in traditional language with flowery excess to underline the importance of the occasion, while the Rex Sole knights the honored person. The ceremony for "The Tordenskjold's Award" is less ritualistic but may even be more of an honor. The Fish Club's awards of merit tend to set the ranking and place in this informal organization.

During the 1920's and 1930's Norwegian shipping in the Pacific region grew rapidly, and a group of young and eager owners' representatives came from Norway to start new lines or to aid in companies' offices in San Francisco. They found the Fish Club to be a fine place for lunch and to socialize and they became P. R. Poulsson's new apprentices. It was obvious that this rather special insurance broker commanded the respect and affection of these youngsters. Among the new shipping representatives during the 1920's and 30's were Christian Blom (of the A. F. Klaveness Co.), Einar Pedersen (Westfal-Larsen), Peter Myrvold (Norwegian America Line), and Harald Muller (Fred Olsen Line).

In time Christian L. Blom became one of the most influential members of the Fish Club and was appointed by P. R. Poulsson to succeed him as the Rex Sole. Christian Blom was born in 1906 in Fredrikstad and attended college in Oslo and university at Oxford. He was a trainee in shipping at Bruusgaard & Kiøsterud in Drammen and moved to California as owner's representative in 1928. He started the Klaveness Line on the Pacific Coast in 1929, and became director of Klaveness in San Francisco in 1937. He resided with his family in New York during the war years. From 1941 to 1946 he led the Liner Division of Nortraship. He and his staff were in charge of all sixteen liner services that Norway had around the world. This modern fleet of liners was the pride of the Norwegian merchant marine. It still amounted to nearly two hundred ships in 1941. Christian Blom has been president and director of numerous organizations related to shipping, business and social life. King Haakon knighted him in the Order of St. Olav for his service to Norway during the war, and he was made a commander in the same order by King Olav. Christian Blom received a number of other honorary awards.

These newly arrived "Soldiers" were given their first test at the Golden Gate International Exposition of 1939. Jens Heyerdahl-Hansen, P. R. Poulsson, Nicholas Gravem and Alfred Abrahamsen cooperated closely with the Norwegian Shipowners' Association in Oslo and the shipping representatives in San Francisco mentioned above, in preparing the Norwegian Exposition on Treasure Island. This project is described fully in a later chapter of this book.

It was this same group that decided to continue to fly the Norwegian flag the following year, for a humanitarian purpose. The German invasion of Norway on April 9th, 1940, made communication with Norway difficult. The country needed help. Many of the coastal towns had been terror-bombed by air and were completely destroyed during the invasion. The need for relief was urgent. Norwegians in the Bay Area converted the New Zealand Pavilion into a Norwegian country house where food was served and donations collected; the whole amount was given to Norway Relief, Inc. after the Exposition's close.

During the war the Fish Club helped their knighted shipowner Lars Christensen to acquire Norway House as a home and refuge for sailors of war that came to San Francisco. This activity also has its own chapter, as does the Seamen's Church in San Francisco.

In the autumn of 1944 the Fish Club decided to document its first thirty years. Three small pages, following a codfish on the front page, recounted the Club's history, concluding by saying that, during the last four horrible years, activity at the Fish Club had been down. Members were scattered all over; Christian Blom, for instance, was in New York to become director of the Liner department of Nortraship, the largest ship company the world had seen until then. He was in charge of 188 of the finest liners in the world, and he made them run as never before. Because of their high speed they could sail independent of convoys and were allowed to do so. They were always fully laden and showed an amazing turnaround. The liners not only helped the alliance with badly needed supplies, they also financed a very significant part of the war material Norway needed to fight the war. Running expenses, supplies and material were not *gratis;* they had to be paid for. Furthermore Nortraship helped the Norwegian Government pay on its loans in dollars. Occupied Norway had no way of producing foreign currency to service these loans.

The five years between 1940 and 1945 were a difficult time in America, even though battlefields were abroad. Norway of course suffered much. It should have seemed an easy task for the *Blitz-Krieg* machine of Hitler's to roll over Norway, being a less militarized nation. But the nation's rugged terrain, few roads, tough climate and long and difficult transport lines were all a great hindrance to German occupation. A few Norwegian soldiers with their precision hunting rifles could stop the Germans in strategic spots. One farmer, very able with his rifle, was commanded to shoot at the Germans; he aimed, fired one shot, and said, "I have never shot at people before. I suppose I'll try one more."

Norwegians, with partly improvised resistance, saved her King and Government from imprisonment and humiliation when they sank the German heavy cruiser the *Blucher.* The Presidency of the *Storting* was able to remove the gold reserves from the country. It was valiant efforts such as these that prompted a now famous remark by President Roosevelt: "Look to Norway." The first allied counterattack came in Norway in 1940 during the Germans' Narvik campaign. A moderate force of French, Norwegians and Polish troops, assisted by the British, forced the Germans to withdraw from Narvik.

The people of Europe did suffer, but few were worse off than the people at sea. At the outbreak of World War II, Norway was believed to have had the most modern merchant marine fleet of the world, and in size, the third largest. The ships of this unarmed fleet were sunk at a rate that no other nation experienced. By the time the United States entered the war, a major portion of this tonnage was on the ocean floor. Thousands of Norwegian merchant marine crewmen lost their lives. Sailors that survived were trapped in ports all over the world. Increasingly, they had a hard time finding a Norwegian ship on which to serve. The options were not many. Those in the United States could join the Army or hire for sea on war-built US tonnage. Many Norwegian sailors continued duty at sea and participated in Normandy and other theaters of war on ships flying the American flag.

It was the Norwegian merchant marine, along with the men in the offices of Nortraship, who made one of the really great efforts for all the allies in the fight for freedom. A British statesman said that the Norwegian merchant marine equaled an army of a million men. He was right. An army can't fight without fuel, weapons, ammunitions and supplies. A major part of these supplies was hauled across the Atlantic on Norwegian ships before, during and after the "Battle of the Atlantic." Britain's Prime Minister Winston S. Churchill said that only once during the war was he doubtful of the outcome. It was regarding the German U-boat peril. During one period U-boats sank twice as much tonnage as all the allied shipyards could build, making the protection of the shipping lanes across the Atlantic the most crucial battle of the war at sea. This remark of his underlines the stature of Norway's merchant marine duty during the war. The history of Norway House in San Francisco recounts how important sailors became in those days.

Consul General Sigurd Steckmest passed away in 1942, and was succeeded by Mr. Jørgen Galbe, Chancellor of the Embassy in Washington, D.C. in 1943. Mr. Galbe served in San Francisco until 1952.

When Christian Blom came back from New York after the war, he found that a new generation of shipping people had arrived. P. R. Poulsson was still presiding as Rex Sole. He named Christian Blom as his Auxiliary Rex Sole. By then Blom was one of the veterans of the Fish Club. Among the most significant and stable participants at the luncheons during the war were Auxiliary Rex Sole Alfred Abrahamsen, the old shipping man Nicholas Gravem, who had been with P. R. Poulsson from the start of the Fish Club, Einar Pedersen (Westfal-Larsen), Rolf B. Schou (ship supplies), Jens Feragen (Fred Olsen), Lyder Bruun (Norwegian America Line), Jacob Andreassen (ship supplies) and Aslak Jensen (Ditlev-Simonsen).

The Fish Club still belonged to P. R. Poulsson. He never failed to show up. He had mastered the Fish Club as an old mariner would command his ship, right from the start in 1914. He presided over the Club for almost forty years, and he still wasn't a very old man. Long before his demise he had become a legendary person in San Francisco. He had an office in Suite 500, Hobart Building, 582 Market Street. He would walk to and from Jack's, the Norwegian Consulate or other buildings downtown that he honored with his visits. His exquisite way of dressing—with a bowler or a top hat, with frock-coat or with tails, perfectly pressed trousers, and polished black shoes with clean white spats—was always finished off with a fresh white carnation in the button hole of his frock coat. P. R. Poulsson had found his style at the beginning of this century and he never changed it. In the early 1950's young people saw him as a relic of old San Francisco when he strolled along the streets of the City. He was one of this city's many special figures and he even left his beloved San Francisco in a special way as well.

This is how it came to pass. Christian Blom had moved into new offices on Sansome at California with his newly started Overseas Shipping Co. P. R. Poulsson, gallant as always, soon paid a visit. He brought flowers to wish Blom all the best for the future. He was returning from this visit, walking along when he was hit by some construction material that fell from a building. He was knocked to the ground and taken to the hospital, but he never recovered from this injury. He faded away and died, knocked out by a tumbling structure in San Francisco that was, ironically, not caused by an

*Christian Blom was the second Rex Sole of the Fish Club, 1953-1980. The picture dates from the 1950's.*

*P. R. Poulsson in his latter years after the Second World War. He was the Fish Club's Rex Sole from 1914 to 1953.*

earthquake. P. R. Poulsson had lived through the 1906 earthquake unharmed.

The powerful and dynamic shipowner Christian Blom inherited the Fish Club's Rex Sole position, while Rolf Schou, and later Jens Feragen became Auxiliary Rex Soles. Changes made by World War II created a new platform for the Fish Club. Life in the latter half of the twentieth century came to be quite different from that of the first fifty years. Long-range military planes made by the thousands had shown the world the future potential of air transport. Airlines across the Atlantic became common. The big and luxurious ocean steamers were doomed. More official visitors from Norway came to San Francisco.

The Consulate General was glad to escort new visitors to Jack's and the Fish Club. Usually the Consul General would accompany them for the walk over to Jack's. It was a grand opportunity for the Club's knights, soldiers and *snyltegjester* (guests) to receive the latest updates on Norway and Europe and to meet interesting people that had come to visit San Francisco.

Minister of Finance and Director of the Bank of Norway, Erik Brofoss, gave insight on the country's financial situation. Director of Health, Dr. Karl Evang, lectured on the health of the Norwegian people. Evang had been in San Francisco before, as a member of the Norwegian delegation to launch the United Nation's Organization in 1945. Managing Director Tom Clausen, Bank of America, giving an address on financial matters, ended it with a devoted speech on the beauty of Norway. Bishop Johannes Smemo was politely reminded that he was lunching in a house where they used to have girls upstairs, and declared that it was his first time in such a place. Minister Svend Nilsen came to the Fish Club, as did Ambassador Paul Koht. Christian Brinck, Hans Jørgen Darre-Hirsch, Olaf Malterud, Christian Mohn, several shipowners, Chief Editor of *Aftenposten* Torolv Kandahl, Ambassadors Arne Gunneng and Ole Ålgård, Mayor of San Francisco Joseph Alioto, and many more post-war attendees too numerous to mention. Recently Admiral Thomas Patterson kept the Fish Club informed on the Liberty ship *Jeremiah O'Brien*'s voyage to Normandy '94. One of the Club's knights, William A. Anders, continues to keep in touch with the Club; having been a member of the Apollo 8 Expedition, he is better known as "Our Man to the Moon."

Even old Ambassador Morgenstierne, who was in San Francisco in 1915, just after the start of the Club, came back and paid tribute to the Fish Club and Jack's. It was Ambassador Wilhelm von Munthe af Morgenstierne and United States Secretary of State Cordell Hull who signed the famous and important Lend-Lease agreement between the United States and Norway in Washington, July 11, 1942. The ambassador is an example of the lasting relations between the official representatives of Norway and the Club.

Over the years the Club and the Consulate General have kept close contact. New Consuls would participate and enjoy themselves. During the Squaw Valley Olympics, all members of the Club were assigned different tasks and jobs. The Consul General's ticket to the Games was to move the snow away from the cabin each morning while staying in Squaw Valley. His young Vice Consul, Thorvald Stoltenberg, had to stay behind in San Francisco and run the Consulate. Stoltenberg later became Secretary of the Embassy in Yugoslavia, Minister of Defense and Minister of Foreign Affairs of Norway, High Commissioner for Refugees of The United Nations, and peace negotiator in former Yugoslavia.

Apart from the Olympic attaché Christian Blom, the Fish Club's treasurer to the Squaw Valley Olympics, Iver Lyche, contributed the most. He knew people who could help the Norwegian delegation, organized accommodations and reserved cabins at the right moment.

Iver Lyche came to California as a student in the fall of 1945 and obtained a master's degree in business from the University of California at Berkeley. Then he returned to Norway to join the family lumber business. Iver Lyche had been in Little Norway, Canada, at war's end and had an outstanding record in skiing competition. He had, however, met a girl from California in school, and in 1950 he finally said farewell to the business in Norway, went back to the United States and his girl in San Francisco.

He started in the paper and lumber business, but in 1952 Lyche joined Shuman, Agnew & Co., where he became a financial broker. He worked his way up and became the president and chairman of this investment company. In 1976 Shuman, Agnew merged with Morgan Stanley & Co., and he became managing director.

Iver Lyche became a director of the New York Stock Exchange in 1976. He was chairman of the Board of the Presbyterian Children's Hospital for many years and remains an advisory chairman for the hospital. He is also a member of several other boards. Iver Lyche has always enjoyed fish at the Thursday luncheon and the Rex Sole found him a great supporter. In financial matters he has acumen, and he has a wide range of contacts and friends. He was an excellent fund-raiser for Norway's involvement in the Squaw Valley Olympics and in the Los Angeles Games, as well as for other activities included in this book.

Consul General Jørgen Galbe retired in 1952 and was succeeded by Bjarne Børde. He was the man that launched the Fish Ball at the Presidio Golf Club that still is an annual event in December. Consul General Børde left San Francisco in late 1958 to assume his new office as Ambassador to Iceland. He was succeeded by Mr. Carl Oddvar Jørgensen, the Consul General in Bombay. Carl O. Jørgensen has so far been the only Vice Consul who has later returned as Consul General. He was a devoted member of the Fish Club.

When Mr. Jørgensen was transferred as Consul General in 1964, he was followed by Mr. Knut Orre, who became the first Consul General to take residence in the government-owned house on Normandy Terrace in Pacific Heights. When Mr. Orre retired, he was succeeded by Mr.

*The Fish Club as guests of San Francisco's Mayor Joseph Alioto at City Hall when Christian Blom received the Key to the City in 1975. Air News Photos, by courtesy Christian Blom.*

Finn Koren. Mr. Koren was one of the most dynamic and colorful representatives Norway has sent to San Francisco. He was an excellent diplomat and a brilliant speaker with a personality that won him many friends. He assisted with the *Gjøa* project and maintained close contact with the Fish Club throughout his stay. Mr. Koren left in 1974 to be Ambassador to Thailand.

The new Consul General to San Francisco in 1975 was Mr. Per C. Prøitz, previously Consul General in Bilbao, Spain. Mr. Prøitz became a devoted Fish Club member from his first day in San Francisco. He is believed to have never missed one single luncheon at Jack's, except when traveling, during his six years in San Francisco. He believed in close contact with local officials as well as those at the Federal and State levels. He did much to improve contact with the Immigration and Customs Authorities, the U.S. Coast Guard and the Armed Forces. It was during Mr. Prøitz' period that His Majesty King Olav V came to America in commemoration of the Norwegian-American Immigration Sesquicentennial, described later in this book. Consul General Prøitz left his favorite city in 1981 to be Ambassador to Brazil, his last post before retiring.

The visit of *Christian Radich* to San Francisco in November and December of 1979 boosted goodwill and promoted more interest along commercial lines. The new Consul General Olaf Solli took this challenge in hand. Mr. Solli came from Minneapolis, where he had served as Consul General. During his term of office the Consulate General was strengthened, first by an Industrial Attache and then by a Commercial Advisor as the Export Council of Norway established an office for the third time in San Francisco. Mr. Solli was a devoted participant at Jack's. After a long life as a member of the Foreign Service, he retired in 1986 and settled in Boston.

Mr. Per Borgen, the new Consul General, came from East Germany where he had served as Ambassador. He too became an ardent member of the Fish Club and its weekly meetings. Having reached the age of retirement he returned to Oslo in 1989.

His successor, Mr. Dag Mork Ulnes, arrived from Edinburgh. During his stay, in 1992, the Consulate General in San Francisco moved from the 28th floor of the Embarcadero Center to Norway Place at the end of California Street downtown. The following year the consular offices added a branch for tourism and travel. Fifteen persons were then employed by the Consulate, including the offices of the Norwegian Trade Council, Norwegian Industry Attaches, the Norwegian Tourist Board and the Consular staff.

Dag Mork Ulnes was the Consul General during the Fish Club's eighty-year anniversary at Burlingame Country Club in September of 1994 with Mr. and Mrs. Lyche as hosts. In December the Club had its eighty-year Anniversary Ball at the Presidio Golf Club. Shortly after, Dag Mork Ulnes returned to Norway and a new position as head of the National Tourist Organization NORTRA. Mr. Hans Ola Urstad was appointed the new Consul General to San Francisco. He came from *Stortinget* where he had held office as the chief of staff of the Foreign Affairs Committee of the Norwegian Parliament.

He was given demanding challenges from his first day in San Francisco, preparing the final arrangements for the visit of the King and Queen of Norway in October of 1995. The consular station in Los Angeles was shut down in 1995, and a new honorary consul was appointed in Los Angeles. Last but not least, Mr. Urstad became instrumental in securing Norway House. He helped closing down the Maritime Directorates engagement in this house, a case where the Fish Club showed the best of its old spirit in discrete involvement to help work out a happy ending.

Hans Ola Urstad was the last Norwegian Consul General to attend the Fish Club with Rex Sole Emeritus Christian Blom still presiding at the Club. Blom had known all the Consul Generals and seen them coming and going since Sigurd Steckmest was promoted the first Consul General in San Francisco this century before WW II.

Mr. Urstad has a more extensive role than anyone before him. The Royal Norwegian Consulate General of San Francisco is today presiding over a district that comprises California and Alaska, Arizona, Colorado, Hawaii, Idaho, Nevada, New Mexico, Oregon, Utah, Washington and Wyoming. Today the station in San Francisco has nine honorary consulates attached.

During the first half of this century, the Norwegian Consular Representation in San Francisco was little more than a "one man show." The start of World War II triggered quite a few changes. The Consulate's responsibilities and the staff grew. More people traveled, the passport became a common document. Still the Consulate was only involved in office activities as a passive caretaker. The Fish Club's role as an extra-consular aide grew accordingly. Contributions had to come from private sources. Not until recent years has the Consulate General received aid—through sources like the Foreign Ministry's cultural budget—to promote culture, which was an all new field for the Consulate to be directly involved in.

The changes occurred as Norway saw a sharp decline in assistance to shipping and maritime-related activities. It was part of a transformation aimed both at building international interest in culture and at expanding areas of business and tourism. New priorities and fields of interest have replaced shipping. Container ships and cruise vessels with international crews usually take care of themselves. The new goals have justified the presence of a costly diplomatic mission covering the vast area of the Pacific Coast including Alaska and Hawaii. California is the key state and San Francisco is this region's capital when it comes to aiding Norwegian interests, in spite of the fact that the Seattle area has a larger populations of Americans with Norwegian roots.

This new national appetite for marketing and promoting all things Norwegian has kept a large consular body busy in an area where Norway has something both to offer and to gain. The main emphasis today is to target groups for investment in Norway, to expand trading and to develop the tourist sector. It is important to present arts, exhibitions, concerts, and to arrange seminars and conferences with Norwegian and American professionals for the exchange of knowledge; all these are fields of work for today's Consulate.

The book will show these to be areas in which the Fish Club has been engaged. The Fish Club has been impressed with the consular development which has taken place over the last few years. In the early part of this century, the Consulate's main work was traditional liaison. Today the Consulate is actively amplifying Norwegian culture, business and trade. The Fish Club salutes and congratulates the Norwegian Consulate on these bold endeavors; it envisions a future with more exchange between Norway and this part of the world.

The Fish Club celebrated its fifty-year anniversary at the Trafalgar Room of Traders Vics on December 5, 1964. It was a remarkable period of entertainment and activity, punctuated weekly by luncheons at Jack's and social contact among both residents and visitors. Among the visitors were members of Parliament, ministers, Speaker of the House, ambassadors, officers, clerical, shipping people, editors, civil servants, and others.

The highlight of the previous era was the Squaw Valley Olympics. During this period Rolf B. Schou was Auxiliary Rex Sole, a position he kept until 1968 when Captain Per Høeg of Overseas Shipping Co. became the new Auxiliary Rex Sole.

Rolf B. Schou had been a devoted member of the Club ever since he came to San Francisco during the inter-war period. He did a great job on the board of the Gjoa Foundation together with Erik Krag, the Dane and once owner of steam

*Per Høeg, Rex Sole 1980 – 1987.*

schooner *Wapama*, a historic landmark of San Francisco. As will be seen in the *Gjøa* chapter, Rolf B. Schou stood by the *Gjøa* all the time and was closely connected to this project until the ship left for Norway in 1972. He died the year after. Captain Høeg was a considerable force in the community and for the Seamen's Church. Per Høeg was promoted to Rex Sole in 1980. That year Christian Blom became Rex Sole Emeritus, while Captain Ole Kalve of Star Shipping Co. became Auxiliary Rex Sole. Sigvor Hamre Thornton was, and still is, Assistant "By-1-bud".

After the death of Per Høeg in 1987, Captain Kalve became Rex Sole. Trygve Morkemo of San Francisco Shipping Service became Auxiliary Rex Sole in 1992. In 1995 Christian Blom died at the age of 88. Ole Kalve resigned as Rex Sole at the end of that year and Trygve Morkemo became the new Rex Sole with Rolf H. Schou as Auxiliary. Ole Kalve is the Club's new Rex Sole Emeritus.

During the last thirty years the Fish Club has kept close contact with Norway House and the Seamen's Church. Devoted members of the Club have been on the boards of these two organizations at all times. Significant activities have been conducted by a group of members that served on merchant marine ships during the war; the war sailors' organizations have been a positive force. A considerable list of devoted diners at the weekly luncheon could be made up of war sailors. The ladies organization *Tabita* has also kept a close contact with the Fish Club, and has been particularly involved in the work for the Seamen's Church, as will be shown later.

The Fish Club has been involved with other major cultural events and achievements, each of which is recounted in detail in chapters following.

Bringing home *Gjøa* could not have taken place without the planning, negotiations, financing, work and administration of the Fish Club. In many of the royal visits to San Francisco, the Fish Club played a major role. The Consul General, Iver Lyche and Christian Blom made a fine team to guide the royal visits and make them representative and successful.

The year following the return of the *Gjøa* to Norway, King Olav V was seventy years of age. A national committee for the King Olav V Birthday Fund was established to honor the Monarch. At the conclusion of this occasion, the Rex Sole, Christian Blom, made this remark to the Fish Club:

*Officers of the Fish Club at the eightieth year anniversary in December, 1994.*
*From the left: Auxiliary Rex Sole Trygve Morkemo, Rex Sole Emeritus Christian Blom, Rex Sole Ole Kalve.*

May I again say how proud I am of the fact that the Fish Club in San Francisco was the only organization in the whole United States to show 100% participation. A real thank to all of you for another fine job done in the history of our little Fish Club.

## SHIPPING AND CULTURE

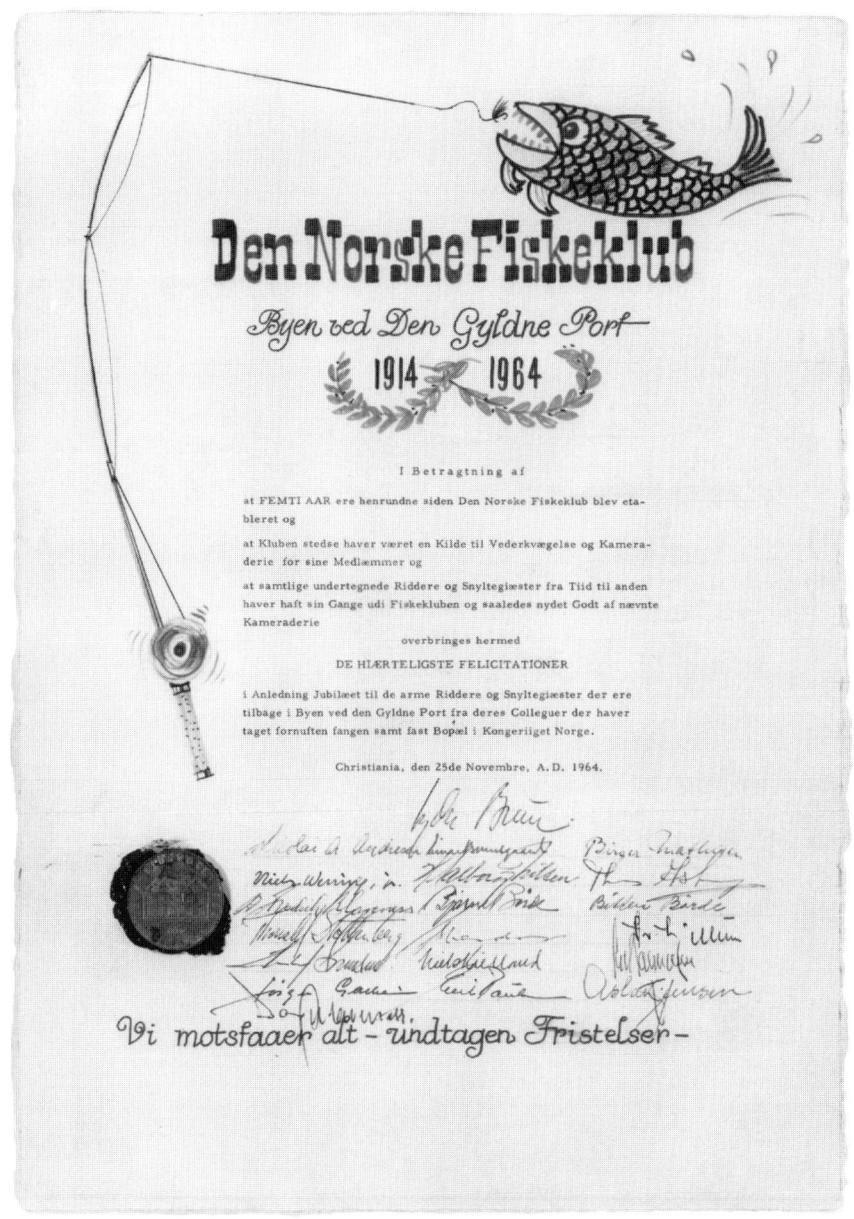

*A greeting from Oslo, Norway for the fifty-year anniversary of the Fish Club.*

The visit of the sail training ship *Christian Radich*, on its longest mission ever was made possible through a joint venture described in a separate chapter. The Fish Club members were essential in assisting the ship, its captain, officers and cadets during the square-rigger's visit to California. They even helped plan the enterprise in Norway before it was launched.

During great sports events like the Winter Olympics in Squaw Valley 1960 and the final preparations at Stanford University for the Los Angeles Games in 1984, the Fish Club played a significant part. Iver Lyche was singularly important in making the athletes' stay at Stanford a lifetime experience. That same year the Fish Club celebrated its seventieth anniversary on December 7, with the traditional Fish Ball at the Presidio Golf Club.

In the aftermath of this event, discussions arose on obtaining a more complete historic review of the years and the time that has passed since it all started with three good friends in 1914.

CHAPTER II

# The Club, Jack's and the City

The long and lasting relationship between the Fish Club and Jack's Restaurant on 615 Sacramento Street started when the Club was ten years old. Since 1924, Jack's Restaurant has been the home of the Fish Club. The Club's weekly luncheon has been conducted for over 70 years in the private dining rooms upstairs. During one period, the Fish Club even had on the walls its plaque, a picture of P. R. Paulsson, and that of the Norwegian Pavilion at the 1915 Panama Pacific Exposition. The famous picture of Jack's during the 1906 fire on Sacramento Street is still there.

Many restaurant guides as well as native San Franciscans consider Jack's one of the finest, if not the very finest, French restaurant in the City. It is definitely not due to a modern interior, grand view or fancy setting.

*This photo of the 1906 fire on Sacramento Street has been hanging on the wall upstairs at Jack's since the restaurant was rebuilt after the quake and fire. Jack's Restaurant can be seen to the right at the sign. It has not yet been dynamited. The fire is closing in on this area of downtown San Francisco.*

The reason is much more the fact that Jack's is almost the only restaurant with the feeling of old San Francisco. The restaurant has a high ceiling, a clean and bright rococo-inspired interior with gold filigree, brass coat hooks around the room, pure white linen and most professional waiters in black tie. They move swiftly and discretely about the room. The kitchen uses old recipes, ingredients of the highest quality and almost no modern kitchen equipment in the preparation of the food. Jack's high scores, according to the columnists and writers on restaurants, are given on its menu, its professionalism, its interior and a history that goes back to the middle of last century. Restaurant life has traditions. At Jack's it is Continental, as is the place itself. In the last century, Jack's was one of the famous French restaurants that were the backbone of the City. It dates back to the days of gold fever, Bonanza kings, attractive girls—and the outgoing, partying city life. Jack's is said to have been the last French restaurant in San Francisco to give up its hotel license. Of course, only a few insiders knew Jack's had a hotel side. Discretion was guaranteed at Jack's, and still is.

Jack's Restaurant on Sacramento was established in 1864. Little is known about the place until 1884 when the Frenchman Jaques Monique purchased the restaurant. He is believed to be the one that gave the place its name. At least he is the oldest recognized Jack of the restaurant. But it could also have originated from the jackrabbits which are still a part of the wall decorations of the restaurant. When Jack Monique was ready to retire in 1897, the restaurant was an old establishment and had a good reputation. Of course, the new owner, Edward F. Blanquie, refused to change the name.

In 1889, Jack's had hired Michael Redinger as a young employee. He did very well and by the time of the 1906 earthquake and fire, backed by his family, he was made a partner with a one-third share. Together the new partners temporarily opened an establishment on Golden Gate Avenue between Laguna and Buchanan, while the demolished Jack's Restaurant in the downtown district was being rebuilt at the same location exactly to its old appearance. In 1907 the partnership moved back to the reconstructed Jack's on Sacramento. Much of the City was still a tangle of ruins and new construction. Jack's quick rebuilding was due to its small size and well known general arrangement of the building. No bigger or more modern structure was to be raised on this particular lot. Monsieur Blanquie was very determined that the old Jack's be restored, down to the details.

Edward Blanquie and Michael Redinger guided Jack's through the turbulent rebuilding period, ending in scandals and cleanup. In fact it was the liquor licenses for the French restaurants, recapitulated in the Norway House chapter, that first unveiled corrupt acts involving top city officials. Edward F. Blanquie died in 1918. Five years later his family sold their remaining interest in the restaurant to the Redingers. Shortly thereafter, the Fish Club moved in.

Michael Redinger, who started working at Jack's eight years before Jack Monique sold his restaurant to Blanquie, was the sole proprietor until his death in 1961. It was possibly the longest tenure of any restaurant owner in San Francisco—72 years. In his latter years Michael ceded interests to his brothers, Paul and Emile. Paul's involvement dates back to 1903, and his son Jack runs Jack's today. It was Paul, searching through the ruins of the demolished building after the 1906 catastrophe, who managed to save a few old sugar bowls and a menu dated April 17, 1906.

Less than twelve hours before the great disaster struck the City, Jack's was offering these specialties for dinner: Green turtle steak, pickled calf's head or ragout of spring duck, including half a bottle of wine. Price: 75 cents. Cognac followed, at twelve and a half cents.

San Francisco is one of the world cities that had a date with destiny. It witnessed a series of earthquakes starting at 5:12:06 in the morning of April 18th, 1906, with a calculated magnitude of 8.3 on the Richter scale. It struck for 65 seconds. For years the official figures stated that 315 persons were killed outright, 352 missing, 6 shot for crime and one by mistake, with the total number of deaths amounting to 674. The cost of destruction was estimated at $500 million, an enormous figure in a time when the best meals cost less than a dollar.

Later research tends to show that the official figures were much too low. The deaths were more like 3000 from the earthquake and fire. San Francisco tried to keep the numbers down, worrying that no one would come if they thought the City was subject to earthquakes. The 353 bodies were recovered from the wreckage and several hundred people were missing. Thousands were injured and not all of them recovered. Figures vary so much that the only conclusion must be that no one really knows.

*The San Francisco earthquake and fire of 1906 left the City in ruins. These images (far left, left, and above) give an impression of how thorough the destruction was. Photos courtesy of The Museum of the City of San Francisco.*

It was a virtually impossible task for the fire department to prevent the City from erupting in fire after the quake. Gas and water lines were broken all over. Hot chimneys triggered fires after being damaged by the earthquake. Other fires were accidentally started when people tried to cook on defective stoves. Wind and the lack of water turned San Francisco into a burning inferno. It lasted for days. Securing the remains of the City was a difficult job. People were shot on the spot when they tried to escap with stolen goods. A greater part of downtown San Francisco was completely destroyed.

fire, even more devastating than the earthquake, burned about 500 blocks, or one third of the city of San Francisco, an area of four square miles with over 28,000 buildings. Fire, a possibility in every city, was apparently more acceptable to the public than an earthquake. One source states that

# SHIPPING AND CULTURE

*In this picture from 1906 the City of San Francisco appears similar to much later pictures of cities destroyed by bombers during the Second World War. Photo courtesy of The Museum of the City of San Francisco.*

Martial law was never declared. But troops were sent in, and the assumption was that the City was under martial law. The Army did a great job in feeding and housing more than 90,000 homeless at the Presidio in the weeks after the earthquake and fire. A large program for help and relief started all over the United States, and even abroad.

Jack's Restaurant was also destroyed, but not by the quake, nor by the fire. According to the owner, the military dynamited the building to stop the fire. So good old Jack's was not entirely gone. After the debris was cleaned out, Jack's was rebuilt on what remained on the site, using the old plan and the common knowledge of how it had been before the demolition. As it appears today, Jack's is the sole survivor in its block of early downtown San Francisco. Today it is standing by itself as stubborn resistance among large post-war office buildings, and with a small open parking lot to the left of the entrance. Jack's is a strong visual symbol of old San Francisco, and has become a famous symbol of any city's little old house in the midst of giant monsters of the new age. Jack's is a strong presence against its background of undistinguished new structures.

Jack's Restaurant is classified as a mid-nineteenth century commercial building, with Renaissance/Baroque ornamentation, the finish trimming showing an influence of the Craftsman movement in the clinker brick window surroundings set in the stucco walls. The construction type is load-bearing masonry of red brick. This landmark is reported to be one of the few remaining restaurant buildings in San Francisco which have the typical small rooms for private dining on the second floor, right

*30*

above the main dining room on the ground floor, which also houses the bar and the kitchen.

The six rooms on the second floor are still named "the Private Rooms." They are often reserved for business luncheons, meetings and intimate celebrations. Entrance to the second floor is through a separate door directly from the street, with an option to enter via the restaurant entrance. The long narrow stairs to the upper floors squeak as they should, and faint smells of old cigars and odd spices still linger. It feels as if one is walking back in time, into the last century. At the top of the stairs a waiter awaits any arrival, for personal escort into the right room. Several parties can be waited on at the same time upstairs. Usually the customers are small groups of men. If the Fish Club gather more than fourteen on Thursday at 12 o'clock, an arrangement will be made to open the next room by sliding away a wall.

A hotel was situated on the third floor, right above the private dining rooms. Each bedroom has a separate bathroom with a tub, and there are intimate dining rooms next door. All the rooms upstairs are still there. Today, this part of Jack's is used as a storage area, except for the two small dining rooms facing the street. They are sometimes used for dining of two to four or up to ten persons. All the rooms, even on the third floor, have a high ceiling typical of the latter part of the last century. Of course, the height of the ceiling increases as one descends towards the restaurant on the first floor, where the height is impressive compared to the size of the restaurant.

*Jack's Restaurant on Sacramento is not much different today than it was prior to the 1906 earthquake and fire. The surrounding area, however, has changed dramatically. Photo Olaf T. Engvig.*

Jack's Restaurant is the place time left. The interior is partly from the start of this century. Jack's is definitely a mature replica of what it was well back in the last century. Until the late 50's the entire house was in operation. The accommodations on the third floor were quite popular, preferable to going to a hotel. After World War II, people started driving to motels. The owner finally decided to close the hotel side by letting his hotel license expire. Jack's is believed to have been the last restaurant with a public hotel license in San Francisco. It was all a matter of courtesy, with a separate entrance for the ladies, and discreet compared to a hotel lobby. Hundreds of John Smiths and John Browns have signed the hotel book at Jack's over the years.

Professionals evaluating the historic structures of San Francisco consider Jack's Restaurant a building well kept and in good condition. Its original use 130 years ago, as its current use, is that of a restaurant. Its design quality is judged as "good," even if the architect's name is unknown. Scales of ratings are always reconsidered, and now this type of structure tends to be upgraded. Jack's has genuine qualities of history and integrity that should place it well onto the list of distinctive landmarks of San Francisco. Indeed, Jack's has changed little over the years. The atmosphere is as much San Francisco as it can be, and as it always was: the old San Francisco gentlemen's club in the Financial District, where a coat and tie still are as natural as wearing shoes. Today, as ever, ladies are more than welcome, even if males dominate as has always been the case at Jack's.

Paul Redinger started at Jack's in 1903. He and his brother Michael were in charge of Jack's when the Fish Club "moved in."

Jack Redinger, Paul's son, is today's owner and manager at Jack's. Jack, his father and his uncle have been the three hosts for the Fish Club since 1924.

When P. R. Paulsson and company decided in 1924 that Jack's was to be their place of retreat, it was because Jack's served the best Rex Sole in the City of San Francisco. A few Norwegians would claim that the greatest knowledge Norway has conveyed to the world is a superb knowledge of fish. It is suspected that the Fish Club also landed where it did because the portions at Jack's are not those fancy little fish dishes, but real king-sized plates of salmon, trout, halibut or almost any other fresh fish on the coast.

Of course, a respectable French restaurant will serve all the basic gourmet dishes. What makes some restaurants outstanding is their kitchen's ability to combine an excellent taste of basic foods with spices and sauces that raise even the eyebrows of sophisticated diners. The top chef is an artist—no written formulas, no spoonful measures. It's instinct, memory.

At Jack's it all starts with a long and detailed menu printed anew each day and dated, an old-time guarantee of fresh ingredients. The customer selects. The waiter, of course, advises if asked. Writers on dining in San Francisco seem to agree that Jack's is the summit. You don't have to be Former Mayor Joe Alioto or Herb Caen, the writer, to get good food at Jack's. The *Chronicle's* journalist prefers grilled steaks and chops, thick, expertly cooked, coupled with a romaine salad sprinkled with imported blue cheese and vinaigrette dressing: "You've got a meal that makes you want to join Jack's club for life." Doris Muscatine puts it this way: "Every day there is filet of sole a la Marguery, a dish I could eat happily for the rest of my days if Jack's did the cooking."

The financier Louis Lurie lunched at Jack's for more than fifty years, not dreaming of eating elsewhere. He had his special corner table and hosted lots of friends and celebrities from all over the world. French actor Maurice Chevalier always dined at Jack's when he was in the City. Jack's was Ernest Hemmingway's rendezvous, and Bing Crosby's restaurant of choice. President John F. Kennedy visited Jack's during his election campaign. A Hollywood producer used the restaurant in one of his films after he dined there. The reason was simple. Jack's looked more like a restaurant than any place he had ever been. Which brings us back to the statement that restaurants have a lot to do with tradition. The Fish Club has been at Jack's for over seventy years. No institution has longer service at Jack's than the Fish Club.

The Fish Club doesn't have to see a menu at Jack's. On an average Thursday luncheon between eight to fourteen persons or so will participate. They will all arrive around 12 o'clock, always greeting each other by shaking hands. After a short standing session the party will be seated. The world's most magnificent sourdough bread and butter will be passed among the guests. After this highly regarded starter, the Rex Sole will give a short welcome, greeting any new visitors and informing if anything in particular is to take place. Then Jose, the Fish Club waiter, will interrupt discreetly but with determination to announce the fresh seafood this way: "Today we have everything!" Or he will say, "Today we have Swordfish, King Salmon, Rex Sole, Halibut, Sea Bass, Petrale, King Crab and Shrimp Louis. Occasionally "he with the black-and-white-striped shirt" and Auxiliary Rex Sole will opt for ox-tail. Old Rex Sole Emeritus Christian Blom always used to order his Shrimp Salad and Rex Sole usually has Rex Sole, the favorite dish.

A surprisingly short time after the orders are taken, all dishes are served. It is plain food with little extra except for potatoes and lemon, which are always present. The big plates with three Rex Soles delicately positioned are burning hot. It is a royal luncheon that needs little else. When finished you feel as though it will be another month before you get hungry again. California Chardonnay is the favorite for this treat.

Later coffee is served and the representative from the Consulate, usually His Excellency, the Honorable Consul General, will read the latest news from Norway.

Visitors will introduce themselves with a short presentation of life and merit. Special topics will be highlighted and discussed. If any activity or initiative is discussed, all—including visitors—will be asked for an opinion. On important matters, an informal voting will take place. That settles a matter. The luncheon is straightforward and simple throughout. The impressive part is that these informal talks can set the course for the great events of tomorrow. Sometimes the luncheon ends at one fifteen, other times at half past one or two o'clock, depending on the party. However, it is not usual to stay for dinner anymore and work the waiter overtime.

For waiters Jack's is their life. Hans Coubler stayed so long that no one could remember when he started. Today, Dominique has more than 35 years, and the youngster, Jose Campos, has 15. The Fish Club seems to be popular among the waiters, "We like this group, they're on time. Always! No problems, they never complain."

*A regular Thursday luncheon at Jack's in 1993, presided over by Auxiliary Rex Sole Trygve Morkemo and Vice Consul Else Berit Eikeland. Photo Olaf T. Engvig.*

CHAPTER III

# Panama Pacific International Exposition

It has not been possible to verify that the Fish Club started as a result of the intensive work of Norwegians in the Bay Area to persuade Norway to participate in the Panama Pacific International Exposition of 1915. But that is how the story is told. Whatever the reason, the time was right. Prosperity and optimism flourished. The City had been rebuilt after the 1906 earthquake on a grander scale than anyone expected. Restoration and development called for a big event.

Construction of the Panama Canal had been successful, and the Canal had opened in 1914. It was the Americans who did it, after the famous French engineering skill, that had created the Suez Canal, had failed. The Canal meant more to San Francisco than to any other city in the world. Ship cargo did not any longer have to make the distant and dangerous voyage around Cape Horn. The U.S. Navy almost doubled its fighting power as battleships could be transferred from one coast to the other in a matter of days.

New inventions and general development of a better standard of living and more luxury made people proud. Life in America was great. The world was invited to see for itself and to participate in the year-long celebration that was to take place during the Exposition. The world came to San Francisco and a world's party it was.

Work on the Panama Pacific International Exposition started in 1910. For a long time it was not likely that Norway would participate. The Government was reluctant to spend needed money on this event so far away from home. The benefits were doubtful. Norway was struggling with a 1914 Centennial Exposition of her own, to celebrate the Constitution of May 17, 1814. When the bill to participate at San Francisco came up in *Stortinget* in the summer of 1913, it lost by two votes.

Americans of Norwegian descent in San Francisco as well as elsewhere in the United States were deeply disappointed. They expected a Norwegian Pavilion at the exposition and would not take "no" for a answer, not even from the Norwegian Government. It would be a disgrace if Norway were absent from this event. All groups and societies with any connection to Norway rolled up their sleeves. Norway's own 1914 Exposition was used as a lever for the Norwegian flag to fly also on the great meeting of nations, in which so many Norwegian Americans took an interest. Every possible argument was discussed, as well as how to collect financial support and voluntary work from Norwegians in the Bay Area.

Shipping agencies and brokers, export and trade interests, art lovers and private persons used their influence in support of the Exposition. The entire Norwegian American community was behind the project, as well as the new Fish Club. Norway's pride was at stake. A campaign was carried out in Norwegian newspapers, assisted

*A general view of the main part of the Panama Pacific International Exposition with the piers at Fort Mason in the background to the right and Alcatraz Island in the distance. Photo courtesy San Francisco Public Library*

and supervised from San Francisco. The arguments made sense. Gradually the sentiment changed. The people of Norway felt *Stortinget's* decision was wrong.

Engineers from the technical colleges were important new professionals of that time. No wonder the Norwegians in the Bay Area looked to them for help. Axel Warenskiold, a mechanical engineering graduate from Trondheim, was known for his engagement in cultural activities and became the chairman of a Norwegian Division of the Exposition. Peder L. Halse from Kristiansund was with the Alaska Packers Company. He constructed the first salmon cannery in Alaska and was called to participate in the Fair Committee.

Jens Heyerdahl-Hansen from Ullensaker, a graduate of Berlin Technical College, worked with the Pelton Water Wheel Company and later, the Pacific Diesel Engine Company. Heyerdahl-Hansen was elected a member of the American World Fair Committee, also called the Main Committee. In the summer of 1914 he was sent to Norway to convince the government of the necessity of participating in the Exposition in spite of the "no" of 1913. He was supported not only by the Norwegian Club in San Francisco, but by organizations of Norwegians all over the United States. The Norwegian Government took up the matter anew, and proposed to the *Stortinget* an appropriation of 100,000 kroner, or about half the cost, which later was granted almost unanimously, on the condition however that all expenses above that amount would be borne by the Norwegian Auxiliary at San Francisco.

Even with so many local Norwegians working for the materialization of a pavilion in the name of Norway, it is today first and foremost the official representatives of Norway that are remembered as the pavilion's officials. It is to the point that the Fish Club later started awarding voluntary work of this type by institutionalizing it under the order of *Tordenskjold's soldater*.

A Norse Castle, symbolizing a Medieval Age Norwegian landowner's chateau, which never existed in Norway, was erected in rugged looking timber with few windows, a boulder foundation and a belfry tower. Its size and appearance were impressive. If re-erected in any Norwegian valley or on the coast, it would have become the tourist attraction of that area. But, alas, all the exposition buildings were to be torn down immediately following the closing night to give room for new housing. Eventually this building was destroyed together with all the rest of the structures, apart for some very rare exceptions, the most famous being the Palace of Fine Arts.

The cornerstone of the Norwegian Pavilion was laid on October 31, 1914, with the usual ceremonies, and work on the site proceeded at an astonishing pace. Norway was located in the southwest corner of the big Exposition area near the Presidio. Around the main structure of the "Chieftain's Castle" and the court, young Norwegian spruce trees were planted. There were no exhibits of Norway in other areas of the Exposition outside the Norwegian Pavilion and the Palace of Fine Arts Annex, where an exhibit of contemporary Norwegian paintings occupied several rooms. They were considered among the highlights of the entire art collection at the Exposition.

Less than four months later, on February 26, 1915, the dedication ceremony of the Norwegian Pavilion was held. In his address from the entrance porch, Norway's Commissioner General, F. Herman Gade, gave an interesting review of the effect of nations upon other nations. His speech on mutual benefits and interaction was quoted and reprinted. It was right to the point on international relations in 1915, with the First World War well on the way. Mr. Gade drew attention to the fact that the number of Norwegian descendants in America nearly equaled the number of Norwegians

*The Norwegian Pavilion on the west side of the Panama Pacific International Exposition recalls a Viking chieftain's castle from the Late Viking Age. Photo provided by the Fish Club.*

at home. The real cause for Norway's participation was to be found in a personal and sentimental attachment to the United States, rather than advantages gained by export, even if important, according to Gade. He mentioned the support that representation at San Francisco might lend the merchant marine, particularly as a new shipping line was started between Norway and the Pacific by way of the Panama Canal. Norway's relationship with the United States is entirely different from that existing with any other country, said Gade. For ninety years Norway has been sending her sons and daughters—pouring a steady stream of her best blood—into this country. That's why the number of Norwegians here today almost equals that of the home country.

The war in Europe was throwing shadows on the Exposition. During the last period before the opening, new problems emerged. Hostilities were escalating. Ship transport became a bottleneck, freight rates climbed sky high, oceangoing tonnage was occupied. This situation profoundly disturbed the business of a nation so dependent on the operations of the merchant fleet; Norway experienced a decrease in national revenues. But there was no turning back on San Francisco, even if the Constitutional Exposition in Norway was reduced to a minimum. The government felt the war to be an additional reason for Norway to appear among the neutral nations of the world.

Daily life in Europe had become difficult, predictions on the future impossible. The story of the art collection's journey to San Francisco is, however, an interesting example of how to solve problems for the benefit of all parties, by networking and improvisation, in time of war and across borders and oceans. An extremely valuable Norwegian art exhibit was on display at the Venetian International Exposition in Italy when the shot was fired in Sarajevo and the First World War broke out. This exposition was closed in October, 1914.

The exhibit was to be secured in Venice pending the conclusion of hostilities, which was the best solution for the time being. No one could foresee the coming events of war, but concern on behalf of the priceless canvases was great. Norwegian art lovers in San Francisco were deeply committed to get these fine canvases out of Europe, to be secured in San Francisco and shown at the Exposition. Their work and cooperation with the National Gallery in Norway, the Exposition's Department of Fine Art, Norway's Commission to the Panama Pacific Exposition, the American Consul to Venice, US Navy and other high federal officials resulted in a solution to all obstacles and secured the long transport in the safest possible way.

The U.S. Navy collier *Jason* left New York in November, 1914, as the "Christmas Ship" bearing gifts for the Mediterranean fleet and presents collected by newspapers all over America for the hungry people of Europe. The U.S. Navy was dedicated to humanity for the occasion, as the war created strict rationing of almost every item in Europe.

*Jason's* arrival in Great Britain and Mediterranean ports with "Yuletide" gifts from America to the children of Europe was an important event for the *San Francisco Chronicle* and other newspapers to highlight, and a fine contrast to the

*A treasure ship. The Navy collier,* Jason, *carried great quantities of fine art and exposition artifacts out of Europe after the First World War had started. The exposition had been in jeopardy because of the lack of available shipping tonnage for the long voyage to San Francisco. Photo courtesy National Archives, Washington DC.*

pictures of young men fighting in the trenches. After unloading, the big supply ship took on 104 cases of statuary from the Greek exhibition at Piraeus, called on Genoa and Marseilles for the artifacts of several European nations, antique French furniture and important post impressionist paintings, which also included the Norwegian art exhibit from Venice—a grand collection of fine art. The ship continued to Barcelona and Bristol where it augmented its treasure with the Spanish and British exhibit material.

When *Jason* finally set course for San Francisco, it had the greatest collection of fine art and priceless exhibit items ever gathered under one deck. The ship's cargo was named the most precious part of the Exposition. Insurance on the art collection alone was $3.5 million, but in reality it was priceless. Many of the paintings were world famous. When the USS *Jason* arrived in San Francisco on April 11, 1915 after a 23,000-mile voyage, it was to the great relief of all parties involved and this relief was reflected in the headlines of the newspapers. Her cargo made the Exposition complete.

Norway had a grand exhibit of paintings in the Palace of Fine Arts. In 1915 Edvard Munch was recognized as the founder of a new modern school called expressionism. Munch's canvases and numerous prints filled a whole room. Never before had California seen art which expressed emotions in such a way. Of course, it drew lots of attention as well as discussion. It ranged from great admiration to very negative description. At times people could not pass by Munch's paintings because of a large crowd of engaged spectators having loud outbursts and emotional discussions on the paintings, widely disagreeing on the quality and art of his work.

Work of other famous Norwegian painters such as Christian Krogh, Erik Werenskiold, Harald Sohlberg, Fritz Thaulow, Olaf Lange, Halfdan Strøm and the bird paintings of Thorolf Holmboe created a width and variety that appealed to all types of visitors. The work of these Norwegians, together with the paintings of Swedish artists, gave the Arts Palace collection of paintings as a whole a significant Northern note that was distinctive and inspiring to art lovers in general, and to Scandinavians in particular.

The Exposition's highest award was given Sohlberg's *Vinternatt i fjellet* for painting, and Olaf Lange for graphic works. Edvard Munch "only" received a gold medal for his graphics, which some art lovers found very disturbing. It was, however, a good example of contemporary taste among the positioned people, and indicated art/political preferences rather than creative and artistic qualities. Politics in painting was very active in those days. Different schools were in strong opposition to each other. Art director J. Nilsen Laurvig, the commissioner to the Norwegian art exhibition, in an effort to calm the most noisy critics, added fuel to the heated discussion by stating to the press that the public had no opinion. Their main task was to accept new art and try to understand. His intention was to underscore that the individuals would need time to adjust to new trends in arts.

The semi-circular Palace of Fine Arts, with its rotunda and lagoon reflecting columns and arches, was designed by Bernard Maybeck, who was inspired by Bocklin's painting *The Island of*

*The Palace of Fine Arts as it appears today, a lasting memory of the 1915 Exposition. Photo by Olaf T. Engvig.*

This page:

WINTER NIGHT IN THE MOUNTAINS, "Vinternat paa fjeldet," was painted by Harald Sohlberg just prior to the exposition. It received the exposition's highest award. Oil on canvas, 160 x 180 cm, 1914. Donated to the National Gallery of Norway in 1918 by J.B.Stang. Photo J.Lathion, Nasjonalgalleriet, 1994.

Opposite page top:

Known today as MADONNA, it was not called so by Munch himself. He called this famous color lithograph "Elskende kvinne," which was translated to AMOROUS WOMAN in the 1915 Exposition Catalogue. © The Munch Museum/The Munch-Ellingsen Group/ BONO 1994.

Opposite page bottom:

The VAMPIRE, color woodcut and lithograph, was one of several of Edvard Munch's pictures that disturbed many lovers of fine art in 1915. Munch's works were shown in California for the first time at the Panama Pacific Exposition. His oil paintings and 57 lithographic works drew much attention. Never before had people in this part of the world seen a painter express feelings in such a way. © The Munch Museum/The Munch-Ellingsen Group/ BONO 1994.

*The lithograph EVA MUDOCCI and BELLA EDWARDS, or VIOLIN RECITAL, showed San Francisco that Edvard Munch had great affection for traditional beauty. These two girlfriends lived together, traveled together and played music together. They were members of the art community in Paris. © The Munch Museum/ The Munch-Ellingsen Group/ BONO 1994.*

*the Dead*. It was located on the west side of the Exposition area, close to the Norwegian Pavilion, and became one of the Fair's most admired structures.

During the Exposition, the decision was made to save this part as a memory, in spite of the fact that the Palace of Fine Arts was supposed to be torn down along with the rest of the buildings. It was not constructed to last.

Today this area is among San Francisco's outstanding landmarks. It had a narrow escape. From the 1920s until the 1960s the structures were allowed to deteriorate to the point where they really came close to their painted prototype—a sorrowful and forgotten edifice, overgrown by old cypress trees, the fog creeping in. After a great reconstruction it was opened again in 1967, and now serves the City in multiple ways and is a great tourist attraction.

The Norwegian Pavilion to the south of the Palace of Fine Arts had a simple carved-and-sawed ornamentation. Within the building was a large "guildhall" for meetings, conferences and concerts, and another hall for exhibits, around an open court where a fountain played. Also opening onto the court was a gallery where visitors could enjoy a luncheon of fish pudding and other typical Norwegian dishes served by young ladies dressed in national costumes. Panoramas of summer and winter scenes under the northern light made the setting complete. The atmosphere of the North was most consistently and distinctly reproduced. For Norwegian-Americans and friends, this setting became their home at the Exposition. Norwegians living in the Bay Area would, of course, act as volunteers whenever needed.

In the exhibit hall was a large model of the vikingship from Oseberg and information on artifacts found during the excavation of the ship only a decade earlier. Sunlight entered the hall through stained glass windows, depicting St. Olaf at his prayers.

The importance of Norway's merchant marine was illustrated by wall charts and models, the most impressive being the two trans-Atlantic passenger steamships for the Norway to New York service. A relief map showed the Norwegian merchant marine arranged according to tonnage. It made an imposing display of shipping in a country with only two and a half million inhabitants. Norway had the fourth largest merchant marine in the world, by far the largest tonnage per capita of any nation. The Norwegian whaling industry was represented by a model of a modern whaling factory ship, with whales on either side and whale catchers in action. Graphics and figures showed that the Norwegians were engaged in whaling in every sea, supplying three-quarters of the world's whale oil. There were models of the lifeboats used by the Norwegian Rescue Service (NSSR), as well as a model of the ultra modern, diesel motorship *Balboa* being completed in Norway for the new Panama Canal service to San Francisco.

Among the leading export items presented were paper, wood pulp, ore and mining industry products, fish and fish products including "tran, or *huile de cod liver*—-well known to kids of all nations even then, and canned goods such as Bjellands sardines.

Above all a brand new industry was presented. It had developed in Norway and had a worldwide potential: the new nitrate production was a Norwegian invention—a means of producing fertilizer from air—that in a very short time had grown into an export industry. It was studied at length by engineers, physicists and electricians. Manufacturing of nitrate products had developed in Norway with tremendous rapidity into a major industry.

New towns grew up in remote areas, clustered about a waterfall with the power-station supplying the huge amounts of electric energy needed for the process. Impressive presentation of this new way to solve world famine by the Norwegian method of producing fertilizers was given much attention and described at length in reports and new books. In 1915 it was honestly believed that this invention once and for all would put an end to starvation and secure a better world for everyone. Fertilizer from animal farming and mines alone could not secure food for the world's increasing population.

The Americans were impressed and delighted. During the planning stage they actually wanted part of a genuine manufacturing plant from Norway to produce the tremendous spark needed and show the "Norse God Thor's domesticated lightning" to the world, but that was not feasible. Instead the products were shown by samples.

Diagrams illustrated the processes of combining oxygen and nitrogen in an electric furnace, cooling the gas, combining oxidized nitrogen with water in oxidation tanks and quartz towers, combining nitrite acid and limestone in the lime tank, and finally the evaporating and packing.

All the different products were present and their importance described: nitrate of lime, nitrate of soda, nitrite of soda, nitrate of ammonia, and refined natrium nitrate; only nitric acid was absent. Pictures taken of Notodden and Rjukan in 1903 and 1911 illustrated how rapidly this development took place. At the beginning of the industry in 1906, the annual world production was valued at $51,500. During the exposition year, nine years later, the annual world production was valued at $11,300,000.

This development was said to be of vital interest to every person. Thousands studied the exhibit with due appreciation, while thousands more learned the important lesson for the first time during their visit to the Norwegian Pavilion.

In 1915 the greatest threat to the future of the world was famine due to lack of fertilizer on a world scale. Birkeland and Eyde's invention to make fertilizers from air was impressive. It was presented in San Francisco at the same time as the last fleet of large German sailing vessels carrying nitrate were ready for their long voyage from Chile around Cape Horn, to take back to Europe the fertilizer needed to keep up food production in the old world. Many of them were arrested because of the war and were later confiscated. They were laid up in ports along the Pacific Coast and sold. Several of these beautiful big windjammers of the last generation of merchant sailing ships are still to be found in different ports as symbols of the seafaring nations' maritime heritage.

"San Francisco invites the world," was the signature phrase for the Exposition. Indeed, the City by the Golden Gate had much to celebrate. Not only was every other state of the union invited, but most of the foreign nations showed up at this world party and brought with them their particular cultural items, samples of specialties, presentations of their countries and fine young representatives.

The Panama Pacific International Exposition was a grand undertaking, and affected almost all areas of the City's life prior to and during the event. A united San Francisco, and a supporting state of California were behind it. It was to be the biggest and best enterprise anywhere until then.

*The central and more spectacular structures that were torn down immediately after the exposition.*

The whole Marina area was redeveloped. Existing buildings were moved or torn down. The area was flattened and enlarged by landfill on the bay side. On this big lot a completely new Exposition city was built, with towers and domes like ancient Venice or Baghdad, with gothic cathedral arches, with structures from Greek temples and Roman courts, with streets and yards filled with fountains and sculptures. Indeed, it was a eclectic mixture of the world's architectural styles over the years, put together in one fairy tale city for pleasure, events, experience, information, education, relaxation, socialization, play and testing as well as celebration.

It became quite a fair with one memorable event following another. One of the highlights was the arrival of The Liberty Bell, transported all the way from Philadelphia, after a discussion whether it was to undertake the journey or not, because of fear that the crack had opened. The bell could be ruined during transport. This symbol of liberty, unity and peace, about which every school child had learned, traveled farther than ever and was greeted by thousands all along the track of fourteen states before it reached San Francisco. It was placed in the Pennsylvania building. The Liberty Bell was believed to be the single most photographed object of the Exposition.

Another important visitor from the East Coast was in jeopardy because of the war. It aroused lot of discussion, even angry newspaper editorials. For the first time in history, battleships of the Atlantic Fleet were to pass over the isthmus of Panama. Then came the message that shocked and stunned the whole world.

On Saturday, May 8, 1915, San Francisco woke up to this headline over the *Chronicle's* whole first page: "Hundreds Perish when *Lusitania* is Torpedoed." There were 2160 persons on board the big ocean liner when it was sunk by a German submarine without warning off the coast of Ireland. More than a hundred American citizens sailed with her. The first headlines on casualties were unfortunately far too low. The next day the number of lives lost was increased to 1198 persons. The world's largest typewriter at the Exposition was used to print headlines of this tragedy.

This disaster immediately put the Navy on full alert, and war appeared to be imminent. Because of the *Lusitania*, the planned visit of U.S. battleships from the East Coast was canceled. But San Franciscans wanted the ships to be there, and so did a great many others. Requests were made, and it took time but finally there came a "go" from Washington. On July 15, the battleship *Ohio* passed through the Gatun locks. Along with the battleships *Missouri* and *Wisconsin* she came, and 650 midshipmen from Annapolis Naval Academy boosted the Exposition.

These were major events that drew more than 100,000 persons per day through the stiles. On San Francisco Day in November, 348,472 was the total, only to be beaten by Closing Day on December 4, 1915, when 459,022 showed up to say "Good Bye" to the Fair and a most exiting year. The Exposition was a great gamble of money that succeeded well. On September 3, a final installment of $110,159.02 had been paid to the banks and the mortgage was officially burned. No one had to pay the bill for this extravaganza but the fair itself. Five years of careful planning and hard work had finally paid off. From that day on, everything was just fun.

The 1915 Exposition is believed to be the first one to witness man in flight. At the Marina

*Art Smith and his airplane were a major attraction at the fair. Photo courtesy Golden Gate National Recreation Area.*

was a large open grass field for outdoor activities. It also became the first airport of an international fair. Art Smith and other daring pilots did loops, "Dippy Twists" and "Jelly Rolls" to the delight of a frightened audience of some 75,000.

The construction of the Panama Canal was called the century's greatest single work. A big model showed how the isthmus looked and how the Canal was constructed and operated. General G. W. Goethals was celebrated; he stated modestly that the construction included no principles that were new. Even so it was a masterpiece of engineering in a really terrible place on earth, replete with tropical sickness, mosquitoes and the death of high French hopes.

In 1915 the kids' big hero was Thomas A. Edison, the inventor, and he came out of his laboratories in New Jersey to see the illuminated fair and the City as well. He was celebrated and gave a speech. At the Exposition's "Inside Inn," he met with Henry Ford. They became the center of interest.

Theodore Roosevelt, twice President of the United States and known abroad as the trust and monopoly killer, gave a speech on peace and war. He was quoted for saying,"It was my good fortune to take the action in 1903," referring to the decision to build the Panama Channel. "It nearly doubles the potential efficiency of the United States Navy, as long as it is fortified and is in our hands."

For the really nostalgic, one of the highlights was Lotta Crabtree, a favorite stage actor of San Francisco's Golden Age of the sixties and seventies. She was brilliant, having started as a child and retired at the early age of forty-four. She never came out of retirement except for this sole occasion when President Moore gave Lotta the Exposition's medal. The Festival Hall had its largest audience since Edison Day a month earlier. The 24-foot cast iron monument that Lotta Crabtree gave the city she loved survived the earthquake and fire, and it is still to be found on Market Street. It is one of the very few original structures older than a hundred years left in downtown San Francisco.

The fair went on with lesser and bigger events. Several committees tried to make every one of the 288 days that the Fair was open into a special day. They succeeded to the point where several occasions had to share days. On Education Day, October 11, a plan was launched to save the Palace of Fine Arts and the Marina, and it was well prepared. The Exposition Preservation Board was founded, funds were needed. Needless to say, it was a success, as this part of the Exposition of 1915 can still be admired to the west of the Marina Green. It houses art and a large theater and museum of science, the Exploratorium, which keeps a few of the winged statues of plaster and gypsum. They look worn today even if inside, but they were not made to last longer than the exposition itself and have managed to survive eighty years and a major earthquake.

*Norway Day at the Fair. Some Norwegians in great spirit for the occasion.*
*Photo courtesy San Francisco Public Library History Room.*

Norway Day was celebrated on June 3. Thousands of Norwegians from all parts of the United States came to San Francisco to honor their homeland and participate in the special Norwegian events that were to take place on that day. The Consulate, the Church, lodges and associations such as the Sons of Norway, *Nord-*

*manns-Forbundet*, the Norwegian Club and the Fish Club, along with shipping people and different auxiliaries and groups like the Scandinavians in the Alaska Packers Fleet were ready to play host for the great number of Norwegian descendents coming in.

Many of those coming from the midwest for Norway Day were born Americans, as were their parents; they came to see the Fair and honor the Norwegian tradition. From Washington and Oregon, where Norwegian immigrants always had been a significant part of many communities, came large groups. Some travelled on the coastal steam schooners of the "Scandinavian Navy." This particular coastal trade was so dominated by Norwegians and other Scandinavians that it carried this name, and has kept it as a significant part of Pacific Coast history. For two days Norway received headlines across whole pages in the San Francisco newspapers. Patriotic speeches, songs from Norway and expressions of loyalty were highlighted by a message from King Haakon VII.

Thousands had crowded along the Marina in the morning hours of June 3 to participate in a strange performance. They gazed out towards the water. On the bright surface of the bay appeared a quaint craft propelled by many oars in the hands of men dressed in the warlike costumes of the ancient Vikings. The ship grew as it came nearer. Sunlight flashed on their arms and armor, spear tips blinking as the rowers bent the oars and the great Viking ship with its high prow and strange figurehead sped towards the landing. In the stern, overlooking the men, rose an heroic figure—the ancient explorer Leif Erickson impersonated by the opera singer L. A. Larsen with his big voice. Most of the Viking rowers and warriors were captains and crew members of the Alaska Packer Fleet's big sailing ships and professional oarsmen and sailors.

*A 20-oared Viking longboat at the Alaska Packers Yard getting ready for a friendly landing at the fair. Years later the longboat was given to San Diego and it finally burned in Balboa Park. Photo courtesy San Francisco Maritime Museum.*

As the proud craft swung into the harbor and approached the landing stage, notes of Edward Grieg's *Landkjenning* sounded shoreward, sung from the ship in strong voice, to be taken up in chorus by the members of Pacific Coast Singers' Association on the landing stage. The song continued as the Viking ship was moored alongside. Leif Erickson in full war armor stepped ashore to a friendly greeting by the Mayor of San Francisco, James Rolph Jr, and Mr. A. Warenskjold, chairman of the festival committee for Norway Day.

A company of local warriors of the first battalion of the United States Marine Corps escorted the Vikings in a grand parade headed by a military band from the Marina to the Norwegian Pavilion, where the Luther College Band participated as well as City and Exposition officials, members of the Norwegian Commission and prominent Norwegian officials. A brief ceremony marked the planting of a Norwegian spruce, brought across from the Royal Garden in Christiania.

King Haakon VII was the subject of the speech made by the Royal Norwegian Consul A. Bjoldstad. A message from the King was read by F. Herman Gade, the Norwegian Commissioner General to the Exposition: "I beg to convey my greetings to all Norwegians gathered in San Francisco to celebrate Norway Day. I express good wishes for their welfare and happiness." It was received with continued applause.

Forceful addresses were delivered on relations between Norway and America. Gifts were exchanged, and President Charles C. Moore extended appreciation for the Norwegian participation. Later that day all the singers gave a grand concert in the Festival Hall together with the Panama Pacific Singing Association. It was followed by a free concert at the Civic Auditorium the day after, with 800 singers participating; it was very well received by the critics. The Norway Day celebration terminated with a banquet in the evening at Scottish Rite Hall. The festival committee made Norway Day into a successful event, according to the newspapers and the official report from the Exposition.

A lesser known product of the Exposition was the great series of congresses, conferences and conventions that stands as an intellectual by-product of the Exposition. Roughly ten to twenty major congresses went on each day in major fields including art, science, education, religion, industry, business, and organization.

In connection with Norway Day the following organizations held meetings: Norwegian Singers of the Pacific Coast, Synod of the Norwegian Evangelical Lutheran Church of America, Federation of Singers of the Synod of the Norwegian Evangelical Lutheran Church of America, Young People's Association of the Synod of the Norwegian Evangelical Lutheran Church of America, Sons of Norway (District Convention District No.2), and Daughters of Norway (Pacific Coast District). Some of the other conventions held at the same time were the Cereal Conference under the University of California and the US Department of Agriculture and a series of library conferences.

The Panama Pacific International Exposition covered everything; new electric propulsion, schools, livestock shows, forestry, mining, steam locomotives, shooting contests, climbing ropes, car races and the spectacular airman in the new invention, the flying machine. There were plays, shows, parades and concerts.

Despite the ravages of the World War and the international conflict, the San Francisco World Fair of 1915 was for the people who experienced it the gayest, most colorful, interesting and educational pageant ever held. From February until November of 1915, people from all corners of the world would meet in San Francisco to see for themselves what strong faith and courage could accomplish. In return the participants experienced the party of their life. Everyone was celebrating, and having such a good time that it would linger on in their minds as long as they lived.

The Henrik Ibsen Lodge of the Sons of Norway produced this post card pointing out the highlights of San Francisco in 1915, namely the Gjøa, the Golden Gate and the Panama-Pacific Exposition Site, all embraced by the American Eagle and the Norwegian Lion. Courtesy The Museum of the City of San Francisco.

CHAPTER IV

# Golden Gate International Exposition

Norwegian-American captains and officers were a distinct part of the crews on the many ferryboats going across San Francisco Bay. During the 1930's they watched the construction of bridges, knowing that in a few years they would all be out of business. From 1936 to 1938 there was even an additional enterprise to share with their commuting passengers. An artificial island was developing on top of what used to be a place only for seabirds—the Yerba Buena Shoals.

One decade of San Francisco's history—the very decade of the great world depression—became the era when the Bay itself was developed. The Golden Gate Bridge was finished in 1937 and the San Francisco-Oakland Bay Bridge just the year prior. They were at that time, and for many years to come, the most outstanding enterprises in bridge construction anywhere in the world.

The Golden Gate Bridge spans the one-mile-wide entrance to San Francisco Bay and

*The Golden Gate Bridge. The most distinctive structure of this era is still in full operation and busier than ever.*  *Photo Olaf T. Engvig*

49

harbor, connecting the land north of the Bay to the San Francisco Peninsula. It became the longest and highest single suspension span in the world. The length of the main span is 4200 feet, with a clearance over high water of 220 feet. The towers rose to 746 feet, highest in the world. The Golden Gate Bridge is a single-deck, six-lane, auto bridge with sidewalks. It was opened in May 1937 after more than four years of construction. Total cost was 35 million dollars.

This masterpiece of architectural beauty and construction design, together with its natural setting, has made the bridge into one of the greatest wonders of the world. Even today there are few man-made constructions more beautiful, functional and beloved, more visited and more documented through film, video and other media.

The San Francisco Oakland Bay Bridge is more than eight miles long, connecting Oakland and the East Bay to San Francisco. When completed, the bridge was the longest of its type in the world. The west crossing is a twin-suspension-span bridge, connected with a tunnel through Yerba Buena Island to the east crossing, with the 1400-feet cantilever span and nineteen truss spans. One pier goes down to a depth of 242 feet, once a world record for a working depth below water.

The Oakland Bay Bridge was a double-deck bridge with six auto lanes and two tracks for inter-city trains on a lower level. Today the lower level is used for eastbound auto traffic. It was opened for cars in November, 1936, after three years of construction, and for trains on the lower level in 1939. Total cost amounted to 80 million dollars, supposed to be another world record.

The state of California and the city of San Francisco had constructed the largest single suspension span—and the largest structure of its kind—in history. Since then the two world-famous bridges have been outstanding landmarks of San Francisco. Admired by millions of visitors over the years, but also subject to damnation by hurrying car drivers who must simply look at the car ahead when faced with a backup and loss of precious time.

*Aerial view of Treasure Island and its Magic City during the 1939 Exposition.
Sand pumped up from the bottom of the Bay filled in Yerba Buena Shoals to create Treasure Island.*

It is not so well known that the work laid down to create a proper place to celebrate these achievements resulted in yet another world record. Out of the bay grew a 400-acre man-made island, the biggest in the world. This third adventure started in the early 30's as an idea in the newspapers, to make a new Fair in San Francisco to celebrate the bridges and tell the world about progress. To find a proper place for the Exposition was not easy. Central San Francisco was all developed. Space was becoming a problem on a peninsula with the sea on three sides.

After investigation and research, the Yerba Buena Shoals were selected as the location of the new fairground. Military engineers found the site ideal as a future airport for land and sea-operated planes, because of prevailing winds, fog patterns, tides, depth, central location and easy access.

Employment was down all over the country due to the great depression that still lingered. The federal administration was looking for new enterprises to help people back to work. Funds were obtained for the new bay project through the Works Progress Administration. The City needed a larger airport for the Pan American trans-Pacific mail and passenger service flown across the Pacific with big seaplanes. An air terminal with service and repair facilities at the final stop in San Francisco could be developed along with the Fair and thereby secure continuing use of the area when the Fair had closed. Raising the shoals from between 2 and 26 feet below sea level to an overall elevation of 13 feet above water was a challenge of significant dimensions. The Army Corps of Engineers laid down a perimeter of rocks more than three miles long all the way around the shoals, to be filled up with sand from the bottom of the bay and secured with stones and rocks from the tunnel through Yerba Buena Island that connects the two parts of the Bay Bridge.

People had a front row view of the development of the island from the ferries. Eleven dredges were used for the work, twice as many as were employed during the construction of the Panama Canal. Their pumps spanned San Francisco Bay, pumping some twenty million cubic feet of sand from the harbor floor one mile through pipes to be discharged at the growing island. Sand was collected from as far away as the vicinity of the Golden Gate and transported to a point where it could be handled further. It took more than one and a half years to dredge the new island out of the Bay.

A highway and a 900-foot bridge was built to connect the island with Yerba Buena and the Bay Bridge. On the inner part of the island a large building was rising, while architects and artists worked on the drawings and design of what would become the new International Exposition in San Francisco. It was a great challenge, it was demanding, it became expensive and it gave the Bay Area new land and much needed space at a good location. It became the City's new treasure. The name could be nothing less than Treasure Island. On Treasure Island was built a Magic City for the world to see and experience.

When Franklin D. Roosevelt's invitation to participate in the Exposition reached Norway, it was followed by information on this new wonderland: it was where the Occident and the Orient will join in festive spirit to create a spectacular "Pageant of the Pacific." The Fair was to be the highlight for visitors to the West's National Parks, and the world's largest bridges in San Francisco.

Carl Joachim Hambro, President of the Norwegian *Storting* and delegate to the League of Nations, came to San Francisco in August of 1938 and was attended by several Norwegian societies, including the Fish Club. On this occasion C. J. Hambro officially informed the Fish Club that the Norwegian Government and the Norwegian Shipowners Association had agreed to participate on the Golden Gate International Exposition in 1939 with a Norwegian Pavilion.

C. J. Hambro was touring the United States on this occasion and was also a guest of The Norwegian Club and the Sons of Norway. There was a grand reception with a dinner following in Oakland Hotel's Ivory Room; guests included four Scandinavian Consuls, the mayor of

Oakland, representatives from the Fair Committee, the Unversity of California at Berkeley, the press and approximately a hundred other guests. On this occasion the president of the *Storting* gave one of his famous speeches: "Collaboration of the North in International Politics." It highlighted the united search for wisdom, peace and creative imagination, while part of the world is only concerned with destruction. Long and explicit reports of the speech were printed in the newspapers.

Once again problems arose for Norwegian participation, but they were different from those of 1915. The country had already engaged to participate in the New York World Fair the same year, and international agreements prevented Norway from participating at two exhibitions in one country in the same year. The San Francisco involvement therefore had to be organized as a private enterprise, and a considerable part of the financing came from the shipping industry and the Norwegian Shipowners Association.

The preference of the Norwegian colony in San Francisco as well as the shipowners was to profile Norway through a genuine Norwegian ski and sports lodge, a small but very special and significant structure. They formed a local committee to take care of the matter.

The pavilion was to be equipped with modern Norwegian furniture and with products originating from the Norwegian home industries, along with decorative art, sporting articles and a supply of preserved food to show the ancient custom in Norway of keeping stores at hand in case of need. The drawings showed connected buildings placed around a yard.

In due time there arrived several traditional Norwegian log structures, usually identified with winter sports and outdoor activities; with it came carpenters to take care of the erection. They had been prefabricated in Norway, complete in every detail and constructed without the use of nails. According to tradition they had sod roofs. The local committee did a splendid job in arranging the construction. On the opening day only two other countries besides Norway were ready. Norway's pavilion was focused on culture and artscraft displays, rather than on commercial presentations of the Norwegian export industry and trade, even with considerable shipping interests behind the enterprise.

The Golden Gate International Exposition was scheduled to be another grand feast, outrunning the one in 1915. From time to time it did. This party lasted one year longer than the earlier one. San Franciscans had every reason to celebrate and entertain the world. The time was ripe for most Americans, as it was indeed for the world. Years of depression and difficulties were coming to an end. The good life was starting again and people wanted a long celebration to forget about the past.

The World Fair—as it was commonly called—opened on February 16, 1939, and for people that participated it was the ultimate party of their lives. It became a fashion prior to the opening for San Francisco males to let whiskers and beards grow. By the opening day the City was full of unshaved and bearded men. They dressed up in costumes symbolic of the West in the good old days of the Gold Rush, and so did the women. Norwegians also turned out for the event with amazing crops of whiskers and mustaches. Costumes were those of prospectors, trappers, miners, cowboys, deputies and sheriffs, merchants and sailors, telegraph operators, gamblers, bankers and even old Spanish padres and monks. The record says nothing about Indians.

Opening day was San Francisco's most hilarious event. Escalating throughout the day, it became even gayer towards the small hours of the morning. The feast went on with full force until the break of dawn. The location of the party was perfect; there was nobody next door to bang the wall or call the police, just a magnificent setting in which to go wild. Only the Carnival in Rio on its best occasions could compete with this San Francisco party.

People in remote fjord communities of Norway, halfway around the world, talked about the new trend in San Francisco. A few brave men

# Golden Gate International Exposition

*Photographers experimenting in color captured images like these during the 1939 Exposition. Photos courtesy the Treasure Island Museum.*

even decided to try the new fashion on a local scale, letting their beards grow for a time just for the fun of it. The Fair started off by making a world fashion.

Unofficially the Fish Club, with its connections to the shipping business, became a significant local host for Norwegian visitors to the Norwegian Pavilion, thus assisting the Consulate and the official committee. For most Americans the Norwegian log structures were peculiar and different. The presentation of Norway in the Official Guide Book stated:

*Probably you won't be wearing ski boots or carrying skis over your shoulder when you walk into Norway's ski and sports lodge, but you'll feel as though you had just come in from the mountain jumps when you see their exhibits.*

*The Norwegian Shipowner's Association and other Norwegian shipping firms were responsible for Norway's pavilion at the Exposition. You'll notice that several buildings are arranged around a court in old-style Norwegian architecture that was known in the days of the Vikings; that the main building is constructed entirely of hand-hewn logs interlocked without the use of nails; and that the roofs are covered with growing grass. You'll notice, too, that the furniture is modern Norwegian, that the tapestries in the living-room or peisestue are copies of old Norwegian handicraft, and that the modern rugs are handmade.*

*You'll see, in the long, low wing designed for a woodshed, toolroom and garage, a collection of sports equipment and clothes, including a pair of Sonja Henie's ice-skates. Next, you'll see a food storehouse or stabbur, built a few feet off the ground as they have them on Norwegian farms, surmounted by a little belfry with a bell such as they use to call the farmhands to their meals. You've heard about the Norwegian bad-*

*Norway's Ski Lodge was constructed in Norway and built of timber in the traditional Norwegian way. It had sod roofs. The Lodge was unusual and drew much attention.*
Photo courtesy the Fish Club/Royal Norwegian Consulate General.

*stue or the steam bath. They're coming into great favor again in Norway, and at the lodge a typical one is shown, big enough for the whole family.*

Indeed, the Norwegian Ski Lodge drew a lot of attention, from the big laugh to deep admiration. It started even before the opening, when the *Call* reported, "Turkish Bath on Isle! Of all places in the Norwegian Lodge Exhibit!" The *Examiner* followed: "As for the Norwegian Ski Lodge, it has a green roof too, but it is not tarnished—it grew there. They call it sod, but it looks like a lawn—and it gives you a good idea of some of the odd problems of home life in Norway. 'For heaven's sake,' we can imagine the typical Norwegian housewife saying to her husband, 'run up and mow the roof. And while you're at it do something about the gophers in the attic.'"

Gophers or not, cold climate and peculiarities in the Viking way of life attracted people from the South Sea who were more familiar with palm huts and coral. The Norway lodge became a success. During the first two days an average of 2000 visitors an hour was recorded. The hand-woven area rugs were completely worn out after the first day, and had to be replaced by rubber mats. The Norwegian version of the Turkish bath was also a must. The passage had to be cut twice as big to get all the people through!

In March the *Chronicle* wrote, "The spread of taste between such horrors as the standing lamps in the court of the Moon and such masterpieces of imagination and functional adaptation as the Du Pont exhibit or the Norwegian Ski Lodge is extremely eloquent, and an analysis of this spread would come to grips with things of far greater significance to our own world than the fifty millionth rhapsody in prose about 'The Birth of Venus.'" The Magic City on Treasure Island had a price tag of fifty million dollars.

One special event during the Fair had a distinctive connection with Norway, even if it had little to do with the Norwegian arrangement. In the nineteenth century, Sondre Norheim, Snowshoe Thompson—the famous mailman of the Sierra Nevada—and other ski pioneers from Norway had taught the world how to ski. In California skiing, the Auburn Ski Club's early history is full of Norwegian names. Jumping on skis was for the Norwegians. This Ski Club was called upon by the Fair to try to

*Never before or after has a "world championship" in ski jumping been arranged at sea level. The jumping hill on Treasure Island was impressive and the upkeeping of it was even more of a challenge, as 300 tons of ice were needed just to cover the hill. It had to be crushed to snow by the machines that were at work almost all the time during the competition period.*

get the ski jump competition of the 1939 World Championship to be sited at Treasure Island, and managed to do so, while the giant slalom and downhill were arranged at Cisco, a small place near Red Mountain not far from Auburn where the elevation drop met international standard.

A hill of championship quality and size had to be made, as Treasure Island was flat as a pancake. The Auburn Ski Club designed and built it of portable steel sections to a height of 185 feet, with a lift. The only competition for tallest structure of the island was the Tower of the Sun. The Union Ice Company provided "snow" from ice. Artificial snow was new to the competitors and proved faster than natural snow. The most able skiers would benefit under such conditions. Reidar Andersen of Norway was the champion,

This ski competition opened the more than 300 sports events during the Fair. It was announced as the first sea-level ski jump in history, and it probably still is the only one. "It will be done in shirt sleeves weather from the highest artificial mountain ever constructed, and at least one hundred miles away from the nearest source of skiable snow, in a city where infrequent falling of crystal flakes calls for dismissal so school children may see them," wrote the *Chronicle* in 1939. It assured that "Despite its freakish nature, the ski jump is sound and authentic. Thirty-five of the best skiers of Europe, Canada and the US will compete with the blessing of the international body governing ski events." The paper also tried to describe those daring men that fly out into space.

*Reidar Andersen from Norway was champion at the 1939 competition. He had a perfect jumping style as this press image shows.*

Norwegian American Alf Engen from California came in second. Norwegians were delighted.

The next governor of California, Earl Warren, and his family were eager participants at the grandstand. His father was born in Haugesund, Norway, and was baptized Mathias Varren. During President Eisenhower's term, Earl Warren was appointed Chief Justice of the Supreme Court.

"From the top of the hill the bird men will ski down a precipitous incline and fly into space, waving their arms to maintain equilibrium like a tight rope walker, and land at the bottom with the breathless velocity of a falling body, meanwhile struggling to avoid cracking up at the instant of impact." The description is given by a San Francisco sports journalist in 1939, as an introduction

# Golden Gate International Exposition

*The Reflection Lake and The Wall were distinct and impressive architectural designs. Together with colors, spotlights and water, the exposition design made lasting impressions on everyone that participated. Photos by Karl Kortum.*

to this entirely new sport for people living at sea level. It was obvious that everyone had deep respect for this daring and dangerous sport.

The ski jumping became so popular that jumpers continued to jump in private tournaments long after the official competition closed. Of course, it was an odd location for a ski jumping championship. Never before had ski jumpers jumped 135 feet, which was a considerable length in those days, next to tropical island settings with palm trees, Hawaiian music and hula girls, fine arts and colorful representatives from all corners of the world.

After the Exposition was over, the management reported back to the Auburn Ski Club that the Jump Competition was the most successful sports event on the Exposition program. One pair of heavy jump-skis from the competition is still in the Navy Museum at Treasure Island.

The Exposition's Magic City was sponsored by the San Francisco metropolitan area and supported by the eleven Western states, an artificial, fairy-like city of joy and imagination. The structural style was modern for 1939, clean and monumental, the architecture a blending of Mayan, Incan, Malayan and Cambodian cultures. The Tower of the Sun in the spacious Central Court was the dominating structure, with rows of imposing exhibit buildings and scores of remarkably beautiful structures. Around and about were breathtaking courts: Court of the Pacifica, the Seven Seas, the Rising Sun, the Moon, the Reflections and Court of Flowers. There were countless statues, fountains, murals, relief panels, arches and other decorative features like lagoons and quiet reflecting pools as well as cascades of sparkling water and evening illumination in all colors. Movement and life were predominant features. It was all magic and unforgettable.

For millions of Californians a trip to Treasure Island meant endless entertainment. The Magic City met all requirements, from intimate concerts to symphony series and huge outdoor shows. Performers included Bing Crosby, Judy Garland, Bob Hope, W. C. Handy and Irving Berlin. Young Ester Williams and her swim-girls did water shows, and Johnny Weismuller or Tarzan was the Exposition dream boy.

Everywhere, the Fair offered girls, girls, girls. They came in bathing suits, in the latest fashion, or in nothing at all. Adults could sketch or photograph models posing behind glass "for art's sake." There was a Cavalcade of the Golden West depicting the 400 years from Balboa's arrival in 1513. Displays, miniatures and dioramas included fossils, useful plants, archaeology and explorations with Magellan sailing the ocean,

*Their Highnesses with a smiling Crown Prince Olav, just behind Crown Princess Märtha, leaving the Norwegian Ski Lodge on May 18, 1939. Photo courtesy The Royal Palace.*

Captain Cook mapping the Pacific and Roald Amundsen at the South Pole. Hawaii and the Pacific, Central and South America and the Far East were strongly represented at the Exposition. Friends from abroad also included many of the old nations of Europe.

On the public wedding day, the mayor gave twelve brides away to twelve grooms. And Joe Sprinz tried to catch a baseball dropped from a blimp 800 feet up. Visitors could learn about art, science, industry and religion, the Navy, foreign and domestic culture and home cooking or American Boy Scouting.

Treasure Island was the site where the Occident met the Orient in what the Exposition called a "Pageant of the Pacific." The world came to see the architecture, the sculptures, landscaping, the color effects and the mural decorations. More than 1.5 million out-of-state visitors spent a total of 212 million dollars in California during the Exposition of 1939.

For the Norwegians, two of those 1.5 million out-of-state visitors brought them the highlight of the year. On Norway's Constitution Day, May 17, 1939, His Royal Highness, Crown Prince Olav and Her Royal Highness, Crown Princess Märtha of Norway, arrived in San Francisco. Their Royal Highnesses stayed at the Fairmont Hotel. After a private luncheon and a press conference, the Royalties went to the Lutheran Church on 19th and Dolores Street, later via Twin Peaks down to Golden Gate Park and the sloop *Gjøa* where there was a brief stop. They then moved on to the 17th of May banquet at California Hall at the Exposition. Music was provided by professor August Werner and the Oakland Singing Society, speeches were offered by the hosts and HRH Crown Prince Olav. The banquet continued into a *folkefest* and Crown Prince Olav and Crown Princess Märtha took seats in highback chairs near the open fireplace in the sports lounge, where guests could pass through the room in front of them.

The next day the royal couple visited the Fair. On arrival, a military salute was given and the troops paraded. The Swedish, Danish and Norwegian pavilions were visited by the royal couple. Higher officials of the Fair attended, as well as the general in command and representatives of the Army and the Navy were present. In familiar settings the royal couple admired the woven wall hangings, the modern version of the old Norse floor mats and other art and craft on display. The lodge had two small bedrooms downstairs and one upstairs, and room for servants. All rooms were fully furnished and ready to use. As mentioned, one wing had the traditional woodshed, toolroom and a garage. This part was used to display winter sports equipment. Next to the storeroom for provisions was the *badstu*, the old bathing form that as mentioned was undergoing a renaissance in Norway.

# Golden Gate International Exposition

Traditional artifacts shown included knitted wool sweaters and Porsgrunn porcelain.

"Never another World Exposition in San Francisco," has become a saying among the superstitious, because then we will have a major war. The First World War broke out just prior to the opening of the 1915 Panama Pacific Exposition. When the 1939 Exposition closed, World War Two had started.

Even so the everyday life in San Francisco did not change. Hostile actions occurred far away and had no immediate impact on Western life. But for some of the nations participating, the war was real. When it was decided to keep the Fair open another year, changes and rearrangements occurred. Norway's decision had been to sell the Ski Lodge in 1939. It was sold and removed according to the plan. One of the buildings is reported to be a cabin near Lake Tahoe–still in good condition. The Norwegian Auxiliary to the Exposition then decided to dissolve, giving the money left over to the Red Cross in Oslo as aid to victims of the war in Europe.

When "The Fair of 1940" became a reality, some Norwegian Americans in San Francisco got together to consider ways and means of having the flag of Norway displayed at Treasure Island. P. R. Poulsson was one of these devoted individuals. A committee was formed, and donations were obtained from a few interested business and professional men in San Francisco. The donations amounted to $528.75, which represented the total working capital of the committee! The Exposition Management, through its Director for Foreign Participants, offered the committee the free use of the former New Zealand building left on Treasure Island as the new Norway Lodge, stipulating, however, that the committee assume responsibility for the remodeling and equipment of the building.

A contract was entered into with A. Svensgaard, who, in consideration of a concession to operate a Norwegian type restaurant in this new Norway Lodge, agreed to assume responsibility for the remodeling and equipment of the building. Mr. Svensgaard further agreed to operate a restaurant to serve a dual purpose; to provide a meeting place for Norwegian visitors and their friends, and to pay the operation expenses of the Norway Lodge. This agreement served its purpose well. The Norway Lodge became very popular. It is estimated that more than 80,000 people were served Norwegian sandwiches during the four months of operation. A truly Norwegian atmosphere was maintained.

*Norway Lodge at the Exposition in 1940. Photo courtesy Royal Norwegian Consulate General.*

In planning participation in the '40 Fair, the committee, after conferring with Consul General Steckmest, anticipated import from Norway of articles representative of Norwegian handicrafts and industrial art. The invasion of Norway on April 9, 1940, made that impossible. An appeal was then made to California Norwegians to contribute articles for display and sale. The response was most satisfactory. Articles donated were sold for the benefit of Norwegian relief, enabling the committee to turn over to the Norwegian Relief Inc. and the American Red Cross for relief in Norway, a total amount of $3,188.50.

The committee obtained the services of Mr. Jens Heyerdahl-Hansen as commissioner. He served in that capacity in 1939, knew the administration, and was in attendance at the Norway Lodge throughout the entire season. Mr. Heyerdahl-Hansen once again did a great job, and served without any compensation. He was successful in enlisting the loyal and efficient cooperation of ladies of the Norwegian community in San Francisco and the East Bay. These ladies rendered excellent service in the sales booths. Mrs. Gudrun Pabst's daily attendance at the Norway Lodge, for instance, was all voluntary work. The San Francisco-East Bay commission in charge of Norway Day arrangements organized the great event and raised the considerable sum for the relief fund. The relations of the committee with the Fair Management was dominated by cordial helpfulness and mutural appreciation. This private and local enterprise for Norway at the 1940 Golden Gate International Exposition was made possible only by President P. R. Poulsson, co-workers of the committee and other local participants, all *Tordenskjolds Soldater* pulling together.

The entire budget for the participation amounted to only the said 528 dollars. Building insurance was the biggest expense at 175 dollars. When other major items like flagpoles, flags, paint, supplies and transport, telephone and postage were paid off, there were 25 dollars left.

The Norwegian "Pavilion" of 1940 was dedicated to the ideas of peace and progress, and for the aid and support of the homeland fighting the Nazi invaders. International sympathy and admiration was showered upon Norway. The remodeled New Zealand building was a success. It really looked like a typical Scandinavian structure. The display of peasant goods of Norway functioned well. It contained Norwegian glass, handmade silver, gold and pewter ware, colorful handpainted wooden ware, and of course, skis. In the textile exhibit were knitted sweaters, socks, wool gloves and other useful clothing for outdoor activities in cold weather.

On Sunday, September 29, 1940, The Golden Gate International Exposition was closed. By then the world was heading into a state of transformation that the alert had already recognized. Times as they used to be were disappearing fast, never to return. All the brave plans for future use of Treasure Island were disrupted. How difficult it can be to look into the future! The brief and extravagant life of this fairytale island, with its Magic City of beauty and joy, was over. Only the memory of the event existed, as war moved closer and transformed daily life, changed public opinion and gradually made San Francisco into an important part of the war machine.

Looking back it seems as if the Fair left little direct impact on the Bay Area. The Pan American Clipper planes, which a few years before were the ultimate new way of transport across the Pacific, soon became a dead end in world aviation. New airfields were built and newly designed, longrange bombers proved the superiority of land-based liftoff. The prestigious Trans-Pacific Clipper Service, that was moved from Alameda during the Fair, was not further developed at Treasure Island, nor did the plans to turn the island into the new San Francisco International Airport materialize. Instead the United States military took possession.

The war was escalating, and the site in the Bay was needed for war purposes. The Navy took command. When the United States entered the war, former Exposition halls became barracks, classrooms and messhalls for sailors and Navy men training for war duty or transfering to new destinations. Treasure Island Navy Station

# Golden Gate International Exposition

*Some of the Fair's architecture and art still exists. Among stored artifacts is an entire fountain. This sculpture is on display in front of the Treasure Island Museum, the 1939 prospective Pan American air terminal building. Photo Olaf T. Engvig.*

became a very important factor in the war theater in the Pacific. Up to 12,000 men per day passed through the island. Out in the Bay an armada of transport vessels were riding at their anchors awaiting sailing orders. Young sailors going through joked that they had to get in line for the next meal soon after they finished the previous one. The fairground of leisure and play, less than a thousand days away, had changed into a crowded military facility, with activities on the run, uniforms, schedules, marching, orders and discipline.

In 1944 the City of San Francisco traded Treasure Island in exchange for the Government land that is today the San Francisco International Airport. The City finally got its new airport but not on Treasure Island. Fifty years later the Navy is closing down its activities on the island.

CHAPTER V

# Norway House, Seamen's Home

During the Gold Rush, San Francisco developed into a major port for sailing ships from the East Coast and Europe. It also became the final resting place for many a fine vessel as officers and crew left the ship to seek for gold, participate in local transportation, or take other good paid jobs in the fast growing communities in this part of California.

Through the latter part of the 19th century, San Francisco continued to grow. It saw a rising number of ships from all corners of the world as the City became increasingly important to ocean shipping. The western United States was rich in different ways. Lumber and grain were usual cargoes for many oceangoing vessels. Scandinavians participated in these trades. Norwegian sailors were quite common in San Francisco. For sailors of all nations, "Frisco" became the ultimate sailor's town.

From the days of sail until the earthquake of 1906, the Barbary Coast remained the spot any sailor had to visit before he could be defined as an old salt of the utmost order, even after completing prestigious voyages to ports like Antwerp, Shanghai, Bombay and Valparaiso. Frisco had an atmosphere of dancing, drinking and hooking, as well as fighting, cheating, looting, and shanghaiing—in which men were sold, often dead drunk and dumped on a departing ship, finding themselves bound for another continent when they woke up, well off to sea.

In this environment there were also humanitarians who established organizations that tried to help and support the sailors and keep them from getting into trouble. People from northern Europe living in the area and their churches often took an active part in helping or keeping an eye on arriving countrymen and sailors. The City itself tried to take action against the worst cases of crime towards seamen without too much success. Although it was a San Franciscan, Norwegian-born Andrew Furuseth of the Coast Seaman's Union who finally secured "the Seamen's Bill of Rights" in Federal legislation, a cleanup of the Barbary Coast never came. In the end, it was the quake and fire of 1906 that did the job. Most of the old Barbary Coast was destroyed, and it was never rebuilt. At the same time international transport changed.

The Norwegian four-masted bark *Alcides* was the last ship to take on board West Coast grain for Europe in 1914. It was the year the Panama Canal opened. It was obvious to everyone that yet another of the last important sailing trades was lost to steamers. The era of Cape Horners was definitely coming to an end.

San Francisco continued to grow. Norwegian shipping lines on the Pacific coast, South America and the Far East were registered, manned and administrated from Norway—on the back side of the world, as seen from San Francisco. Quite a few sailors adopted San Francisco as their homeport when sailing, and especially between ships. Some would know fellow countrymen and stay with them. But many did not have friends living in the area. They would be subject to stays in boardinghouses, leaving valuables in odd places where they often disappeared. They received little help in need. In certain periods, such as during the 1939-40 Golden Gate Exposition, hotels and boardinghouses were crowded and sailors arriving from a long voyage had to be put up in the slums and flophouses.

During the inter-war period, Norwegian shipping people, the consulate and local organizations like the Fish Club discussed the possibilities of trying to establish a center for seamen in San Francisco, but it never materialized. The outbreak of the Second World War complicated this picture. Seamen who wanted to go home could not do so because of the war in Europe.

*San Francisco became an important port for Norwegian sailors. The four-masted bark* Alcides *belonged to the large fleet of big sailing vessels that traded between Europe and San Francisco by way of Cape Horn. She disappeared in the Atlantic with all hands in 1917. Photo courtesy San Francisco Maritime Museum.*

The occupation of Norway in April 1940 made it necessary that shipping offices abroad deal with matters that ordinarily would be handled through the shipowners' offices in Norway. Nortraship was established to administer the Norwegian merchant marine fleet of more than 800 modern oceangoing vessels. The headquarters were in both London and New York. Nortraship became the largest shipping organization in the world. Qualified people were needed. Many of them had to be found outside Norway. A worldwide body was established to conduct and serve the world's third largest merchant fleet, an important instrument in fighting and winning the war.

In San Francisco a new hiring hall, named the Scandinavian Shipping Office, was established to help sign on sailors, and the Norwegian Seamen's Union started a branch office in San Francisco. The old idea of getting a home for the sailors finally materialized.

A welfare board within the exile government's Nortraship office came forward in support of the idea. Shipowner Lars Christensen Jr. of Thor Dahl in Sandefjord, Norway, who had a shipping line on the Pacific, visited San Francisco and had talks with different local people. Alfred Abrahamsen, who presided as Auxiliary Rex Sole at the Fish Club, was requested to help in finding a suitable property. Among the suggestions was a house on Vallejo Street in Pacific Heights at a price of 10,000 dollars. However, the welfare board could not produce the necessary funding. Then shipowner and consul Lars Christensen Sr., who was a member of the welfare board, took action. He decided to buy the house himself and give it to the sailors of Norway as a seamen's center named Norway House. On May 6, 1941, he sent a short telegram to Alfred Abrahamsen, San Francisco. It read: "Accept the house" and was signed by Lars

# Norway House, Seamen's Home

Christensen. Norway House became reality. It was a gift from Lars Christensen Sr. and his wife to Norwegian sailors and would be owned and run by them.

The large and prominent property on the corner of Vallejo and Pierce is a four-story building of wood. From the upper floors there is a magnificent view towards Alcatraz, the harbor and Marin County on the far side of the Bay. In the foreground is the Marina with Fort Mason to the right and the Presidio to the left.

This impressive family mansion was constructed in 1905 by contractor J. A. Deneen for Eugene E. Schmitz, the accomplished violinist, composer and conductor of the Colombia Theater Orchestra. He was also the local musician union's leader, and he became the City's mayor under Abe Ruef's Union Labor party ticket in 1902. It was during his period as mayor of San Francisco that Eugene E. Schmitz moved to his newly built and expensive home on Vallejo street, today's Norway House, together with his thrifty and strong-willed wife, Julia. The house was located on the hill where the slope plunges towards the bay, overlooking a swamp soon to become an exposition site, and now called Marina District. Boss Ruef, an old fashioned extra-legal figure—the city boss—guided San Francisco into a era of graft and corruption, with franchises for the favored in the telephone system, street railways, water supply and real estate, as well as extortion related to liquor licenses.

People who suspected the existence of bribery usually took it for granted, as part of politics. Since late 1906 newspapers had asked how the mayor could build such an expensive home, insinuating that the contractor had helped him in exchange for special favors in contract work. After all, the cost of building the mansion was $30,000, when Schmitz' salary was only $6000 per year.

Mayor Schmitz was re-elected twice. He had all the different qualities demanded of a mayor and received broad support. After his handling of the City through the earthquake and fire of 1906, he enjoyed high prestige in San Francisco. In the reform movement during the rebuilding period in 1907, Schmitz and Ruef were charged with acceptance of bribes, extortion, and other corrupt acts. Investigation of the liquor licenses for the notorious French restaurants, landmarks in the City since the 1850s, showed bribery. A series of graft trials nailed Abe Ruef and ended Schmitz' mayoralty. Schmitz was sentenced to five years at San Quentin.

The conviction was overturned by a higher court and Schmitz was later elected to the city's

*Lars Christensen, Sandefjord, was engaged in the welfare of sailors. In 1941 he bought the house at 2501 Vallejo Street himself and gave it to the Norwegian sailors ashore in San Francisco. It became Norway House. The photo, dated 1941, is dedicated to P. R. Poulsson, Rex Sole of the Fish Club.*

*Norway House in San Francisco as it appears today. It was built for San Francisco's Mayor Eugene E. Schmitz in 1905. Photo Olaf T. Engvig.*

Board of Supervisors, a position he held for many years. He was, however, not able to keep his beautiful home at 2501 Vallejo.

In 1911 Schmitz had to borrow on the house to pay for lawyers during the graft prosecution. He was never able to pay back what he owed. In 1916 the home was sold by trustees to W. L. Waldron. Between 1923 and 1941 the house was sold eleven more times. In 1941 the California Pacific Title & Trust Co. was the owner and they formally sold it to Norway House Inc., on November 18th, 1942, according to the Assessor's Office records. By then the Norwegians had used the house for almost a year.

Nothing about Schmitz suggested a trade union man. He was the complete opposite of the Sailors Union's acrimonious, Norwegian-born Anders (Andrew) Furuseth. Moving to the newly built mansion with a superb view seemed a natural step for the congenial Mayor Eugene E. Schmitz and his Julia.

The address 2501 Vallejo Street belonged to one of the finest mansions in that area. This shingle house was modern for its time, with three-part windows, exposed beams, and the "flying buttress" arches at the roofline which were characteristic of the First Bay Tradition or Shingle Style, in vogue in the early years of this century. The house is painted natural dark brown with scrollwork ornaments in red, white and blue, matching the Norwegian and American flags flying from the front of the second floor of the building. The structure's many gables, the trimming and the church-like pointed arches expand the house and add great movement and life to its exterior.

Inside, the house has an impressive entrance, a flight of stairs leading to the different floors. It is decorated with solid wood paneling of mahogany. In spite of remodeling and adaptations over the years, it still has an old and exclusive appearance that must be very close to the original.

Usually the manager's residence has occupied the bottom floor, above the garage. Up the stairs is the main floor with a big and beautiful reading room and library with an open fireplace, exquisite wooden paneling, big windows in niches, and impressive wall and ceiling trimmings. This floor is used for conferences and for extended dining. Next to this room is the dining room, which easily seats thirty people, with similar wood paneling and another huge fireplace. Doors between these two rooms can be opened to enlarge the area for larger dinners or receptions. During Christmas parties, "17th of May," and other special events, some 150 persons can be accomodated. Adjacent to the dining room is a restaurant kitchen. On the next two floors up are the bedrooms.

The house was acquired to provide room and board for sailors who needed to stay in San Francisco for some time, as well as a news and information center with a reading room for sailors in port. Remodeling and furnishing became a problem as the Social Welfare Board for Seamen declined to equip anything but a reading room. Once again Lars Christensen helped out. Alfred Abrahamsen was given funds to acquire furniture and other necessities. He owned a dry-cleaning store downtown and knew lots of people who could help in getting everything set up, from linen to hardware. The rooms upstairs were rearranged for boarding purposes, and a new kitchen was equipped.

Consul Christensen even guaranteed the running expenses for the first six months. The seamen's center was opened before Christmas 1941. Alf A. Jacobsen became the manager. In November of 1942 it became "Norway House Inc.", with Abrahamsen, Myrvold, Svanevik, E. Petersen and Consul General Steckmest on the board. About the same time the government welfare board was more formally reorganized into *Sjømannsorganisasjonenes Velferdskomite*.

The upper two floors were planned for a capacity of eighteen lodgings from the start, but during the war and shortly after as many as thirty persons would be put up for the night in Norway House.

Norwegian sailors finally had their own home in this part of the world, a nice residence where they could retire from hard work and strain at sea during wartime, or from the wild life on shore if they had chosen to participate in the nightlife of San Francisco.

The waterfront, or the old "City front," was always important to the City. Most of the activities concerning travel and transport, communication and information were connected to the City front. It was the city's meeting place with the outside world. East Street—today's Embarcadero—ran next to many a fine ship. It had all the saloons sailors from the seven seas ever needed. It was the place where sailors easily could run into fellow countrymen of the Scandinavian Navy. The coastal steam schooner fleet was so full of Scandinavians that it got its nickname from them. San Francisco was the number one dream for sailors battering along in a convoy to Murmansk, in the dark Arctic winter, or standing watch in a blistering cold north Atlantic storm. This waterfront was also the right place to get a ship to the South Seas with its fine climate and sunny, easy life and lovely hula girls who fancied blond-haired and blue-eyed Scandinavians.

The Audiffred Building on East Street and Mission, from where Andrew Furuseth led the

Sailors' Union of the Pacific during the famous waterfront strike in 1901, had its Bulkhead Saloon on the corner. Adjacent to the Front and a short walk up California Street were the shipowners' and agents' offices; some of them are still there. On nearby streets and alleys were all the services any ship, crew or captain would need, be it a dentist, decorative artwork, provisions, or getting new crew members from a crimp or the union.

Andrew Furuseth's union was the first organization for sailors. It fought for sailors' rights not only in San Francisco but everywhere; it was at war with any American shipowner, master, crimp, boardinghouse runner, tailor or anyone taking unfair advantage of sailors. In this respect the Sailors' Union of the Pacific set a standard for treatment of sailors all over the world.

Places for refreshment were found all along East Street, but not many prostitutes. They were to be found a little further up in the City and were not only in business because of the sailors. They served local people, military personnel and all types of landlubbers as well. Romantic notions of old time sailors with a fine life in the tropics and girls in every port are, of course, only partly true. Sailors were workers in a transport system that brought them to major world ports. Those ports were of great military importance, usually rich, with a wide variety of activities and a lot of people coming and going.

Norway House was off to a flying start. Within this first year the seamen in San Francisco met with Crown Prince Olav and Crown Princess Märtha at 2501 Vallejo Street. Several ministers of the Norwegian Government came visiting, as well as prime minister Nygaardsvold. His Majesty's Medal of War was given to honored seamen. The house became a popular place not only to mariners. Ambassador Morgenstierne, Washington DC, recommended to the Norwegian

*His Royal Highness Crown Prince Olav, in general's uniform, to the left, and Crown Princess Märtha to the right, talking to Norwegian merchant sailors during their visit to Norway House in 1942.*

Foreign Ministry that the house be used for some of the activities of the Norwegian delegation to the United Nations Conference in 1945. It was also used for international receptions.

The Big Alliance, a union of 26 nations formed in January 1942, held a series of conferences during the war in an attempt to improve world government after the Second World War. President Roosevelt referred to the alliance the "United Nations." After the Dumbarton Oaks meeting in 1944, a new conference was scheduled for San Francisco in 1945.

For this conference, held during the last victorious weeks of the war in Europe, the allied nations sent delegations for the most part headed by their foreign minister. Many famous and important people from the different war administrations came to San Francisco with large delegations including specialists, typists and clerks. The City's hotel capacity was put to the test. Norway's delegation stayed in the Fairmont Hotel together withrepresentatives from five other nations, including the United States.

The newspapers took pride in printing the names of all delegates. Even in the smallest type it filled the better part of a whole page. The intermingling of world leaders and social contacts were popular material for the press. Different personalities, peculiar names and cultural differences were discussed. During the conference one column ended this way: "...Well.., then I want you to meet a great guy. Fellow named Trygve Halvdan Lie, Norway's Minister of Foreign Affairs."

That summer a new international organization was born in San Francisco on June 26, 1945. The event took place on the stage of the Veterans Auditorium, today's Herbst Theater, and the name of the organization was the United Nations. The 51 nations represented signed the charter. Trygve Lie was elected the United Nations' first Secretary General in London on February 1, 1946. Within a few months Trygve Lie was back visiting in San Francisco. On June 27, 1946 he entered his name into the Visitors Book of Norway House.

Norway House has a central location and became a convenient gathering place for state officials and other Norwegians visiting San Francisco. But from the start it was first and foremost a boardinghouse for sailors coming to San Francisco. They stayed from one single night up to half a year or more. Receptions, dinners and meetings were held on the second floor. In the late 1940's it became a tradition for members of the Norwegian colony in San Francisco to meet at Norway House for the annual 17th of May celebration and other social events.

The seamen were well respected during the war. The Norwegian merchant marine was considered important for the outcome of the war. One of the world's largest fleets of modern and fast vessels became a major factor in the supply service to the different war theaters, especially on the North Atlantic run. This was the lifeline providing fuel, ammunition and other war materiél and supplies for the war on the Eastern front, and for the buildup for the invasion that came in Normandy in 1944.

No nation had more tonnage per capita, and few nations lost more ships than Norway. The sailors were on the front lines all through the war. Norway House was used to decorate seamen with His Majesty The King's War Medal and other medals for distinguished service. A number of the high speed Norwegian cargo ships produced awesome achievements, making more than 50 round trips across the Atlantic by the summer of 1943. The motor tanker *Stiklestad*, a San Francisco-operated vessel until Nortraship was established, hauled gasoline and other fuel oil products from the first to the last day of the war. This one ship alone kept hundreds of military vehicles rolling and airplanes flying. The Norwegian merchant marine World War II saga is full of heroic incidents but also of tragedies and disasters.

*His Majesty King Haakon VII of Norway was the national symbol for all Norwegians fighting the war. This picture of the King was made in London during the war and presented to Norway House in San Francisco.*

Norway House Inc. was legally registered in Sacramento on November 24, 1942. Leif Svanevik of the Scandinavian Shipping Office had been acting manager. In 1942 Alf A. Jacobsen was hired and administrated the house until F. Johannessen took over as manager in 1946. He was followed by Otto F. Elmar in 1951.

The welfare committee supported the reading room and reading material. The board was also responsible for administrative tasks, and controlled a recreation fund for seamen. They arranged sightseeing and country tours as well as parties and other gatherings. During the war years many sailors stayed at Norway House recovering from rough sea duty or after having been hospitalized. As they slowly recovered they liked to do their part, as sailors often do, by running errands and giving a helping hand in the house.

The Norwegian Government Seamen's Service (NGSS) was established after the war, replacing the former welfare committee. F. Johan-

*The spacious living area and the adjacent dining room on the second floor of Norway House.* Photos Olaf T. Engvig.

nessen continued as manager, his salary now being provided by the *Velferdstjenesten for handelsflåten* (NGSS).

From 1947 on, the formal owner, Norway House Inc., were relieved of their administrative duties as long as the NGSS kept the premises in good condition for the benefit of Norwegian seamen. In 1951 the board gave NGSS the full financial and organizational responsibility for Norway House and all the employees were on the NGSS payroll. Sailors and other maritime people were supposed to be, and have always been, represented on the board of Norway House Inc. They have also been members of the Fish Club. Some of them are war sailors of the merchant marine. The Norwegian Consul General is the chairman and conducts the board meetings.

During the first five years after the war the Norwegian merchant marine, which suffered a fifty percent loss of tonnage, was rebuilt to pre-war size and continued to grow. It passed pre-war size, even with a state-enforced stop in the contracting of new ships built abroad. Most of the post-war tonnage was new first class cargo ships and tankers. The Norwegian Government Seamen's Service expanded as the number of Norwegian sailors increased. The house's original function as a boardinghouse and reading room was supplemented with services—the latest newspapers from Norway, films, books, materials for sport and games—to all Norwegian ships in port.

In 1954 Otto Elmar was followed by a new manager, Hans Berge. He did a great job in managing the house and developing new services. In 1959, Hans Berge was followed by Erling Settlie. Six years later John Pedersen was hired as a cook. In 1970 he became temporary manager.

The Norwegian Government Seamen's Service was closed down in 1990, and almost all foreign stations were abandoned. Norway House in San Francisco was owned locally and could not be sold. It was kept in operation as a joint venture with the Norwegian Maritime Direc-

torate that had taken over the remains of the Norwegian Government Seamen's Service. Under John Pedersen, Norway House pioneered new services to seamen like telephone calling cards and a video library for ships.

The post-war period up until the late 1970's was an era of great activity and expansion. The staff usually consisted of four persons employed by NGSS. Local helpers were hired for special events. By this time the were usually two managers, a couple, who ran the day-to-day operation of the house, servicing ships in port, arranging parties, sightseeing, gatherings and room service. A full-time cook provided meals for the guests and the staff, and a maid did all the housekeeping.

From the start during the war, there were four beds to a room, and one bath on each floor. At that time the maximum capacity was thirty guests. After the war the rooms were remodeled several times. Since the late 1980's there has been a suite on the top floor, and on the other floors there are three double rooms and one single room for rent at Norway House, all with bath and all the usual facilities including cable TV. At the beginning, Norway House had eight bedrooms all together on the third and fourth floors, and a billiard room on the corner of the third floor towards the front street. The administration offices for the Seamen's Service used to be on the third and fourth floors. The dining room and the large sitting room on the second floor have not been altered or remodeled.

The Norwegian Government Seamen's Service grew out of the need to aid seamen. It was started during the war, and was administrated by Nortraship. No professional group of Norwegians experienced more anxiety, suffered more or gave more lives for freedom than sailors.

After the war the head office of the Norwegian Government Seamen's Service was located in Oslo. It shipped out material to as many as fifty different stations all over the world, as well as many local stations in Norway. The stations would call on all ships when they reached port. The newspaper, library and film services were always important for seamen who had been at sea for weeks, often coming from strange and distant ports. Different games and sports equipment for activities on board could be ordered from the station. Some stations had bikes, skis and other sports items for free use.

"Sports Weeks" and a world-wide soccer tournament between ships of all nations was arranged each year. The soccer tournament was believed to be one of the world's largest. A thousand different ships—teams from some 70 nations—would participate in the annual tournament. Some results were impressive. One year, the winner of the men's 100 meter run, Class I, was clocked at 10.9 seconds, and the longest jump measured more than 6 meters. To cover all these sports events an annual sports magazine named *Sport of the Seven Seas* was published in English by The International Sports Committee for Seafarers (ISS), an instrument of ILO, the UN Labor Organization. It was distributed to all ships through Norway House and to other foreign stations.

*The team from M/S* Thorsgaard *became the winner of the 1969 Frisco Cup in soccer.*

The Information Department of the NGSS also issued the monthly magazine *Frivakt*, a Norwegian magazine for seamen. Most of the issues were shipped to all corners of the world, and ended up on board a ship, taken there by a local representative of NGSS. In San Francisco, of course, the local representation was Norway House. *Frivakt* was highly appreciated by the seamen who viewed it as their own magazine.

Going ashore has always been what a sailor wants to do when in port. Norway House conducted "Sightseeing in San Francisco" and "San Francisco by Night" and those excursions became very popular. In the 60's it included a visit to Haight Ashbury. A visit to North Beach with its vibrant nightlife was also popular. For ships with a long stay in port, Norway House arranged an evening ball, a shrimp or crab party, with a dance in which several ships' crews would participate. Girls were invited for a free evening in an international setting and had the opportunity to make friends with people from abroad. They would come from nearby hospitals, from the *au pair* colony, or from the Young Scandinavian Club. With the development of container shipping and the shorter stay in port, these social events came to an end in 1985.

Gradually services to ships in port declined. Ships' calls became less and less frequent. Their stay in port was often very short, and they often moved between different terminals. It became more efficient to serve a ship by making a parcel of what the crew wanted, sending it with the agent or a parcel service instead of showing up in person. Sometimes it was even hard to find any Norwegians on a ship flying the Norwegian flag. Telephone card service and video rental came to include ships that never came to San Francisco. These services were not profitable, and were finally closed down when they threatened the existence of Norway House itself.

The major function of Norway House is still to rent out rooms to seamen and maritime personnel. People working for the cruise lines make up a large part of the maritime personnel stopping over. Representatives of Norwegian ship companies are another group. In addition, state and department employees, Norwegian students, military personnel, musicians, artists, and business people also visit the seamen's home in San Francisco.

From time to time local organizations have used the premises for different gatherings. The Fish Club has some of their Thursday lunches at Norway House, and the War Sailors always gather at Norway House for their meetings and celebrations. Since 1942 it has been used by the Consulate General. A typical example of a joint venture was the Thursday luncheon December 14, 1961 to commemorate the fiftieth anniversary of Roald Amundsen's reaching the South Pole. Hosts were the Consul General, the Gjoa Foundation and the Fish Club, and a formal invitation was used. Among the guests were city officials, representatives from the maritime museum, shipping people, and Norwegian mariners.

The house that started its life as the residence for the mayor of San Francisco has over the years been visited by people from all strata, including consuls, ambassadors, a prime minister, other ministers and the first Secretary General to the United Nations. On several occasions it has also been visited by royalties.

Crown Prince Olav and Crown Princess Märtha visited Norway House during the war. Olav later came back twice as the King of Norway. His son, King Harald, lived at Norway House during the world championship for the one-ton sailboats in 1988, when he was still a Crown Prince.

Since Norway House became a sailors home it has first and foremost been their home, and always offered special rates for seamen.

Lingering on in Norway House are memories of the 1906 earthquake, and the even more turbulent times during the heydays of high society, mayoral parties and community fraud. Did Julia and her Mayor keep undetected secrets or hideaways in their home? Some time ago a manager was asked by an elderly neighbor if he ever had discovered hidden valuables in the walls or in secret compartments at Norway House during later renovations? Wild stories would, however, surface if the walls of Norway House could talk.

# Norway House, Seamen's Home

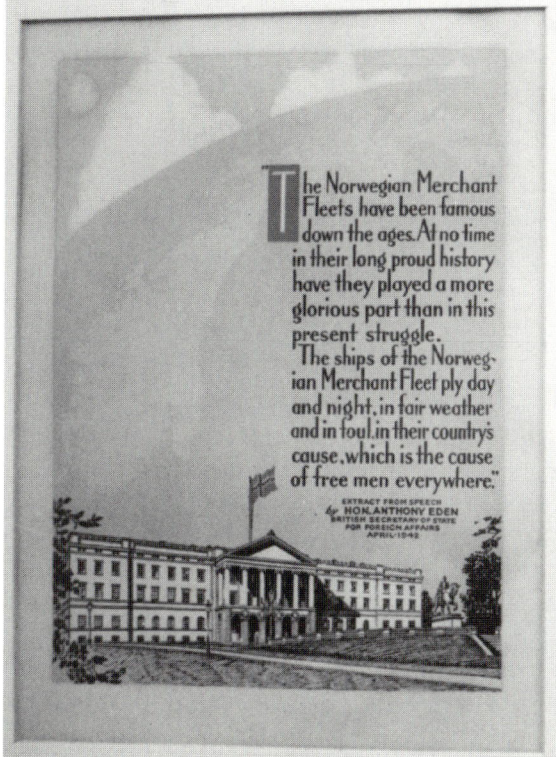

*Typical and important icons from the troubled years of World War II. They have been on the wall of the living room at Norway House ever since that time.*

CHAPTER VI

# The Norwegian Seamen's Church

A new Mission in San Francisco. It sounds so natural, and still, in 1950 it was a little strange. A reminder of times long gone. Of Spanish missionaries and old Indians, of mission fields in India, and poor tribes in Africa and Madagascar. Yet, the Seamen's Mission is a true mission, like any other mission, a timeless ordeal, to follow the orders of Christ. It has been an active force for almost two thousand years, since the first apostles set out from Palestine. Two years after the United Nations was born in San Francisco, the Norwegian Seamen's Mission established a church committee in the City. This committee's main goal was to start a mission for seamen in this major world port.

This decision didn't mean that Norwegian sailors were left alone in the Bay Area until after the Second World War. Back in the days of the Gold Rush, missionary activities had been helping sailors of every nation entering port. In 1890 a Scandinavian Lutheran Seamen's Mission was established to serve the sailors from this part of Europe. Of course, parish churches usually welcome sailors, and a couple of them were established for and by people from Scandinavia. The Salvation Army also had a special unit close to the Ferry Building called "The Salvation Army's Scandinavian Corps." They always helped seamen.

The usual procedure to establish a local church was for the seaman, or any other group of people for that matter, to take the initiative. A true missionary activity, on the other hand, would be to go out and address the sailors at the place they were staying, on board the ship or on shore.

A Norwegian Seamen's Church and Mission in San Francisco had been an old dream that in 1934 led to the establishment of the women's organization called *Sjømannsmisjonsforeningen Tabita*. Though only about 25 members, they worked very well together and by the end of World War II they had raised some $6,000. Obviously this group of ladies needed more support

*2454 Hyde Street just after it was converted into a Norwegian Seamen's Mission in 1951, with the old cable car rattling by. Photo courtesy Seamen's Church.*

75

to realize their dream. By the late 1940's, *Tabita* had managed to involve the Norwegian Seamen's Mission, eager individuals, and different clubs and shipping interests in the City. Many sailors were in San Francisco at any time. The number of Norwegian ships calling into the port was increasing. The Norwegian Seamen's Union, as well as a shipping office, was signing on about a thousand persons a year on Scandinavian ships. Norway House was in service to house seamen ashore and see to their welfare.

A Seamen's Church was established on Barton Hill in San Pedro during the war. Consul Lars Christensen bought a small church in 1941, and it became the first church of the Norwegian Seamen's Mission to California. The church was a really tiny one, and could not function properly as a mission. In 1950-51 the Seamen's Mission Headquarters in Norway build a new and proper station in San Pedro to serve the needs of sailors in port. The church in San Pedro was also called upon to do missionary expeditions to San Francisco in the 1940's—"to spend some time on this work-field." This system didn't function well.

In 1947, Seamen's Mission representatives from Norway had a formal meeting with appointed local representatives in San Francisco and formed a church committee, "the main goal being to erect a missionary station." A. H. Thorsen became the committee's secretary. He had been the last minister of the Synod's old Norwegian-American Scandinavian Lutheran Seamen's Mission at Mission Street #9, which was closed down in 1946. In a joint effort $20,000 was collected, including the value of a vacant lot uptown on Fell Street, bought in 1948 by the committee. This lot was later used as part payment for refitting of the new station closer to the harbor.

Birger Mathisen, the assistant pastor in San Pedro, was offered and accepted the head of the new station in San Francisco. He came with his family before Christmas of 1950. He had to borrow churches for his services, as he had no church of his own. The Norwegian Lutheran Church at Mission Dolores and 19th was the church mostly used while the hunt for a new church took place.

Pastor Mathisen used the best part of spring 1951 to walk up and down the streets of San Francisco looking at properties for sale. Captain Aslak Jensen, chairman of the committee, went with him when he found a property of interest. The committee favored the area near Russian Hill, as access to the harbor was good. This was a popular residential area, and few houses were for sale. Finally the committee settled for the property on 2454 Hyde Street as the most suitable. But it was an expensive home, far beyond the means of the committee.

Visitors from the Headquarters in Norway liked the property and its fine view, and promised to support the project. The final offer was $47,500, the owner accepted, and the deal was closed after all necessary permissions were given by the City to use the house for its new purpose. The Norwegian Seamen's Mission had found a home in San Francisco.

Then conflict broke out. The neighbors' organizations decided they did not want a mission and sailors coming into their residential area. They held protest hearings and engaged a lawyer to throw the Norwegians out of their building. There was little they could do as all formalities had been observed.

The problem with the mortgage was still unsolved, when some of the no-name Fish Club members insisted on a meeting with the pastor. They asked quite frankly to see the budget. When they got the numbers, they started working, assuring Pastor Mathisen they knew nothing about running a Seamen's Church, but had experience in financing. They immediately stated that the high interest loan of $22,000 the pastor had been pursuing was not the way. "It is too much! We will get a loan of 15,000 dollars," they said, "and the rest we will try to get from elsewhere. Give us thirty days!" After this period, the three men returned with $6,000 in cash, which they had collected among friends in the shipping business, and two private loans for the rest of the amount, on extremely good terms, with a 2.5%

interest. If possible, the loan was to be paid back over a five-year period. Today we can reveal that those three men were Aslak Jensen, Christian Blom and Jens Feragen.

Furniture, items for the station and other artifacts were donated or collected through separate campaigns. Contract work on conversion of the building had to be paid for. Well known ship companies and shipping individuals were the good Samaritans behind several donations as well as the "loans" needed for the Seamen's Church to get started.

It is a superb location and it has a grand view of San Francisco and the Bay. The house is on the upper corner lot of Francisco and Hyde Streets, one block above Bay Street, where the cable cars climb up the steep hill of Hyde. From the grand terrace there is a breathtaking view of the area between San Francisco's two great bridges. To the left is the Golden Gate Bridge, with the Pacific Ocean behind. Marin Headlands, Sausalito and Tiburon are on the far side of the Bay. The Presidio, Marina and the dome of the Palace of Fine Arts are distinct landmarks on the City side. The St. Francis Yacht Club is easily spotted right underneath the south tower of the Golden Gate Bridge. There are Fort Mason and North Point, and closer still, Aquatic Park. Straight down the street, at the bottom of the hill, is Hyde Street Pier with all the historic ships. It is possible to observe people walking the deck of the full-rigged ship *Balclutha*. Straight out into the Bay is Alcatraz Island.

Big merchant ships entering the Bay through the Golden Gate will reveal their destination by turning after passing Alcatraz. If they are headed for San Francisco, Oakland, or Richmond or they are going towards Carquinez Strait and the ports beyond, the people at the Norwegian Seamen's Church will know. Norway House sometimes used to call over to get this crucial information, to know where to intercept the ship. Looking to the right there is Treasure Island with the Coast Guard Station and the Bay Bridge closing off the view on that side. Fisherman's Wharf and the old City front and all the piers from Hyde Street almost to the Ferry Building are within short range of the Church.

Visitors not interested in piers and big ships get their amusement from watching Hyde Street, which is always full of tourists taking pictures, climbing up the sidewalks, or hanging from the cable cars. This last sight seems to be timeless.

The original building permit for this property was issued to F. Dudley Tait on June 9th, 1914. His permit was to build a three-story structure with basement, three lavatories and fourteen rooms. The architect was Ralph Warner Hart, who was a very good architect, and the builder H. A. Klyce. Mr. Tait had bought the lot from J. O. Greenwood. The estimated cost was almost $17,000, and the proposed size of the building 40 feet by 79 feet. It was to be used as a residence for one family. Today we know that all those involved did a very good job, creating a beautiful and strong building. It has survived the evolution of architectural design, earthquakes and the "teeth of time" very well.

The home at 2454 Hyde changed owners several times over the next thirty years, but it was not until 1951 that the building changed from being a single-family house. When Karen Erika Mathisen, the pastor's wife, saw the house for the first time, it still had an enormous double set of stairs from the hall leading up to the top floor, and even a separate ladies powder room next to the stairs. This room is today the pastor's office. The whole top floor was converted into a nice flat for the pastor and his family, new and modern for its time. The previous owners had a large bedroom upstairs facing the Bay. It became the pastor's living room. The old-fashioned bathroom finally became a TV room, regretted by people knowing how beautiful an old bathroom could be. The stairs from the main floor runs in the back.

The main floor lost its old-fashioned hall appearance with the stairs. The livingroom facing the Bay is still much the same, with its fireplace and big windows. But the part closest to the kitchen in the back has been altered a few times, first into a small chapel, and later when the

*The seamen's reading room at the time the Mission opened. Photo courtesy Seamen's Church.*

chapel was moved downstairs, it became a library and reading room with a billiard table. Today it also has a kiosk. The entrance area and hall function as a reception area, and are used for different purposes. A lot of modernizing, in 1951 considered a necessary face-lifting, took place. Basic parts of the house remained untouched. Early in the 50's, the room downstairs, that was later to become a chapel, was just a large playroom for children, with a garage underneath.

When the Norwegian Seamen's Church in San Francisco was established, the church Committee was dissolved. The enterprise was now the responsiblity of the board of trustees. As for Norway House, the Norwegian Seamen's Church was established as a formal body incorporated within the laws of the State of California. New by-laws were adapted from St. Olav's Church in San Pedro. Articles of Incorporation were filed with Secretary Jordan in Sacramento on March 29, 1949.

Converting the new house into a Seamen's Mission with a church was quite a challenge, and it became a very busy time for all persons involved. The Grant Deed is dated June 25, 1951. On July 17, all formal papers were approved, and the adapting and remodeling started the next day. Less than three months later, furniture, equipment and supplies for the new station arrived with the Fred Olsen Line from Norway. By a coincidence it was brought on the fine Norwegian liner with the proud American name *Abraham Lincoln*. The ship arrived at San Francisco on October 12. For once, longshoremen were met not only on board, but outside the harbor, helping to carry furniture and equipment to 2454 Hyde. Freight, handling, landing and custom charges were all free. Late the next day everything was in place. The following day was October 14, also named Columbus Day; it was scheduled to be the inauguration day for the Norwegian Seamen's Church of San Francisco, making the following day the first ordinary day of work at this mission.

A procession of six ministers participated in the inauguration ceremony. Aslak Jensen, chairman of the board, gave the key to Pastor Mathisen, several speeches were given, and telegrams were received from His Majesty, King Haakon of Norway, from the Government of Norway signed by foreign minister Halvard Lange, and many more. The event was given publicity through several newspapers. Later that day a reception was held for about sixty specially invited Americans and Norwegians. San Francisco's Mayor Elmer Robinson managed to leave the Columbus Day Celebration. He made a fine speech in which he highlighted the Norwegians as a seafaring people; they came on sailing ships and did much to develop San Francisco not only commercially and culturally but also spiritually—as this Church proves, he said. He added that the Norwegians were of good breed. During his thirty years of practice as a lawyer and judge, he couldn't remember one incident with Norwegians involved. "You are good law-obeying citizens and I wish you all the best. You should feel at home in San Francisco," said a smiling mayor, as he wished each one a welcome to the City.

Three Norwegian ships had arrived in port during the day, and the seamen participated in the grand opening feast that same evening with much good food, cakes and coffee, more telegrams, more speeches and entertainment.

The Seamen's Church proved an immediate success. Sailors felt at home, they found recent issues of their local newspapers from Norway, met old friends, wrote letters and got personal help and comfort when needed. Part of the downstairs area soon became a locker room for sailors wanting to leave trunks and suitcases with valuables ashore. People sailing in the Pacific and to the Far East were always very far away from home and wanted to keep things in San Francisco until the time came to go home to Norway. Even the old system of keeping money for the sailors was still in service. Seamen would leave considerable amounts with the Church until they returned home. This service was closed during the 1960's as expanded banking services were developed in Norway to handle the sailors' savings. The Church cashbook for seamen was kept up until 1966.

With many ships in port there was lots of work to do, and the pastor was more or less left alone with the work. At least he was the only person employed. Like some presidents of the United States, the pastor had a helping hand in the devoted work by his spouse. This effort did not show up in official records or on any payroll. Sailors stopping over often became good helpers and assistants. One of them, Øyvind Laundal, became the first assigned assistant to the pastor.

It was needed. Several ships could arrive in port the same day, and it happened that as many as 230 persons gathered on the premises. It was a higher number than anyone had hoped for, and really too many at one time. The house was after all designed to be a one-family home. The board

*Serving seamen in port has always been an important part of the duty of the Seamen's Church. Photo courtesy Seamen's Church.*

feared it might collapse and immediately started plans to reinforce the structure.

The first period was, of course, a time of improvisation and preliminary adjustments. The pastor and the board showed great skill in this respect. If major tasks were to be accomplished, it happened that a whole ship's crew would get a day working on the church instead of on their ship. Captains, first mates, bosun and crew, steward and cooks would be happy to help out. The cooks on some ships calling regularly into San Francisco would provide the Church with fresh *Wienerbrød* —Danish pastry— for the visitors.

People from the colony would help in finding solutions to difficult matters. The ladies club *Tabita* was an active and close supporter of the Church and the pastor's family. Visitors other than sailors stopped by to say hello. On the "17th of May Celebration" in 1952, Norwegian-born Colonel Bernt Balchen showed up without notice and gave a nice speech. He piloted captain Richard E. Byrd's plane, the first to fly to the South Pole. The next year Bishop Johannes Smemo, Prime minister Oscar Torp and Ambassador Morgenstierne came visiting from Norway.

When Christian Blom and Fredrik Klaveness met Pastor Mathisen for the very first time; he was in overalls, busy moving cement, and making the foundation for the new station in San Pedro. Blom got the impression that construction of churches was the pastor's great hobby. Indeed, it was.

Five years after the inauguration of the first one in San Francisco he started all over again, with overalls and shovel. With the help of many voluntary hands from ships and ashore, the pastor dug out the space downstairs where the children's playroom used to be, to make a new church. He got steel beams from Bethlehem Steel with able assistance from Captain Arne Kiønig. Contractor Andrew Berwick, who did the work in 1951, put in the beams with sailors to assist along with the professional people from Bethlehem Steel. Before long the new church was on safe ground.

It was in 1956 that the chapel moved downstairs. That gave the station a larger permanent chapel, with a proper entrance directly from the street, and more room upstairs next to the reception area. The local colony was impressed. For his sixtieth year anniversary, Christian Blom suggested that he, Fredrik and Dag Klaveness give the new chapel an altar-piece, a beautiful wood-carving, crafted by the famous Norwegian artist Dagfin Werenskiold. This was only one of the many private donations the Church has received over the years.

Birger Mathisen was called to the Norwegian Seamen's Church in London in 1958 and moved back to Europe. Before he left, like the chief mate of a fine ship, he saw that every bit of the station was in perfect condition. The roof, pipes and chimneys, scuppers, outside woodwork and terrace were reviewed and approved. An overall repair of the building had taken place in 1956 when the chapel was moved. The original loans were all down to zero by then.

In 1960 the Church got the revenue left after the Squaw Valley Olympics, and the next year barber Anton Lie left a considerable sum to the Church. Mrs. Wilson Meyer is another of the testamentary benefactors. Funds have been established in the Church with the donors' names. Chimes, a new robe for the priest, old icons, even a church ship model of the bark *Augusta* have been given to the Church. A Hammond organ and pianist Tora Bratt Buchanan's grand piano were donated to be used upstairs in the living room.

His Majesty King Olav V visited the Seamen's Church on May 1, 1968, the Norwegian Labor Day. He was received at the entrance by Pastor Dagfinn Kvale and the head of the board, Christian Blom. His Majesty was escorted to the altar. The congregation sang the Royal Anthem. The King responded in a spontaneous speech that he knew how important the Seamen's Church was to people away from their native country, and what it meant as a gathering place and for the feeling of togetherness among fellow countrymen. He was convinced that the Church in San Francisco filled these spiritual and material needs. He hoped that the place would continue to be one of joy and benefit to all that came to San Francisco. Afterward the King and his company went upstairs and greeted the corps of Scandinavian consul generals, the pastor's family, sailors and students. Three hundred people from the local community were gathered at the Seamen's Mission. The highlight of the King's visit was a grand luncheon given by the city of San Francisco in the City Hall Rotunda, with Mayor Joseph L. Alioto as the host. Pastor Kvale gave the invocation.

Seven years later King Olav returned to San Francisco and the Seamen's Church. It happened during the celebration of the 150th anniversary of Norwegian emigration to America—the commemoration of the "sloop-people" back in 1825. They sailed across the Atlantic in the small sloop *Restauration* to settle in the New World. This royal visit had a form similar to the prior one. Pastor Ole Elias Holck was the host. King Olav made his speech upstairs in the reading room. The night before a formal dinner was hosted for the King on board the cruise ship *Royal Viking Sky*. The revenue from this event was given to the Seamen's Church.

H. R. H. Crown Prince Harald came to the Seamen's Church on August 21, 1988. During this stay he unveiled a bust of his grandfather King Haakon VII of Norway.

King Olav first visited when Dagfinn Kvale was pastor. He succeeded Pastor Worren in 1966 and stayed in San Francisco until 1975, but not long enough to meet King Olav on his second visit in October of that year. Pastor Ole Elias Holck had arrived prior to His Majesty's visit. Holck stayed for four years. He was relieved by Pastor Jacob Frode Knudsen who lived in San Francisco from 1979 until 1984; Pastor John Arne Lund covered the rest of the years until 1990. When Pastor Jon Albert Ihlebæk came in 1990, it was obvious that the old system of sailors' welfare belonged to the past. The three last pastors before Ihlebæk saw the distinct decline of ships and Norwegian sailors coming into the Bay, as Norwegian tonnage was sold or transferred to flags of convenience. Establishment of a Norwegian International Ship Register, NIS, did not serve to bring the sailors back.

*The Norwegian youngsters met with Crown Prince Harald. Photo courtesy Seamen's Church.*

*In 1988 Crown Prince Harald visited the Seamen's Church and unveiled a bust of his grandfather King Haakon VII.*

One of the sparks of innovation in international shipping was the war between Israel and Egypt. This led to the closing of the Suez Canal, and mammoth tankers were needed to carry oil around Africa's Cape. During the rest of the 70's and most of the 80's world shipping changed on all levels. Many a fine old shipping house went insolvent. The Norwegian Government Seamen Service closed, but no major changes occurred at the Seamen's Church. Pastor Jon Albert Ihlebæk came to San Francisco in 1990. A year later the Church celebrated its fortieth anniversary. Four decades had passed since the inauguration of 2454 Hyde Street. Many developments had occurred in the work of the seamen and their way of life at sea.

When the mission started in 1951, sailors had to stay on board for two years before they could get a free ticket home. Sailing was a traditional way of life. Cargo ships would stay in port for many days. Everything was unloaded by manpower with winches or cranes. Major ports had thousands of longshoremen employed. Even if a 15,000 ton tanker could be filled to the mark in fewer than twelve hours, life was slow going. A good-sized tanker of 19,000 tons would carry a crew of nearly fifty. Six ABs, the bosun and carpenter would maintain the ship, only occasionally being called to the bridge for other duty. Those ships had almost the same number of mess halls as S/S *Norway* has today, every one with its own personnel. Reading was the main occupation off watch; there were no movies or other entertainment, very much as in the old days of sailing life in the doldrums. Letters could take months to reach the ship. Latest newspapers could often be two months old, except when the ship came to a port with a Seamen's Church or the Government Seamen Services.

Before the end of the period 1951-1991, crew size was down by half and the ship's size was considerably larger. Large tankers were twenty to thirty times the size of the average tanker of the early 1950's The ships sailed faster, the stay in port was shorter, the crew worked harder and had achieved many of the same benefits that people on land have. There were current letters and newspapers, there were telephones and entertainment. They shared one common cafeteria, each had his own cabin with shower, spent a short period on board, and had a free ticket home.

The seamen of today are used to bigger units, machine handling of containers, and sometimes much shifting of berths in harbor with bow-thrusters eliminating the need for tugs, as well as easy line handling—no more wet and lead-heavy nine-inch manila lines. With short terminal stays, the crew must stay on board. With oil products, containers and other dry cargo shipments like cars, ore or chemicals, it is now a matter only of hours before a ship has unloaded its cargo, loaded another, and is off for a new port, sometimes halfway around the world. Even the huge passenger-carrying cruise ships are operated this way. Tourists are just another part of an industrial production in which the ship is the operative word and the sailing crew are employees.

It is impressive to see how well the Seamen's Mission has adapted to this constantly changing environment. Even today the Norwegian Seamen's Church manages to do a lot for the sailors. The need for spiritual guidance and support remains the same. This is one important reason why the Seamen's Mission will always be needed in port.

Much happened in Norway as in the rest of the world during the 1950's that affected the church's history. It was a period of building and expansion. Scandinavian ships kept coming to San Francisco. The rate of rebuilding Norway's merchant marine after the war was astonishing. The fleet passed pre-war numbers and size less than six years after the war ended, and continued its rapid increase. Only the United States and Great Britain had more tonnage than Norway. This small nation of fewer than four million was a merchant marine giant.

Most of the world's transportation is by sea. Because 75% of the world's surface is water, a floating hull is the best way to move large quantities of goods around the world, no matter what the commodities might be: fuel (solid or liquid), ore, other raw material, fertilizer, food or automobiles—even the major bulk of furniture and clothing is sent by sea. By 1957 Norway was the foreign nation with the most ship arrivals into the port of San Francisco and the Bay.

The Norwegians' ships showed off. Most of them were new tonnage, swift, clean, tidy and well kept, often painted in light colors despite the usual appearance of rust stripes and stains from rugged sea voyages. In the days before sandblasting and modern two-component coating, the first rust would start showing after a few days at sea. The maintenance crew would be over the side as soon as the ship was berthed, followed by the watchmen when the voyage had ended. The deck gang would be picking, scraping and painting any bad spots.

The berths in San Francisco, the Bay Area and the inland waterway system in the Delta are unique, unlike most major ports of the world. Even the enormous port of Rotterdam is easier

*The Church as it appears today with the beautiful wood-carved altarpiece and the traditional Norwegian church ship. Photo Olaf T. Engvig.*

for a Seamen's Mission to work than San Francisco's. There are great distances within the different harbor areas, several bridges and up to thirty miles of traveling inland to meet a ship. Under such circumstances, sailors need time and help to get to the Church. If San Francisco is the first American port of call, the ship's crew might have seen twenty or thirty days of sailing since its last port in the Far East. Nowadays it also happens that the next port may be in Europe. Going through the Panama Canal only means a short day of travel inland.

Transportation became a primary concern for the Church. The first pastor used a station wagon when seeing ships, delivering newspapers and inviting the crew. Sailors had problems getting to Church because the car was too small.

After 1960 the Seamen's Church got a new car and then a bus. The Fish Club decided that it was the only way of getting a whole crew to the Church. With the aid of several shipping lines the Fish Club bought a beautiful big bus of 38 seats and gave it to the Church. The first trip it made was when the pastor came over to Jack's on Sacramento, loaded up the whole luncheon party, and took them over to the Seamen's Church for coffee. It was a fine introductory test ride and a nice way for the Church to say thank you for the bus, but some found it a disgrace that pastor Worren himself should have to do this kind of work, driving around the harbor and taking sailors to and from their ships. They didn't know that the good pastor in his youth used to be a professional bus driver for *Sogn and Fjordane Fylkesbilar A/S*, taking American tourists along the hair-pin turns and "pig-tail-turns" on the difficult, old and narrow roads to Geiranger and other tourist spots in Western Norway. It was the money Worren earned as a bus driver that paid for his studies to become a pastor. He was happy to practice his old skills in hilly San Francisco in getting seamen to the Church.

During the 60's the Church also had a smaller fifteen-seat bus. The Mission was rather well equipped with personnel in those days. It took an active part in the sports events and football games that the *Velferden* at Norway House were arranging. In San Francisco there was always a first-class relationship between these two Norwegian organizations: the state-operated Seamen's Service (NGSS), and the old voluntary organization *Norsk Sjømannsmisjon* that had to rely on fundraising and private gifts. The soccer games between ships were the most popular of all sports events. The ship was the seamen's miniature nation and patriotism was often great. For many sailors it was important to be on the ship with the best football team.

During one period there even existed a *land(s)lag* or shore-based team, called "Frisc," pronounced as the Norwegian word *Frisk*, a good team name. It became active when a ship did not have another ship in port to compete with. Some of the pastors were devoted football players. To see your minister on the team was quite common in those days. Many sailors called them the football priests. Pastor Dagfinn Kvale was one of the more famous, as was Torsten Malmestrøm, a Swedish pastor working with the Church.

San Francisco seems to have been very lucky in getting pastors and other staff members well fitted for these special mission duties. Pastors driving buses, building churches and playing soccer, what more could sailors ask for? Except, maybe, meeting a good friend

*Photo previous page: People from the local community and the Fish Club help pastor Ihlebæk with voluntary work in keeping the premises nice and tidy.*

*This page: Sigvor Hamre Thornton, also called Mor Norge, has been a strong supporter of the Church for more than forty years.*

from the past. This happened at the Church, when two old friends met in the gathering room, their hair gray, both still sailing. Their last time together was on a liferaft, after their ship had been sunk during the war. They made it through the war and finally met again at the Seamen's Church in San Francisco. Both surprised that the other one was alive and sailing, they had a lot to catch up with since that last day on the raft in the middle of the war.

Pastor Ihlebæk moved to Norway in 1993, to a new position in Fredrikstad. Birger Mathisen, retired Dean of the Cathedral in Oslo, came back to San Francisco to assist his old station over the winter, awaiting the new minister Dagfinn Kvale. He arrived in the spring of 1994, another pastor who returned to his old Seamen's Church. It seems hard to forget San Francisco.

In addition to sports, which always played an important part for a ship's crew on shore, the Church also took sailors on sightseeing and shopping trips. Ex-sailor Rolf Jamvold had a property in Burlingame where the Church took sailors for a day at the swimming pool, with a barbecue and music.

Schedules for the station have changed some over the years, but the basic framework has always been the same. On Sundays it was church service, just like home. Every day the mission is open from around noon until late evening. Sailors and others would come in for a chat, a cup of coffee and waffles, and questions, or they would write letters and postcards or read the latest newspapers from their home towns, new magazines or books. Talking and exchanging information were always important parts of any sailor's life, whether it was with the crew from another ship, the Church staff, or local visitors.

Twice a week a feast would be arranged, starting at 8 p.m. During Christmas, Easter, the 17th. of May Celebration, *vår-fest* and Bazaar, there would be much activity around the Church. *Ad hoc* gatherings or fiestas would also take place if some ships in the harbor called for it, or if a prominent person was visiting. The Church has conducted special evenings and gatherings for students, *au pairs* and other groups of young Norwegians. During one period some couples from the colony arranged parties at home and private sightseeing for sailors, assisted by the Church.

For the Seamen's Church, the ship visit was the prime target. As soon as a ship arrived in port the Church would try to be there as the missionary service it is. Meeting the ship was always considered the single most important event. In San Francisco, Norway House and the Seamen's Church would try to cooperate to the mutual benefit of both parties. On many occasions several ships entered the harbor and were cleared about the same time.

For many years San Francisco sailors had an extra helper. He was the minister of the Baptist Seamen's Mission, established in 1946-47, and the pastor's name was Thorbjørn Olsen, or "Vaffel-Olsen," as he was called locally. Vaffel-Olsen was a devoted man that met all the ships he could, personally visiting the crew, bringing waffles, newspapers and information. He was on good terms with many a salty dog that didn't mind much what the first name of the church was, as long as it served the purpose. Pastor Olsen made a good name for himself among sailors. Many of the old sailors are still out there today on ferries and coastal steamers back in Norway. If you tell them about San Francisco, they will start inquiring about Vaffel Olsen to see if you really know the place and its waterfront.

The Norwegian colony in San Francisco supporting this mission understands that the Church is there for the sailors, as do, of course, the devoted people running the station. The number of sailors changes over the years. But sailors are always out there. That is why the Seamen's Church in San Francisco is such a nice place to be. The colony is its backbone.

The Norwegian Seamen's Mission to San Francisco has become the primary church for the Norwegian colony in the City. They see the Church as a good substitute for the old congregational church they left in Norway. The colony uses the Church for all types of services from baptisms, confirmations, and marriages to memorial gatherings.

The Seamen's Church has been the Fish Club's fondest devotion since the Church was founded in 1951. It is still a close concern of the Club. The guardian angel of the Seamen's Church, however, is a small women's group called *Tabita*. This women's organization was started on April 17, 1934, long before the Seamen's Church was born. For many years the group was headed by Mrs. A. H. Thorsen, wife of the minister to the Scandinavian Lutheran Seamen's Mission. *Tabita* is keen on keeping a Norwegian church in San Francisco, a cultural and spiritual center, that would serve the colony as well as sailors and other visiting Norwegians.

*Tabita* meets regularly once a month for a luncheon. The ladies of *Tabita* do knitting, embroidery and other traditional Norwegian handicraft. Occasionally there will be a lecturer or some other type of cultural or spiritual participation during the meetings. *Tabita* arranges an annual fundraising event in the spring, and the great Bazaar in the Church in November.

Well-known brands of food from Norway, not on sale in the United States, are annual favorite items to be sold, along with chocolate, magazines and other specially imported items. *Tabita* will sell hand knittings and other traditional handmade crafts, and there will be a raffle and an auction of donated major items, from a TV set to cruise tickets. The *Tabita* Bazaar is a great annual event of the community and the Seamen's Church. It produces good revenue for the Church. In 1934 it produced $150. In 1985 it produced $11,000. In 1992 revenues were more than twice as much, and in 1993 it was $30,000, a reflection of the continuing popularity of the event.

The Norwegian Seamen's Church of San Francisco is the spiritual center and a prime meeting place for all Norwegians in the area. The mission has been the bridge of contact for sailors, residing countrymen and short-time visitors. Today it is even a well-established "tourist drop-in." When tourists spot the Scandinavian flags on Hyde street, they enter the building ready to speak a Scandinavian language again.

Since the days of sail, shipping people and shipowners always believed that a Seamen's Mission was to the benefit of the crew of any ship, helping this small and intimate social system to function better and to achieve a safer and better voyage. Officers and masters always look forward to a port with a Seamen's Mission. Dropping by the Church on shore leave meant seeing other Norwegians, perhaps old friends from other ships, reading the latest papers and asking for news from your local community in Norway. The sailing people, the shipowners and the shipping industry helps and supports *Tabita* and the Church.

From its beginning in 1951, three members of the Fish Club have served as presidents of the Norwegian Seamen's Church in San Francisco: Captain Aslak Jensen (1951-59), Shipowner Christian Blom (1959-82) and Captain Ole Kalve (1982-). They have been, and still are, a close and reliable support for the local field workers and the station in San Francisco as well as for the Norwegian Seamen's Mission Headquarters in Bergen, Norway.

The Norwegian Seamen's Mission, founded in 1864, has recently adopted a new name. The organization's name is today *Den norske sjømannsmisjon / Norsk kirke i utlandet*, which is translated "The Norwegian Seamen's Mission / Church of Norway Abroad."

# The Norwegian Seamen's Church

*Forty-five years and little has changed on Hyde Street. Even the age-old cable car keeps running by. This property has become the main gathering place for Norwegians in the San Francisco Bay Area.*  *Photo Olaf T. Engvig.*

## SHIPPING AND CULTURE

*Norway's contingent to the Olympic Winter Games in Squaw Valley 1960 on opening day. Photo by courtesy of Johan Brun.*

CHAPTER VII

# 1960 Squaw Valley Olympics

*To be a speed skater is not a life profession. It belongs to the youth, one day it is over. What then? "You could be a leader," said my coach, "and continue to be boss for new youth," or he would say, "Years from now you walk into our union office and ask for a ticket to a race. When you have left, the board members would ask me, 'Who was that?' Then I'll say, 'Don't you remember Knut Johannesen, or Kuppern, he was great a couple of years ago. He was very good once!'"*

*Being a world champion, and the God of that time, is soon forgotten.*

Translation of Knut Johannesen; *Fra Kampen til Squaw Valley*, Oslo 1960, p.160.

Squaw Valley's Winter Olympics is history. But in 1960 it was a major international event. For the Fish Club of San Francisco, Squaw Valley became the most enjoyable sporting event in the Club's history. Participating Norwegian athletes remember Squaw Valley as the most memorable competition of their careers; they have even formed a Squaw Valley Club in Norway that meets regularly.

Fifteen years after the Second World War, the world was riding a wave of optimism, good will, prosperity and happiness. Young and old, east and west, most people felt the United Nations would resolve conflicts. There were few concerns. Pollution, environmental balance, ozone holes, global warming, general depression, homelessness, migration, education problems, hostility and violence were not issues. The United States was the world's leading nation, a country everyone wanted to visit, see and experience, and for the first time in years the Americans were hosting the Olympic games.

When the International Olympic Committee (IOC) selected Squaw Valley for the Eighth Olympic Winter Games, few outside Lake Tahoe had ever heard of the place. Most maps weren't helpful. It was a remote, unpopulated little valley in the "Californian Alps." In the 1930's, a skier, Whyne Poulsen had bought 1200 acres of land in the Sierras to develop a ski resort. In 1948 he teamed with Alexander C. Cushing to push the project ahead.

It was Alex Cushing's great talent for publicity and organization that persuaded the International Olympic Committee to vote for Squaw Valley. Cushing convinced the IOC in Switzerland that Squaw Valley was much more than the world's first chair lift, two pony tows and fine downhill tracks. What was missing, Cushing conjured up. His impressive model of Squaw Valley suggested a fine jumping hill cleverly outlined as if it were there. Skating arenas shown appeared to be in place. The IOC was impressed. Alex Cushing gambled and won.

Squaw Valley has indeed a magnificent location in the high Sierras northwest of Lake Tahoe, 200 miles northeast of San Francisco, at an elevation of about 7000 feet. This little valley is surrounded by mountains rising another 3000 feet. In February it is usually covered with snow,

89

*A high Sierra overview of Squaw Valley. Photo Johan Brun.*

basking in spring temperatures, much like the mountain ranges of Northern Europe in April.

After IOC's selection of California as host for the Games, the Americans set about creating an unparalleled Olympic setting. There were plans and drawings, boards, committees and subcommittees, architects and artists, hardware and horsepower from electronics to big bulldozers. Every aspect of Squaw Valley would supersede anything the world had seen.

The Fish Club's involvement in the Olympics emerged out of a Thursday's luncheon at Jack's. The Norwegian Athletes Association (*Norges Idrettsforbund* or NIF) and the National Olympic Committee in Oslo knew that Norway was faced with one of its greatest sporting challenges ever.

With the high exchange rate of the dollar, the high cost of living in the United States, the long trip, and the time needed for athletes to adjust to high altitude and time differences, NIF was afraid that Squaw Valley alone would demand more than the organization's entire budget for 1960, even if they reduced the size of the team.

Before World War Two, the Olympic Winter Games had been a rather provincial affair with few nations outside Scandinavia and Central Europe participating and a small number of competitors. To host the Winter Olympics became increasingly prestigious after World War II. The Games grew rapidly in size as teams grew larger and new nations and more events were added. The expansion which started in St. Moritz in 1948, particularly the number of participating athletes in each competition, shocked the host of the 1952 Olympics in Oslo. This trend continued at Cortina, Italy in 1956. The Olympic Winter Games had become a world event.

Norwegians in the Bay Area showed great interest in the coming Games. The Consulate's involvement and NIF's search for help and support coalesced into a search for an organization that could help prepare the Norwegian team for Squaw Valley. The organization would have to have people with time and ability to fundraise and administrate on behalf of Norway and the Norwegian participants.

According to the Consulate the answer was obvious. They, as well as the Olympic Committee in Oslo, felt that the Fish Club under its Rex Sole, Christian Blom, would be the best agent to be in charge of this enterprise.

Early in 1958 Mr. Blom was asked by the Norwegian Olympic Committee if he would be Norway's official attaché. After consulting the Fish Club, where everyone agreed to roll up their sleeves and share the different jobs, Mr. Blom accepted the engagement. In September of 1958 after international consultation and approval, Christian Blom was appointed "Attaché for the Norwegian team to the VIII Olympic Winter Games at Squaw Valley" by the Norwegian Olympic Committee in Oslo and the US Organizing Committee in San Francisco.

From the fall of 1958 until the games started, the Fish Club was fully engaged in preparing for the Norwegian athletes, their leaders, internationally appointed Norwegian judges, sports journalists and radio reporters, photographers, film teams and general visitors from Norway.

A major part of Mr. Blom's job was fundraising. This work was not to interfere with fund-raising in Norway or among shipping lines outside the West Coast of the United States. The archives show that Christian Blom and Iver Lyche did an excellent job in securing financial support for the enterprise, largely from the local shipping industry. Articles of Incorporation of the Norwegian California Olympics Committee (NCOC) were registered in Sacramento, February 10, 1959. The Seamen's Church performed bookkeeping and was promised the balance of funds left after the games. The venture was a financial success and the Church received substantial proceeds from the event.

The local committee chair handled requests from numerous businesses trying to promote their products, as well as Norwegian-Americans wishing to give parties for the Norwegian athletes. The Norwegian Athletes Association, however, did not want the team to participate in any kind of advertising. It was the committee's responsibility to say a polite "no" to different promotional ideas. The committee's job was to protect the integrity and welfare of the team. The Fish Club decided to arrange a farewell dinner dance party in San Francisco after the games was over. The local people could then meet with all Norwegian participants in the Olympics.

The Fish Club also maintained close contact with two sub-committees, one in Los Angeles and one in New York. Everyone involved felt that the athletes should get the opportunity to see the United States and bring home memories of more than just the Olympic Village, the arenas and the airport. In 1960, going to America was something quite different from what it is today. Most likely it would be the only time they would come to the United States. The team was scheduled to go home via Los Angeles and New York. The Olympics was the last major winter sports event that season. The athletes should be given time for sight-seeing, shopping and socializing in San Francisco, Los Angeles and New York. The two

*Gun salute and hoisting of flags at the Fish Club cabin. The jumping hill can be seen to the left. Photo Johan Brun.*

sub-committees were given the task of taking care of the team while it visited these cities.

Almost two years before the games, the Fish Club's Financial Chair, Iver Lyche, managed to rent a fairly large cabin in the heart of Squaw Valley, facing the jumping hill and the skating arena. The price was at that time considered to be very expensive. But less than a year later, it was obvious that the Fish Club had remarkable foresight. Requests for housing rose sky high and with it the rental prices, as new nations and far larger teams than expected signed up for the Games.

To pre-test the site, California invited skiers and skaters from Europe to try out and judge the arenas in a pre-Olympic competition in 1959. For competitors from Northern Europe, it was an unusual environment to compete in, high altitude, sudden changes in weather and wind, high temperature, soft ice and wet snow. It was clear that preparation and starting times would become major issues as conditions might change drastically during a race.

For Norwegians coming back to Squaw Valley a year later, the most impressive change was the transformation of the old, narrow and bumpy road from Reno to the Valley. It was unbelievable that the Americans had managed to build a beautiful highway in less than a year.

Of all the Olympic winter games held after the Second World War, Squaw Valley was probably the most exquisite one, because architects and developers could start with almost virgin ground. It was compact, a dream situation, with no villages or shabby barns in the way, nor a local township with its own ideas and agendas.

The area is not unlike a valley in Norway, a little more level at the bottom, but with the same towering mountains on all three sides. There were those same green pastures and woodlands and the trout stream in the middle. Steep mountain slopes, mainly naked and white, the perfect setting for numerous downhill and slalom runs. No wonder the architects were estatic with such a site: pure white snow, bright light, deep blue sky, a creek, dark green forests, and thousands of icicles everywhere.

The developers created an impressive Olympic Valley. The architects won awards in both design and construction. The United States carved new dimensions for the Eighth Olympic Winter Games, a setting the world had never seen.

Spectators to the games approaching Squaw Valley and looking towards the bottom of the valley would see the arena for speed skating and figure skating in the middle just outside the giant main arena where the opening took place and the hockey teams played. Here in the nave of the valley bottom was the flame of the Olympic torch, next to the emblem boards of all the 31 participating nations. Close by was the stand where the Olympic winners were awarded their medals. The ski-jumping hill was on the far side of the valley with its landing area stretching out into the area next to the speed skating arena and the parking. Further in from the jumping hill towards the bottom of the valley lay the finishing line for the downhill and slalom events. The housing area for the international judges and the staff servicing the games was close to the slalom arena. Next to this housing complex were the Olympics admin-

*The Norwegian team leaders paying homage to "Snowshoe Thomson," the famous "Mailman of the High Sierras." Photo Johan Brun.*

istration headquarters, the data center and the press and information buildings.

To the right were the houses for leaders and the village for the participants. They lay more towards the central right side of the valley and a little withdrawn, only a short walking distance away from the competing arenas. In the front of them was a huge parking lot. The main entrance for all spectators as well as others entering the Olympic Games was close to this parking lot. Every venue of this Olympics lay within a short walking distance of one another. The Fish Club's cabin was right across from the jumping hill and a few hundred yards away from the speed skating. A wide-angle camera in a helicopter could include every aspect of the Eighth Winter Olympic events in one single shot, except for cross-country skiing and the biathlon, a first-time Olympic event, both of which were performed outside Squaw Valley.

The story told is that this was not how it was intended. The meadows next to the jumping hill were originally to be used as the cross-country ski arena, but a dispute arose involving property lines and cutting of trees without permission. The cross-country races were moved out of the valley to a place called McKinney Creek close by Lake Tahoe, where the terrain was more suitable than the location inside Squaw Valley.

Once more Iver Lyche managed to help. He himself owns a five-bedroom cabin on the shore of Lake Tahoe, next to McKinney Creek. Here the cross-country skiers stayed free of charge. They could do their final waxing, and test the skis on the snow before anyone else got there. Best of all, the Norwegian competitors didn't have to get up at 4 in the morning to travel from Squaw Valley by bus. The Norwegians coming out of the Lyche cabin could sleep two more hours in the morning. Years of training and sacrifice is at stake in an Olympics. Most competitors have a hard time sleeping the evening before an important competition, so accommodations are important. Olympic games always involve nerves, "secret weapons," new equipment, new training methods and new clothing. Norway's secret was obviously the cabin at Tahoe. The skiers of the other nations greatly envied the Norwegians who had a Fish Club to help them.

Prince Bertil of Sweden clearly expressed this sentiment when he said that this time Norway was clearly superior, with better solutions. Prince Bertil came to be a regular visitor to the Fish Club cabin in Squaw Valley, sharing the Norwegians' joy when they had an Olympic champion. The Prince, who had an affection for cooking, invited the Norwegians over to test his culinary skills, and he created wonderful soufflés, but the guests didn't have much chance to see the Prince, as he was too busy working in the kitchen.

A blistering snowstorm just prior to the opening ceremonies threatened to ruin the Squaw Valley Olympics, a warning to everyone that nature itself was still in charge. Old photographs show snow-covered Knut Johannesen carrying the Norwegian flag and his fellow athletes hoisting their shoulder to the weather, as the athletes were marching in. The stormy overture had an elevating effect on the ceremony, for suddenly the sun broke through the clouds and the valley sparkled with light reflected from millions of snow crystals. Nature herself had prepared a more perfect setting for the opening than anyone could have anticipated.

Down the long slopes of the valley came a sole skier at full speed, with a torch in hand, making wide turns on her way. The figure was joined by others. Norwegians watching were particularly touched by and proud of this prelude. It had associations with Sondre Nordheim—who taught America and the world to walk on skis—and with Snowshoe Thompson, the man who for twenty years managed to carry mail and medicine on skis across the Sierras in those early days when the West was sealed off from the East during winter. They both came from Telemark in Norway, the cradle of modern skiing.

The torch to light the fire at Squaw Valley had come from Telemark, from the open fireplace at the Sondre Nordheim farm in Morgedal where Sondre, the "father of today's skiing," was born. The torch was carried across the yard and then downhill to the next station on an endless relay that in fourteen days took it through nine time zones. From Oslo the Olympic flame was transported in a special container across the North Pole on the SAS transpolar flight to Los Angeles, California. Olympic champion Parry O'Brien carried it for the first leg in the United States. The flame was brought to Papoose Peak above Squaw Valley where Andrea Mead Lawrence, slalom Olympic Champion from the Oslo Olympics in 1952, carried it down.

Slalom skiers made a guard of honor and joined in, making patterns in the snow as they approached. Andrea skied to the opening ceremony, where the torch was delivered to speed skater Ken Henry, also an Olympic Champion from 1952. He had the honor of carrying it to the large bowl where it would burn during the

Olympic Games from the 18th until the 28th of February, 1960.

The opening ceremony was conducted in a most impressive way. Visual and sound effects, illuminated flags, drumbeats and music from brass horns backed and supported the recitation and speakers. The Olympic hymn was sung by 2645 students from 52 high schools in California and Nevada. The band consisted of 1285 instruments.

*The torch from Norway has arrived. The flame is lit. The games are about to start. Photo Johan Brun.*

Avery Brundage, president of IOC, gave the welcoming speech. Vice President of the United States of America, Richard M. Nixon, declared the eighth Olympic Winter Games to have begun. On behalf of 988 athletes from 31 nations, young figure skater Carol Heiss, silver medal winner from Cortina in 1956, recited the Olympic Oath, promising to participate honestly and in the best possible way. She became an Olympic champion a few days later. Two thousand white doves were released, to signal that the games had opened, followed by a kaleidoscope of fireworks and colorful balloons, all to the delight of more than 20,000 spectators. In 1960 it could not have been more magnificent. Reporters from all over the world reported on beautiful and touching performances; they said it was almost right out of one of Walt Disney's marvelous fairy tales.

Those who attended the 1960 Olympics agreed that Alec Cushing was right to promote Squaw Valley to the IOC. It was the perfect setting for the Olympics Games—compact and glorious. The architecture was greatly prized and admired. The open structure for the ceremony won international acclaim. Europeans found the A-frame cottages charming. They were probably among the most characteristic structures of the Olympics and can still be found at Squaw Valley today.

Ice sculptures symbolized different winter sports, a gift from various Californian cities and crafted by Walt Disney. For the Norwegian visitors well used to snow-removal equipment, the American snow-moving machinery was most impressive. Their size, power, and efficiency were greatly admired.

Less than one month before the games, there was very little snow, which caused great concerns. But the weather changed just in time. Several consecutive snowstorms in a row packed the valley full of snow. Houses, roads, cars—everything had to be dug out. The huge machinery and military personnel did a great job in cleaning up all the tracks and arenas for the competitions.

For those from Northern Europe, cross-country skiing, speed skating, jumping and the combined events were of greatest interest, where they had hopes for medals. Downhill, slalom, figure skating and hockey had, for some time, been dominated by central European countries, the Soviets and the Americans. Military skiing had now found an international version, called biathlon.

Norway's first gold medal was probably the most intriguing and for many the least expected. Prior to the Olympics Norway's top skier for years, Haakon Brusveen, was not among the those chosen to go to Squaw Valley. He had not performed well enough in pre-tests. An extra run was orchestrated, Brusveen won, and was sent on a plane to the United States the day after the other skiers had left.

The selection system is nerve wracking and often many good athletes are left out; only the best physically fit and mentally strong get through. Then they are faced with challenges on an international scale. What were other nations doing? Media initiates discussions of new training systems, new equipment, techniques, tactics and strategies, so-called "secret weapons."

One Norwegian strategy, as mentioned, was to possess a cabin at Lake Tahoe. Another that proved useful was to catch an early ski lift to the peaks above the valley to train at an even higher altitude to get adapted. It didn't take long before Sweden's Sixten Jernberg discovered that the Norwegians made use of this technique, and decided to try the same thing. Jernberg was considered the world's best cross-country skier at that time and became the skiing ace of these Games.

An extremely tall young Norwegian participated in the Olympics for the first time. Haakon Brusveen leaned over to Sixten to advise him about Harald Grønningen's high speed along the track. "You better watch out for that youngster, just look at his extremely long legs." "Yes," Sixten said, "I am sure they can outrun anyone when they work, but I am happy I don't have all those legs when they start hurting and aching."

The 15 km cross-country competition became the fastest and most thrilling race in the Olympics. Haakon Brusveen, arriving in the United States after all the others, skied the race of his life and outran everyone, in an extremely clever and well conducted run, and became the Olympic champion. The two favorites, Sweden's Sixten Jernberg and Finland's Hakulinen, started later than Brusveen, but could not beat his time of 51 minutes and 55 seconds. They received silver and bronze medals respectively. Only 75 seconds divided the 12 best skiers, among them all four Norwegians. With that result the Norwegians became the favorites for the relay.

The starting lap of the relay was Harald Grønningen's. He did an outstanding job on this difficult leg where all teams start together and fight for position. Only a Swede finished ahead of Harald and with just a few seconds. Grønningen sent Hallgeir Brenden off. He soon took

*The Fish Club cabin was a convenient place for the athletes to relax, have a coke or a coffee and friendly talks. Photo Johan Brun.*

control of the lead and completely exhausted his Swedish competitor with several sprints. Once he was out of the way, Brenden concentrated on the Finn and managed to stay ahead of him, sending Einar Østby out first on the third lap. Østby gave an outstanding performance and shook off Finland's Mäntyranta. Everything looked safe before the last lap when Haakon Brusveen, the new Olympic champion, set off twenty seconds ahead of Finland's famous Hakulinen. But for the Norwegians the race turned into a nightmare. Shortly after starting, Hakulinen caught up to Brusveen after an enormous sprint out of the arena. Somehow he managed to stay there. Haakon tried in vain to shake him off, but the Finn kept coming back. Downhill Hakulinen managed to sit on his skis and regain whatever lead Brusveen had attained. Hakulinen kept close to Brusveen through the race and passed him on the last hill, but then Brusveen came back and had to switch over to the reserve track approaching the arena. The world experienced the closest finish ever in a relay. One moment Brusveen's skis were inches ahead, then the Finn's. Only fifty yards from the finishing line it definitely looked like Brusveen had the stronger legs, but then Hakulinen changed tactics. With his great arm strength Hakulinen managed to pull himself inches ahead and secure the gold medal for Finland. The four Norwegians got the silver medal, beaten by 2/10 of a second after competing for two hours and 18 minutes. It was a thriller the world had never seen before. The "smallest defeat possible," as some newspapers put it.

A similar scenario took place in the speed skating competition, and once more, Norway was involved. Senior skater Roald Aas, with an Olympic bronze medal from the Oslo Olympics eight years earlier, told reporters that the only trophy he was missing in his huge trophy collection was an Olympic gold medal. He was a good 5000 meter skater but decided to race in the 1500 meter, his favorite distance, since the two distances were on consecutive days.

When Roald Aas' turn to race came up, the situation was not the best with strong gusts of wind in the arena, but it didn't seem to bother Roald Aas much. He skated a well planned, tactical race and turned in 2.10.4, a very good time indeed. Several top skaters from different countries challenged his time, but in vain. It was too good. Roald Aas was expected to get gold when the Soviet Union's Evgeni Grisjin started. This eminent sprinter already had the gold medal from the 500 meter race, and the 1500 meter was considered a little too long a distance for his capabilities. As usual, Grisjin got a very fast start and had an amazing race. He had more than 3 seconds on Aas at the last lap. But as expected, his energy was overextended, and he stiffened. Nevertheless, he managed to maintain some speed and with his last efforts sailed across the finishing line. Grisjin got exactly the same time as Aas, losing more than three seconds during the last two to three hundred meters of the race. Both skaters were awarded the gold medal and the Olympic Championship.

From the Norwegian viewpoint the most impressive competition in the 1960 Olympics was the 10.000 meter speed skating race. It produced a new world record that stunned the world. Experts on skating anticipated that the new artificially frozen arena in Squaw Valley would be one of the world's fastest speed skating tracks, perhaps faster than Davos in Central Europe and Alma-Ata in Kazakhstan, both world famous high altitude arenas. This was the first time in history artificial refrigeration was utilized for Olympic speed skating events. Speculations were numerous, especially that the wind and rapid changes in weather conditions would produce differing—unfair—conditions over the course of a race.

The 5000 meter race was to prove those speculations to be true. Norway's Knut Johannesen was a favorite for the 5000 meter race together with Jan Pesman of Holland and Ivar Nilsson of Sweden. None of the favorites was happy with his run, apart from Pesman who managed to slip in 2/10 of a second before Torstein Seiersten's finishing time. He won the bronze medal Seiersten had hoped for. Under difficult conditions Knut Johannesen made the run in 8 minutes and was awarded the silver medal. He was beaten by a good Russian, Victor Kositsjkin, who started later when the conditions had improved.

The day of the 10.000 meter race, two days later, conditions were good: blue sky, little wind, pleasant temperatures, and fine ice. Hjalmar Andersen's eight-year-old world record from Hamar's post-Olympic race in 1952 of 16.36.6. seemed ready for replacement. Knut Johannesen and his trainer Kaastad decided to show the world how a 10.000 meter should be run and pulled out the schedules for a new world record. They both knew this could be the day. But how good the new world record was going to be no one knew. A run of fifteen minutes or less was still unthinkable to many.

Halfway through this sensational 10 km race the skating world was astonished. In Norway, late at night, people could hardly believe what was radioed across the world from Squaw Valley, California. Knut Johannesen managed to skate the first half of the race six seconds faster than his previous 5000 meter that had given him an Olympic silver medal two days before. And he continued round after round, at a pace unheard of in 10.000 meter speed skating. The clock stopped at 15.46.6, which was 50 seconds faster than Hjalmar Andersen's old world record. Knut Johannesen, or "Kuppern" had run two consecutive 5000 meters, one at 7.54 and one at 7.52.

"Unbelievable" was the world's first reaction. The commentator at the scene said plainly that "he smashed the old record". This was skating history. "Kuppern's" outstanding run became the new world record.

Afterward questions arose on how fast a 10,000 meter could be performed, and many suggestions and many guesses arose. When asked by a radio reporter, old champion Hjalmar Andersen said plainly, "I only can say that they can't run a 10,000 meter in no time at all."

Squaw Valley Olympics had other surprises: good for some, bad for others. As Cortina had shown four years earlier, the Norwegians had definitely lost their hegemony in ski jumping, which they up to that point had dominated. The German Helmut Recknagel won. The best Norwegian finished fifth. Ski jumping was the closing competition of the Eighth Olympic Winter Games.

The winter sport that used to be the highlight of competition in the old days was the cross country and ski jumping combined. These Olympics showed clearly that new nations would challenge the Norwegians, and did so with good result. Georg Thoma of Germany

*Speed skater Knut Johannesen's 10,000 meter run was an unbelievable endeavor. No one had ever experienced anything like it. Photo Johan Brun. Courtesy Knut Johannesen.*

was the big surprise and managed to win, whereas Tormod Knutsen of Norway barely came second. He struggled to keep the next two competitors behind him.

For Americans more interested in figure skating, slalom, downhill and hockey, it was gratifying to see how well their own nationals could compete with those from other countries. Competition was hard and the Soviets did especially well. As usual, athletes from Central Europe took a good share of the downhill races. The greatest

*The Fish Club's team preparing for the celebration of a gold medal. Photo Johan Brun.*

victory for the United States was in ice hockey. It was the country's first Olympic hockey gold and its first World Championship. The hockey team became the wonder boys and great heroes, overshadowing Carol Heiss and David Jenkins who both secured gold medals for the United States in figure skating.

For the first time in Olympic history, men competed in the biathlon. Hollywood reproduced some of its ideas in the motion picture *The Heroes of Telemark*. In this discipline the Soviets were expected to win. Surprisingly, a Swede became the winner, a Finn second. Norway hoped to do well in this venue, but the best Norwegian came in seventh.

In other ways Squaw Valley differed from previous Olympics. Some of these were strange things such as the plastic figures, or a musician wearing knitted gloves with exposed fingertips, playing live organ music on the inner track during speed skating. A marathon performance, indeed, during the long and demanding 10.000 meter event. This same organist actually stopped playing and jumped up and down cheering during "Kuppern's" record breaking run. Who could believe fifty military men taking the ski lift up to tramp down the hill until three feet of snow were compressed? That amazed reporters and competitors from Europe. In other parts of the world skiers still had to trot up hill on their own to make the run down. In 1960 Squaw Valley had four double chair lifts and a rope tow. Today the area has 27 lifts, including a Super Gondola and a Cable Car. The latter can carry bikers, babies in strollers and disabled persons.

Most impressive was that all results were handled by punch cards and electronic computers and were ready in seconds. In 1960 this was very advanced. Elsewhere around the world people still used paper and pencil to record every digit, calculate by head and compile all the different results. These had to be checked for errors before the confirmed results could be handed out, often several hours after an event had ended.

The Olympic Village where all competitors lived together was new. The shops, many smart arrangements and, above all, the American food were highlighted in letters going back home. Many competitors tasted hamburgers for their first time. The food was unbelievably good, plentiful and reasonable. The Winter Olympics in Squaw Valley were the first Olympics to be televised nationally in the United States.

Memorable as well was nature itself, the beauty of the Sierra Nevada, the creation of a fairyland world of make-believe, but it was not Hollywood; Squaw Valley was real. It was also a delightful surprise that so many world celebrities showed up to watch the games in person.

After all, the world's best athletes have many things in common with famous movie stars. They are heroes for millions of people around the world. For competitors from overseas, it was a dream come true to meet Danny Kaye, Jayne Mansfield, Bing Crosby, Walt Disney himself and others, or just to see them or be seated at a table near by. One of the Norwegian competitors said before his departure from Oslo that his greatest wish in life was to meet Marilyn Monroe.

The Fish Club's cabin became the natural meeting place, not only for the athletes and their leaders, but also for the press and everyone else who dropped in. Christian Blom, his wife Lissi and other members of the Fish Club like Iver Lyche, Jens Feragen, Lyder Brun, Rolf Schou and Per Høeg, in charge of the cabin, and Kjell Lund, who was responsible for transportation, the cabin at Lake Tahoe and all the cooking there. All did so much to make everyone feel at home. Laura Jensen, originally from Finmark, was the cook. She got up at five in the morning to bake cakes, waffles and Norwegian *bløtkake* every day there was a birthday or medal to celebrate.

The Fish Club's NCOC had printed a special welcoming program including every aspect of the Olympic Games, for the aid of the Norwegian participants. It listed the different events and days, with blank space for personal notes. It had information about people in charge and whom to contact in each and every case. It even had a section for the activities after the games, including a schedule of the events in San Francisco and Los Angeles. This program was handed out to the entire Norwegian team.

Reporters were impressed. The media in Norway raved about the committee's work, its activities and services at the cabin. Pictures of Fish Club members at work accompanied the daily reportage. Everyone appreciated the work of Rex Sole and his team in making the Norwegian team feel at home in Squaw Valley. At the Fish Club's cabin right across from the arenas, athletes could read papers, drink soda or coffee or just relax and learn more about life in America.

When a medal was won by the Norwegians, a special celebration followed the official one at the arena. Everyone gathered at the Fish

*Athletes, leaders and people from the Fish Club celebrating a birthday party at the Fish Club cabin. Photo Johan Brun.*

Club cabin. A salute was fired and the Norwegian flag was hoisted together with a pennant in gold, silver or bronze, depicting the medal won. Since this was performed close to the main road and right outside the arenas, it was easily observed by others. The cannon blast made people pay attention. Soon everyone knew the Norwegians had another medal celebration. Christian Blom would open one of his famous magnum bottles of champagne for everyone to share with the medal winner. Lissi and Laura would serve *bløtkake*.

Expeditions to Lake Tahoe and Reno were arranged for athletes who had finished their competition. In Reno, the gold medal winners and their friends were photographed trying to win more gold in the casino, checking out western outfits and guns, and embracing some good-looking and scantily clad show girls, perhaps to tease the girls back home. Some of these pictures were used in popular pictorial magazines, the media's form of the visual before TV became common in Norway.

The "Fairy Land Olympics" came to an end. After all the excitement it was suddenly over. The many Olympic medals had been awarded. New friends and international contacts were made. Squaw Valley would rest peacefully again. Only some military units and clean-up teams would remain.

The closing ceremony was even more touching than the opening. It was time to part, say goodby to new friends and return home from a dream. Everyone gathered at the arena where they had met only ten days before, though it seemed so long ago. The flags were lowered, the poles left bare, and the flame slowly faded away.

Thank you, Squaw Valley—and farewell!

Early the next morning the Norwegian team left by bus for San Francisco, only stopping for lunch at the Nut Tree west of Sacramento. The Norwegian Seamen's Church hosted a reception where the participants met their respective hosts. All were to stay in private homes and experience the well-known American hospitality. Everyone gathered afterwards for the gala celebration, when the Fish Club hosted a formal dinner dance at the Presidio Golf Club for the Norwegian team and more than a hundred invited guests from the Bay Area.

It was a memorable evening with speeches and rewards. The athletes were congratulated for their achievements. Christian Blom and the Fish Club were praised for a job well done, and received roaring applause. All the medal winners were gathered at the head table. Haakon Brusveen was asked to give a speech in appreciation of all the good food they had. Brusveen

*The main structure of the 1960 Winter Games as participants remember it. The roof caved in after a heavy snowfall many years ago. Photo Johan Brun.*

*"Kuppern" Johannesen admiring Sonja Henies' trophies, during the Olympic athlete's visit to her home in Beverly Hills on their way home. Photo Johan Brun, courtesy Knut Johannesen.*

stated in a broad Norwegian Vingrom dialect that he found it a little difficult to comment on the food, as he didn't know what he had been eating. But it really didn't matter, because the food was very good. He found it strange, he remarked, that the smallest and skinniest man on the team got the assignment to make a speech on food. It should have been the leaders; they had, he continued, been mainly eating and doing little else while staying in America! The whole speech was hilarious, according to Norwegian-Americans not too familiar with that particular type of Norwegian dialect. Brusveen later became a popular radio sports reporter in Norway.

The streets of San Francisco, the steep hills, the Golden Gate Bridge, the Alcatraz and the Oakland Bay Bridge were admired by the team, as was Amundsen's famous ship *Gjøa* at Ocean Beach in Golden Gate Park, a ship known by any schoolchild in Norway.

Several of the athletes, having worked in the forests back home, wanted to view the enormous redwood trees in Muir Woods. Shopping downtown and a visit to Chinatown were parts of the second day's excursion. The next morning the Olympic team left for Los Angeles, and at Burbank Airport the local committee in Los Angeles took over. There the team visited Disneyland at the private invitation of Walt Disney himself, a close friend of a committee member. In 1960 Disneyland was the top attraction of visitors to Southern California. The Norwegian athletes were just as excited and impressed as everyone else. Disneyland still is one of the highlight memories for athletes of this Olympics. The Disneyland visit was followed by a lunch at Disneyland Hotel and a tour through Hollywood and the film studios.

Three-time Olympic Champion and ten times World Champion Sonja Henie, and her husband Niels Onstad, gave a cocktail party for the young competitors at their home in Beverly Hills. Some of the athletes had impressive collections of trophies, but had to confess that they were no match for Sonja's collection. Her skating trophies also included six European Championships, several Norwegian championships, and many other medals, cups and other trophies. It filled a whole room in the couple's big house.

In fact, it was Sonja Henie's trophies, together with the celebrated couple's outstanding collection of fine art, including great works of Bonnard, Gris, Klee, Léger, Matisse, Miró, Munch and Picasso, to mention some, that were later moved to The Henie Onstad Center outside Oslo. Today that center is a major tourist attraction in the Oslo area. It is visited by many Americans that remember Sonja Henie as a film star in Hollywood and her famous "Holiday on Ice" shows.

The Beverly Hills' visit concluded with a dinner at the new and luxurious Beverly Hilton, a tribute to Conrad Hilton's father, Gus or Augustus, as he was baptized in Norway. The old Hilton farm lies only a short distance from Olympic combined medalist Tormod Knutsen's home near Eidsvoll. After this dinner the team was off to the airport and New York, including an unexpected detour to Montreal, Canada, due to bad weather and fog on Long Island. After hectic days and sight-seeing in New York, the team enplaned for Oslo. Just after departure, the stewardesses started serving dinner, but by then, most of the athletes were sound asleep. The cabin crew told reporters in Norway that the Olympic team members returning from Squaw Valley were the most exhausted passengers they had ever had on an airplane.

The 1960 Olympic extravaganza, as some European sports organizations felt it was, became the point of no return for the Winter Olympics. The three post-war games prior to Squaw Valley set new trends that really materialized at Squaw Valley. Lovers of sport feared that in the future the idea of amateur sports would be lost. Squaw Valley meant much more than competition to see who was best. In these Olympics even the loser had good things to remember. To become part of an Olympic team became a victory in itself. Norwegian reporters clearly understood that without the help and financial backing of Californian friends and the shipping business, everything would have been much more difficult.

Editorials from those days are worth reading. They are filled with understandable worry. Later in 1960 during the Summer Olympics in Rome, Italy, IOC actually discussed whether winter games should be abandoned after the next games in Innsbruck in 1964. Individual World Championship competitions were proposed as a substitute. One editor stated that Norway's participation in Squaw Valley cost as much as the Norwegian state funding to all sports for two years. Some nations were accused of an arms race in sport, for the showdown at the Olympics. It was feared that other events and activities would suffer, and that the true amateurs would be the losers.

Norway was still, at that time, a country of true amateurs. It was not a mass consumption society. One of the skiers brought an electric razor to Squaw Valley and his team mates would line up to borrow this new device that even worked on US voltage. In Norway, soap and water were still the way to shave. It was better to save money to repair the fence at the farm, or to save it for a rainy day.

Plain bread and brown cheese had for generations been the basic fuel for the body, even in Olympic competition. The athletes from 1960 still

*Two A-frame houses are the most significant remaining structures from 1960. The jumping hill has been reclaimed by nature, trees growing up all over the area. Photo Olaf T. Engvig.*

remember the American food as very tasty and plentiful more than thirty years after the games. The participants think of Squaw Valley as the most memorable sports event in their sporting career. Even today some rank the 1960 events among the most efficient and successful Winter Games ever conducted.

Harald Grønningen from Lensvik was 23, and in the Olympics for his first time. Everything had a magnitude and impact that was lasting. Grønningen came from a little place by the Trondheimsfjord, not used to much. He was a farmhand and worked the forests during winter. He discovered for the first time that he could outrun men from all over the world. "In Squaw Valley I finally understood that I could compete and get all the way to the top. Everything was great with America. I watched TV for the first time in San Francisco. The food was fantastic. Blom and the Fish Club made the stay just perfect."

Later Harald Grønningen became one of Norway's greatest cross-country skiers ever and participated in several Olympics, winning a series of medals including Olympic gold. But his silver medal from the relay at Squaw Valley was the one that made him realize he could become an Olympic Champion. He has never been back to Squaw Valley.

Haakon Brusveen was considered a veteran in 1960. Crossing the finishing line at McKinney Creek and receiving the gold medal was the greatest moment in his whole life. He was asthmatic as a child, little and thin, and the doctor did not recommend his participation in the school's annual skiing event because he was so weak.

Brusveen went back to McKinney Creek some years ago. Everything had changed, but he managed to find the finish line he crossed in 1960, locating it by a big tree where Hakulinen passed him at the end of the relay. There was a house built right on the finish line, so Haakon walked straight into the house and told the man sitting at the kitchen table, surprised by Haakon's intrusion: "'You are sitting where I experienced the greatest moment of my life,' I told him. He must have thought I was nuts. He came from another state and had never even heard of the Winter Olympics, nor the cross country event at McKinney Creek, so I told him, in his own kitchen, coming all the way from Norway. He was stunned.... Now he knows."

For most of the participants at the 1960 Games, the memories of California linger on. The Squaw Valley Club meets on a regular basis. Christian Blom was until he passed away the club's honoree member. Iver Lyche is also

*The 1960 Norwegian Olympic medal winners.*

*From left Haakon Brusveen (Gold+Silver), Roald Aas (Gold), Hallgeir Brenden (Silver), Harald Grønningen (Silver), Tormod Knutsen (Silver), Einar Østby (Silver) and Knut Johannesen (Gold+Silver).*

*Photo Johan Brun.*

remembered, and the ladies, of course. It was an unique experience, "Kuppern" says, unlike any other skating competition. For ten years after the Hjalmar Andersen era, "Kuppern" Johannesen was the "boss" among world speed skaters.

In those days, speed skaters were the gods of winter sport. Even a pre-Olympic qualification run, in Oslo like the one held at Bislet in 1956, would draw more than 20.000 fans in freezing cold weather; they were there to see and cheer on their great heroes. The World Championship in Moscow, 1955, drew 60.000 the first day and around 80.000 on the last day. For generations in Europe, speed skating was the ultimate competition.

Today, that's no longer true. Only the most devoted will come to an outdoor arena in biting cold weather to watch two skaters compete round after round against time. To watch such competition on TV is not the same. It tends to be repetitive so TV producers prefer other sports. Ski jumping works well on the screen, as does figure skating and hockey. Fans can enjoy the sport from the comfort of chairs. There is no need to find parking, lose time, freeze and spend large sums of money. Why bother? The heroic spectators of yesterday are an endangered species. Only a few remain.

"It is soon forgotten," Knut Johannesen wrote in 1960. Brusveen experienced the letdown in the kitchen at McKinney Creek.

Squaw Valley never became California's Innsbruck, Holmenkollen or Thunder Bay, a lasting place for winter sport on the world championship level. Instead, the Olympic Valley was adapted to leisure winter sports. The true amateurs have reclaimed this famous location for the fun of the sport and as a vacation spot for all seasons.

Today Squaw Valley is both different and yet the same. The jumping hill is full of trees. Most of the arenas are gone, converted into parking space, but the two A-frame houses remain. So do hotels like Squaw Valley Inn. The Fish Club cabin also remains intact. Areas for off-season sports activities have been developed above the valley. A big cable car takes people up the mountain to go biking, skating or just to admire the wonderful view of Lake Tahoe from on high. In winter the downhill slopes are still the most popular meeting place in the Sierras.

A significant sense of a great past lingers on at Squaw Valley. The Olympic housing that remains, the signs and souvenirs tell of the hectic days in February 1960 when the world for a brief moment listened in to one of the greatest Winter Olympics in history.

*Today Squaw Valley depends on leisure and tourist activities, rather than major sports events and international competition. Aerial view of Squaw Valley from the gondola lift.*
*Photo next page: Olaf T. Engvig.*

# 1960 Squaw Valley Olympics

# Prelude to the 1984 Los Angeles Olympics

More than two years prior to the 1984 Summer Olympics in Los Angeles, President Arne B. Mollén of the Norwegian Olympic Committee in Oslo sent a letter to Iver Lyche in San Francisco and asked the Fish Club for advice on when and where the Olympic Team could best adjust and pre-train for the 1984 Olympic Games in California. The Committee in Norway believed that the team should stay away from Los Angeles until right before the Games.

Iver Lyche, still today a director of Morgan Stanley & Co. Inc., discussed the matter with the Fish Club and sent Mollén his report. Iver Lyche was then asked by Norway to be an attaché for the Team. However, objections arose from Los Angeles. It was decided that the Norwegian Olympic Team should stop over in San Francisco for about two weeks prior to going to Los Angeles for pre-Olympic training at Stanford University.

Again the group from the 1960 Olympics in Squaw Valley came through and made arrangements for a workout session for the athletes in the Bay Area. As in 1960, Iver Lyche teamed with Christian Blom, Per Høeg and the rest of the Fish Club. In a personal letter to Arne Mollén in 1982 Iver Lyche expressed it in this way: "To me it is an opportunity to pay back what Norwegian competitive sport gave me when I was young."

The 78-year-old Christian Blom was still the work horse he has always been, writing numerous letters to potential donors. Together with Ole Kalve, Erik Salbu, Jeffrey Meyer, Per Høeg and the staff at Overseas Shipping, he raised $40,000 for the athletes' stay at Stanford. The Seamen's Church received the remainder of the funds.

Christian Blom preferred to called this arrangement a lucky combination of sports and the church. When he grew up in Fredrikstad, Norway, before the First World War, a minister was per definition not interested in sports. Later in life he found out that seamen's pastors were among the most eager sports enthusiasts. This was to him a pleasant surprise he often liked to talk about.

Approximately 50 athletes stayed at Stanford University from July 16 until 28, and used this famous University's excellent premises for their final training and adjustments. Per Høeg was once again a key coordinator.

In the fall of 1984 Per Høeg received a letter from the housing manager at Stanford University, a very sincere thank you-note which ended as follows:

> All of us in the Housing and Food Service areas want you to know that we consider the Norwegian Olympic Team members to be the nicest group of persons that we housed this summer, and we housed 12,780 people. The Norwegian team members were so well loved with their pleasant and friendly attitude by all of our staff on campus. The Stanford students were also very pleased to be able to interact with and meet your team members.
>
> Lois E. Fariello,
> Manager of Conferences,
> Stanford University.

CHAPTER VIII

# Gjøa, The Ship in the Park

*The exploration sloop Gjøa ending her perilous voyage, arriving under tow in San Francisco after the Northwest Passage was completed in 1906. This was the end of 34 comprehensive years of sea duty for this famous Arctic vessel.*

When the old and battered expedition sloop *Gjøa* entered San Francisco Bay on October 19, 1906, it became the Norwegian colony's pride and problem. For more than half a century the Fish Club would be one of the ship's watchdogs. *Gjøa* developed into a major challenge for the people of Norwegian descent who gave her to the City of San Francisco. She became the City's bad conscience and her supporters' biggest headache. It was the Fish Club that finally saved the *Gjøa*. Little *Gjøa* became one of the world's most famous ships after her successful transit through the Northwest Passage. Her struggle for survival added to the fame. Her sailing days, however, started in quite an ordinary way.

The sloop *Gjøa* was built in Hardanger, Norway in 1872 by Knut Johannesson Skaala for her skipper, Asbjørn Sexe, and named for his wife Gjøa. *Gjøa* was an ordinary Norwegian *jakt* of her days, serving as a freighter on the coast of Norway and in the herring fisheries. She was only 69 feet long, with a beam of 20 1/2 feet and a depth of almost 8 feet, drawing three feet of water unloaded. *Gjøa* was originally measured to 61.5 net tons; when Amundsen had her, she was less than 50 tons. She had a sloop rig and carried a fore-and-aft mainsail, three staysails, a gaff topsail and a squaresail. *Gjøa* proved to be an excellent sailing vessel.

When ten years old, the *Gjøa* was wrecked in northern Norway and declared a total loss. The wreck was sold, repaired, and went to skipper Hans Christian Johannesen in Tromsø. He took her to the Kara Sea and up the coast by King Carl's Land, to Greenland and Svalbard and many other islands in the Arctic. The *Gjøa* had quite a reputation as an Arctic sloop when Roald Amundsen purchased her in Tromsø March 28, 1901. Amundsen then became a sloop skipper, but in fact had never sailed such a small vessel before.

Roald Amundsen was an ambitious and experienced Arctic seaman. He bought the *Gjøa* for the purpose of sailing through the Northwest Passage, the last passage of the world still unconquered. Explorers of leading seafaring nations had long before abandoned this project due to grave problems with ice.

Since ancient times, Europe's connection with India and the Far East was the slow and difficult caravan trek of thousands of miles across mountains and deserts with little payload and many obstacles along the way. That made impossible the profitable import of large quantities of exotic and desired goods. Vasco da Gama opened up a new seaway to the East by way of the Cape of Good Hope. Christopher Columbus thought that India could be found by sailing westwards. Indeed he discovered new land to the west, but it was not India. After Magellan sailed around the world via Cape Horn, explorers concentrated on the final challenge—to find a way north around the same land mass. If there existed an navigable passage to the north of Patagonia, it would shortcut the distance from Europe to Japan and China. It would be half the distance of sailing around the Horn. Commercial interest was the driving force.

Expensive and well-equipped expeditions with several ships set out time and again only to be stopped by the Arctic winter. The search went on for more than three centuries. It started with John Cabot, Sebastian's father, upon whose 1497 voyage England's claim to North America rested. Martin Frobisher charted Frobisher Bay. Muscory of London fitted out two vessels under Pet and Jackman with the goal of negotiating the passage. Henry Hudson, William Baffin, James Cook, John Ross, W. E. Parry and Sir John Franklin were some of the more famous explorers who tried to find the Northwest Passage.

At the beginning of the nineteenth century, motives became imperial and explorative rather than strictly commercial. Lives were lost. Franklin disappeared with two ships and 129 men in 1845. Twelve expeditions were launched just to find Franklin, and even rescue expeditions were lost and searched for. In 1850 the remains of Franklin's party were found, and the idea of a Northwest Passage was given up due to the severity of drifting ice, though all reports suggested the possibility of a navigable passage.

When Amundsen, then an unknown Norwegian ship's mate, fifty years later refloated the idea that he could find the Northwest Passage, nobody was interested in putting up money for the effort. Over the centuries suitable ships had been developed to sail the long voyages around Cape Horn and the Cape of Good Hope. The 1855 railroad across Panama had improved transportation to the Pacific, as did the railroad across the United States in 1869. In 1867 the Suez Canal opened. Demands for exotic goods from India and the Far East were met successively by Dutch and English company ships, clipper ships and ocean steamers. Amunsen's plan came too late to open a new navigation route. If successful, however, it would be the final victory in man's longest, most costly and disastrous exploratory struggles—the struggle to find a navigable passage around the globe north of America.

Because there was no longer a viable commercial purpose for the expedition, Amundsen knew that to obtain financial backing he would need to incorporate a scientific purpose for the expedition. During most of last century, studies of earth magnetism, magnetic mapping and be somewhere in the area of the Northwest Passage. Only when Amundsen promised to determine the exact position of the North Magnetic Pole did he receive international attention and some of the financial backing needed. That was in the year 1900, and it was in the following spring that Roald Amundsen bought the Hardanger sloop *Gjøa*. During the summer he tested the

*Captain Roald Amundsen and his six men on board the Gjøa just prior to the start of the expedition from Oslo in June 1903. From left: Roald Amundsen, Anton Lund, the pilot taking the Gjøa out of the Oslofjord, Helmer Hansen, Adolf Lindsrøm. Seated in front: Godfred Hansen, Gustav Wiik, Peder Ristvedt. By courtesy of the Norwegian Club.*

magnetic poles were given great international attention, as was the problem of using a magnet compass in an iron ship. One of the international names in geomagnetic research was professor Christopher Hansteen, the father of empirical science in Norway. He had been the teacher for the first group of young Norwegian scholars. Fridtjof Nansen was a younger scholar fascinated by Hansteen's work. He was an established scientist by the turn of the century, specially known for his Arctic explorations.

Nansen encouraged Amundsen to search for the North Magnetic Pole which was known to ship while performing oceanographic work in the Arctic Sea. The *Gjøa* passed the test, and refitting was accomplished. The hull was strengthened by an extra floor and frames, and she got another three-inch oak skin outside her hull and iron straps to strengthen her bow. In addition beams were laid above the bilge, secured and fastened to a row of stanchions between keel and deck beams. All this work improved the vessel's ability to withstand the pressure of the Arctic ice.

*Gjøa* also received an auxiliary engine, an early type of a two-cylinder 13 HP *Dan*, semi-diesel engine. Starting it required a blowtorch to ignite the fuel and make it run. It was a very simple and reliable machine, but with lubricating oil and an open torch in the wooden engine room of a small and rolling vessel, the fire hazard was extreme. This little engine performed very well, and could drive the *Gjøa* at about 4 knots. A fuel tank of 20,000 liters was also installed in the ship. The expedition members were as follows:

Roald Amundsen, expedition leader and captain of the ship, a former mate with a new master's license. He was self-trained and ambitious, an experienced skier and well prepared for the hardships such an expedition would face;

Godfred Hansen, chief mate, was responsible for navigation, astronomy, geology and photography;

Anton Lund, first mate, shipmaster and harpooner from the Arctic fisheries;

Helmer Hansen, second mate, experienced in Arctic navigation and fishing;

Peder Ristvedt, first engineer and meteorologist;

Gustav Juel Wiik, second engineer, was in charge of magnetic observations;

Adolf Henrik Lindstrøm, a veteran Arctic explorer, was responsible for the zoological collection and the cooking—the main food for the explorers would have to be selected from zoological species collected in the area explored. He is believed to be the only man that has worked his way on sailing vessels all around the American continent. After the *Gjøa* expedition he signed on a ship that took him around the continent by way of Cape Horn. He was a marvelous cook and even got credit for a beef entre he didn't invent.

*A large painting on the first floor of the Merchant's Exchange Building on California Street shows Gjøa struggling through an Arctic gale. It is called "Northwest Passage 1903–1906" and is painted by Nils Hagerup. Fritz Olsen of Fred Olsen Line ordered the picture and presented it to the Exchange. Photo Olaf T. Engvig by courtesy of First Interstate Bank of California.*

"Beef a la Lindstrøm," served in restaurants all over the world is said to originate from Sweden or Russia but is often credited to Adolf Henrik Lindstrøm, the *Gjøa* cook.

This company of seven men was *Gjøa*'s crew on her three-year long Arctic expedition through the Northwest Passage. It became one of the greatest voyages in history, undertaken in one of the smallest expedition ships ever used on such a long and exhausting enterprise. The main quarters aft measured only nine feet by six.

After refitting the *Gjøa* and arranging for supplies to be picked up at Greenland, funds began to run short. Amundsen had hoped for donated food and supplies, but that did not materialize. Finally he ordered the food and supplies, but some creditors—fearing they would never get paid—demanded payment within 24 hours or the ship would be arrested. The whole expedition was in danger of falling apart. Amundsen, in a great dilemma, decided to trust his companions and asked them to set off under cover of darkness. On June 16, 1903, around midnight and in a pouring rain, *Gjøa*'s hawsers were cast off and she was towed down the Oslofjord, heading out into the Skagerrak by morning. She sailed on to the North Sea and the Atlantic. *Gjøa* did not make a landfall until she reached remote Disko Island on the west coast of Greenland on July 24. By then the ship was quite safe from arrest. Amundsen had dogs, sledges, and other deck cargo waiting at Disko—all needed for the Arctic winter. From Disko, the *Gjøa* sailed north to Dalrymple Rock, an old Scottish whaling station, where arrangements were made to refuel, and top off with provisions and water.

Every square inch of *Gjøa* was packed with special crates and the deck filled with all kinds of goods. Leaving Dalrymple Rock, the *Gjøa* looked like a floating moving van. On the deck of the 69-foot-long vessel, even some twenty dogs had to be accommodated.

Their first station was set up on Beechey Island where they took a series of bearings of the true direction of the Geomagnetic Pole. Then *Gjøa* continued along Peel Sound and Franklin Strait. No ship had ever gone beyond this point and the expedition now sailed into virgin waters. Great precaution was taken. Amundsen was often at the masthead in the crow's nest. Even with great care, the *Gjøa* struck a reef. It took a lot of unloading and maneuvering to finally refloat her, only to discover that the rudder was about to come off. By sheer luck a sea from behind pushed it back into place. The vessel also had an engine room fire, a highly feared hazard. It was extinguished before great harm was done. West of Boothia Peninsula the ship ran into a gale described as the worst her experienced crew had ever seen. Amundsen was sure he would lose the *Gjøa*. Anton Lund took charge; he was a most experienced Arctic captain. He managed to take the *Gjøa* through the storm until the weather calmed down.

It was September and the Arctic winter would soon close in. The expedition had to find a sheltered bay for winter quarters if they were to survive. A small cove on the south coast of King William Island was chosen and named Gjøahavn, today's Gjoa Haven. The sea froze on October 1. The men built the camp from wooden material stored in *Gjøa*'s hold. During the stay in Gjøahavn, the team determined the approximate location of the North Magnetic Pole. Amundsen's studies established that the magnetic pole moved. He found it frustrating to be on target one evening, only to observe being off target when they tried to verify it the next morning. He learned that the Earth's Geomagnetic North Pole is not a particular point like a geographical pole, but shifts around in a given area.

The Arctic winter is long and demanding. The expedition's field trips, recording work and hunting parties were good therapy for dogs and men. Amundsen was particular about special events. The expedition's ultimate luxury was a small phonograph and some recordings. They were played during "the concert" on Sunday afternoons or on holidays. All hands were required to dress properly on such occasions. This and Lindstrøm's culinary variations made the holidays special. Not long after the winter quarters were established, some Inuits arrived at Gjøahavn. They had never seen a white man, but some of their ancestors had met with British explorers more than seventy years before.

The Inuits were impressed with the tools and equipment the expedition carried. Metal

*The only known picture of the Arctic trader Charles Hanson of San Francisco. She was built in 1881 by the Danish-American Hans Bendixsen who later built the historic schooner, C.A.Thayer. On August 26, 1906, the Charles Hanson met the Gjøa in the Beaufort Sea. Repeatedly, Amundsen recalled this first encounter with a ship from the west: "The Northwest Passage was conquered. My dream from boyhood - in this very moment it had materialized." Photo courtesy San Francisco Maritime Museum.*

tools and weapons were like miracles to them. What their elders had recounted had happened again. This time the Inuits were more determined to stay and learn, when Amundsen made them welcome. A whole village of Inuit igloos arose, and the Gjøa expedition suddenly had the company of some two hundred men, women and children—a dream for any anthropologist. Through barter Amundsen obtained several sets of Inuit artifacts, showing every phase of their daily life in this untouched and hostile part of the Arctic. These artifacts are still on display in the Museum of History in Oslo as well as in other Norwegian museums.

The Inuits were eager to learn. Much information was exchanged. Amundsen and his men managed well by adapting to the hostile elements in the Inuit way, a good lesson later to be used by him when reaching the South Pole and returning. The old problem of white men offered the liberties of native women arose. According to Amundsen's records, he had a serious talk with his crew and urged then not to yield to this temptation.

The temptation lingered on, however, because Gjøa was stuck in Gjøahavn. Amundsen and his men were offered female favors as a part of many bargains. The summer of 1904 was a bad one and the ice never opened up enough for the voyage to be resumed. The ice froze again in September before Gjøa could get under way.

Amundsen made several long sledge expeditions to the vicinity of the North Magnetic Pole, recording all the time. By April 1905 Gotfred Hansen and Peder Ristvedt explored by dog sledge the coast of Victoria Island and a gulf later to be named Queen Maud Gulf in honor of the new Queen of Norway. They returned on Midsummer Day after a 800 mile journey. Only three days later the ice broke up around Gjøa and she could once more get under way to sail the Northwest Passage after 22 months in Gjøahavn. When they left, on August 13, 1905, Gjøa continued west on a course untried by man. But the research done during the stay had given the party all indications of navigable water when the sea opened up. Gjøa stood across Queen Maud Gulf. The weather was ever changing in the short Arctic summer, from beautiful sailing in bright sunlight around the clock to difficult and demanding conditions including fog and ice.

The expedition met new problems, struggled with fog and finally reached a strait that became more and more shallow until the point where *Gjøa* was barely floating. Amundsen lowered the boat, and for days he rowed around sounding, through a wilderness of floating ice and uncharted, twisting channels, nearly without sleep, trying to take the *Gjøa* through. They succeeded, and on August 26, 1905, Amundsen reached the area mapped by former expeditions coming from the west. Then Amundsen knew that the *Gjøa* had sailed the unknown part of the passage north of America and resolved the old search for the Northwest Passage. The expedition continued west by sail and engine towards the gulf which is today named Amundsen Gulf.

On September 4, the watch of the *Gjøa* sighted the first ship since Greenland, a schooner far to the west. She was the *Charles Hanson* of 183 tons from San Francisco, skippered by Captain James McKenna, a famous Arctic trader. After a brief meeting with the ship, Gjøa continued westward to reach the Mackenzie River delta, not dreaming that the relatively simple remaining voyage out of the Arctic would take yet another year. The ice formed, and by September 9 Amundsen and his crew had to admit *Gjøa* was stuck for another long Arctic winter. The vessel was exposed but found an anchorage at King Point behind a big stranded ice floe. It was only a few miles away from Herschel Island, the whalers' winter stopover, an American/Inuit whiskey-and-fur trading station. Several other ships were also caught in the early winter ice. Herschel was an isolated place far from law and order located in Yukon on Canadian territory, it was abandoned by the Americans a few years later.

In March 1906 Gustav Wiik died after being exposed during a blizzard. He was the youngest of the *Gjøa* crew and also the last person to die in the search for the Northwest Passage that had taken such a heavy toll of life over the centuries. Amundsen was on a dog-sledge mission to send telegrams about the expedition's achievement when Gustav Wiik died. An Inuit boy Amundsen had brought along on the *Gjøa* to be educated in Norway drowned in an accident at Herschel later the same spring.

*Amundsen's successful voyage was first celebrated when the expedition reached Nome in Alaska and local representatives entered the ship. There is a considerable group of ladies in the party.*

At last, the ice opened up on July 11, 1906, and *Gjøa* set sail along the Beaufort Sea, passed Point Barrow and sailed through Bering Strait for Nome in Alaska where the first celebration took place. Then the weary and weather-beaten little ship sailed all the way down the Pacific Coast to San Francisco. By then she had covered 3.460 nautical miles from Disko Island on the west coast of Greenland where the scientific part of the voyage started.

*Gjøa*'s arrival in San Francisco was not without complications. The City had hardly recovered from the earthquake when a cyclonic storm struck the coast and the ill-housed City. Off the coast, the same storm struck *Gjøa* so hard that the crew had to pour oil on the sea in an effort to reduce the buffeting of the waves that threatened to engulf her. A passing schooner gave her tow until the bar pilot could get her safely into Bonita Cove. Gjøa arrived unheralded on October 19, 1906, and was towed through the Golden Gate to an anchorage in Sausalito by the Revenue Cutter Golden Gate. Here Roald Amundsen, who had traveled ahead from Nome, joined his crew.

Two days later was a Sunday, the sun had returned, and the City in ruins rose to the occasion and prepared a royal welcome for the Norwegians. It started with a naval parade on the Bay to celebrate the herring sloop that conquered the Northwest Passage. As Gjøa passed the U.S. battleships Chicago, Wisconsin and Princeton, she was saluted by a grand dipping of flags and great cheers from the crews gathered on deck. At the end of the parade Gjøa was tied up at the Mission Street wharf in downtown San Francisco. Amundsen and his men were taken in carriages drawn by horses through the City to the Norwegian Club on Pine Street where the men were graciously welcomed.

Most of the following week became a continuous celebration with receptions and banquets in honor of Roald Amundsen. The festivities were capped by a banquet given by the City for 250 guests at the St. Francis Hotel. Guests were still living in a temporary structure built in Union Square, but the banquet halls and kitchens were already in operation. After these events Roald Amundsen left by train for Washington, D.C. to meet with President Theodore Roosevelt.

During the celebration week, discussions arose as to what to do with the Gjøa. The president of the Norwegian Club suggested that the Gjøa should be placed under the government's care at the Mare Island Navy Yard in order to become the first vessel to pass through the locks when the Panama Canal opened. She would then be the first vessel to circumnavigate the North American continent. In 1906, however, the Panama Canal was still well in the future. Would good old Gjøa after much suffering through the three years in the Arctic still be seaworthy when the canal finally opened sometime in the future? Amundsen lacked money to finance new projects. Even if he would have liked to take her home around South America, Gjøa was in no condition to undertake that much longer voyage without considerable repairs and new funding.

The Norwegian colony in San Francisco had mixed feelings about new enterprises for the Gjøa. They knew she was old and weary, and they felt she would be better off if she remained in San Francisco as a memorial to her voyage. They started raising funds to purchase the ship. Roald Amundsen was always hunting for money to pay for debt or for new expeditions, and he would sell her to the highest bidder, especially if it would include recognition that would strengthen his career.

Before Christmas of 1908, the Park Commission of San Francisco was advised by the Norwegian Consul that the Norwegian Colony was ready to place the Gjøa in the City's custody. On June 16, 1909, Gjøa was formally turned over to the City of San Francisco by the Norwegian Consul on behalf of the Norwegian residents in the area. The ceremony was held on board the vessel moored at Pier 1, and old Gjøa became U.S. property under the San Francisco Park Commission. She was said to be shipshape, but she had not undergone any major repairs, and it was obviously for good reasons that she was hauled ashore rather than left in the water. She had lived a tough life so far and was a tired 37-year-old wooden vessel.

On July 4, she was made ready for her final voyage at Mare Island, and was towed out through the Golden Gate and past the Cliff House. Lines, horses, winches and a large crowd waited for her on the beach. Gjøa's last voyage on her own keel ended on Ocean Beach in the northwestern corner of Golden Gate Park, where a berth was prepared for her. Gjøa was beached bow first at high slack water with many people present to see the operation. It was part of the July 4 celebration week for the year 1909. The sloop's last crew of six were "rescued" by the U.S. Life Saving Service's breeches buoy after they had hooked her to the lines from the shore. Then the Gjøa was slowly hauled up on the beach on an even keel with mast and yard standing. Her bowsprit pointed northwest as a symbol of the last chapter of more than three hundred years of exploration and human struggle to find the waterway to the north of the American Continent.

During the next decades the *Gjøa* deteriorated. Wind, sun, rain, sand, termites, fungus, rot and vandals took their toll until it was

*Gjøa's last voyage on her own keel was a short one. After being laid up for three years she was towed out the Golden Gate to Ocean Beach and pulled ashore. It was a great occasion with hundreds of spectators. Courtesy San Francisco Maritime Museum.*

*Slowly she emerges from the water. It took time, and most of the people had left before she reached her final resting place. Erik Krag collection. Photo courtesy Rolf H. Schou.*

obvious that something drastic had to be done to save her. The City was occupied with other and bigger problems and for a long time didn't seem to get around to the *Gjøa*. Partly it was lack of organization on the side of the donors of the ship and ship enthusiasts in general. Through the San Francisco *Chronicle* and other newspapers they tried to make the City aware of the problems. As it turned out, all efforts simply turned into another review of the subject. For people familiar with the Ocean Beach area, it was no secret that

the decision to put the *Gjøa* in this location was a bad solution from a conservation point of view. The location is extremely hostile towards wooden structures.

A few years after she was placed in the park, the first article appeared warning the City that *Gjøa* was rotting and advising that a proper housing should be provided as soon as possible to envelop the whole ship. By 1932, and in spite of numerous repainting jobs, it was obvious to everyone that she was in a very bad state. Dry rot

*The bow of the Gjøa. Behind the anchor, the ship looks badly deteriorated. The protective three-inch oak planking outside her hull is in place. Even the beaten-up bow with some loose iron strappings is clearly visible. She was, indeed, an old and weary vessel when this picture was taken in 1910. Photo courtesy San Francisco Maritime Museum.*

had made holes in her hull planking, and the first restoration took place. Well underway it showed that decay was much deeper than the surface planking. The old ribs, fashioned of bent tree trunks together with the massive keel were infected with rot and worm-eaten. The first restoring only postponed the problems temporarily, although the Park Commissioners in a letter to Consul Bjølstad of February 14, 1933, wrote,

*San Francisco's first historic ship soon became a landmark. "The Ship in the Park" was often used as a location for advertising purposes such as showing new cars. The above occasion celebrates a motor vehicle that has accomplished a coast-to-coast drive, arriving from New York in the early 1920's. Photo courtesy the Museum of the City of San Francisco.*

"The restoration of the *Gjøa* took about five months to perform and was completed some three months ago. The Park Commissioners deplored the possibility of this historic little sloop entirely disintegrating and took it upon themselves to restore it, as nearly as possible, to its original condition."

Five years later a letter from Director Isachsen of the Norwegian Maritime Museum in Oslo to the Consulate General in San Francisco stressed that something should be done to restore the *Gjøa* and put her inside a building if she was to be saved for the future. A meeting in October of 1938 at the mayor's office launched plans to get her out of the sand dunes and move her to Aquatic Park, restore her and put her inside a building.

A letter from the Park Commission to the Norwegian Legation in Washington, D.C. on the *Gjøa* states that "A throughout inspection of the ship *Gjøa* discloses almost complete deterioration. Repair is entirely out of the question…The proper procedure would be to rebuild completely the ship."

However, *Gjøa* and her voyage did not lack attention, in spite of the fact that she was kept inside a fence, keeping spectators at a distance. The "Ship in the Park" appears on post cards,

paintings, and other souvenirs and was frequently visited by tourists and local people. She was one of the landmarks of San Francisco and the City's first historic ship.

Roald Amundsen himself helped a great deal in making San Franciscans proud of the *Gjøa*. In 1911 he and four companions with three dog teams became the first men to conquer the Geographical South Pole, and returned safely to the *Fram* waiting at the Ross Ice Shelf. From 1918-1921 he sailed his new ship *Maud* through the North East Passage. Later he tried to fly to the Geographic al North Pole from Svalbard. It was a hasty venture, but he reached 88 degrees north and managed to return with all crew members after three weeks working around the clock to escape from the hostile Arctic environment, an outstanding achievement. In 1926 he headed an expedition in the Italian-built airship *Norge* from Kings Bay, Svalbard across the North Pole to Teller, Alaska, piloted by Umberto Nobile from Italy and sponsored by the American, Lincoln Ellsworth. It was the first trans-Arctic flight, and Roald Amundsen became the first man to have reached both the North and the South Poles, together with Oscar Wisting, a loyal companion for many years since the South Pole expedition. After the flight in the *Norge* he retired from polar expeditions at the age of 54. It was the only profession he had known.

In 1928 Roald Amundsen came out of retirement to aid Nobile, who had crashed in the Arctic with the airship *Italia*. Nobile had a radio on board, and had called for help. Several rescue missions were launched to find him. Amundsen headed a French-Norwegian expedition in the French airplane *Latham*. They took off from Tromsø in northern Norway on June 28, 1928, and were never heard of again. Roald Amundsen vanished in the polar sea where he had started his career on an Arctic sealer 34 years before. His tragic death triggered new histories of his heroic life and a re-publishing of his books.

In San Francisco a tall granite stone with the inscription "Roald Amundsen 1872 - 1928" and a

*Gjøa appears with different coatings over the years; the rigging and other details were altered at times. Shortly after she arrived in the park, her name-boards were moved forward to the position shown. Photo courtesy the Museum of the City of San Francisco.*

bronze relief of his head was raised in front of the *Gjøa*. It was dedicated in 1930. Poems and articles on the historic ship and its epic voyage were printed over and over again. Color postcards with *Gjøa* in Golden Gate Park went all over the world. She continued over the years to be a symbol of bravery and perserverance.

Only occasionally were persons permitted on board. Fashion models used her deck, fittings and ropes to present the new collection of beach and sportswear in a manner that today's *VOGUE* could envy. To new generations the *Gjøa* was presented as one of the world's most famous ships still existing. Her humble size, her long voyage and explorer Roald Amundsen were all part of that lesson.

Little did all this attention preserve her. The ship continued to suffer from little or none of the

*In April of 1927 Roald Amundsen returned to San Francisco for the last time and was photographed by the Gjøa, his first command. He had retired as an explorer after a remarkable life investigating and mapping many of the last unknown parts of our planet. During the first three decades of this century the polar regions were still more unknown to men than the face of the moon. Photo courtesy San Francisco Public Library, History Room.*

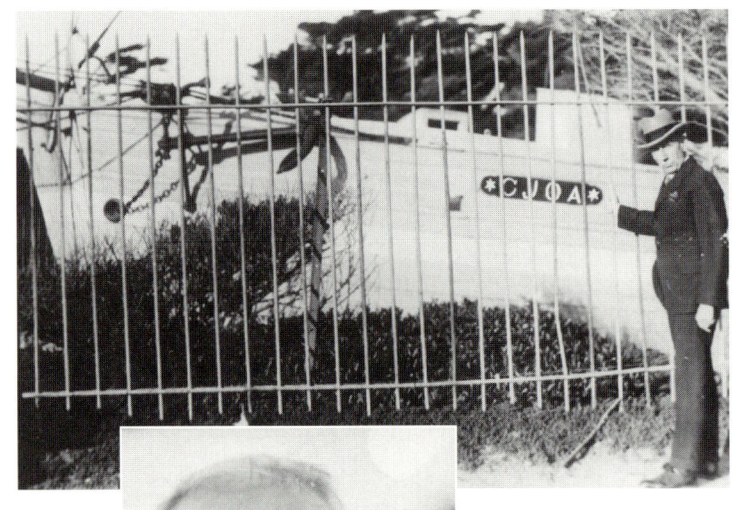

*This picture of Captain Roald Amundsen was taken in San Francisco in 1927. It is believed to be one of the last portraits made of the polar explorer who vanished with the seaplane Latham in 1928 on a rescue mission to aid Umberto Nobile. Photo courtesy San Francisco Public Library History Room.*

maintenance and care that all wooden ships so urgently need when they are exposed to the wind and weather.

An editorial in the newspaper entitled "The Shame of the *Gjøa*" in 1939 triggered off a new avalanche of articles and comments on the City's years of neglect. New demands were voiced for proper housing and restoration. "The city's shame is long-standing. If sufficiently strong demand is made on the City Hall, something will be done. Thus far the only formal protests have been made by citizens of Scandinavian birth residing here. Why should we leave it to them? Where are our Native Sons and first families?" said an angry San Franciscan in the paper.

Among people of Norwegian descent, this situation was especially difficult. They were partly responsible for *Gjøa*'s stay in San Francisco. The Fish Club and the Norwegian Club did not know what to do. Opinions were divided in the matter. After all the vessel belonged to San Francisco. However, when years passed by and the City failed to take proper action, the Norwegian community finally acted in 1939.

Five determined men including the Norwegian Consul General assembled on April 15, 1939 to form a non-profit, cooperative organization under the California laws, to be known as "Gjoa Foundation." The purpose of this organization was to assist in the preservation of the ship under the supervision of the Park Commission of the City, and to promote interest in the ship without gain or profit. The five men were S. Steckmest, E. Petersen, A. Abrahamsen, E. Krag and C. Hexberg. At the first regular meeting May 23, 1939, A. C. Storen, H. R. Higgins, P. R. Poulsson, C. G. Graham, Christian Blom, A. F. Pillsbury, E. J. Cashin, W. C. Empry, Harald Muller, C. R. Page and D. A. Webster also attended.

The bold action to form a group to help the Park Commission grew out of the general belief among people of Scandinavian decent that this would be the last chance to save anything of the *Gjøa*. California's Secretary of State Frank C. Jordan certified the foundation on May 19, 1939, and the Gjoa Foundation immediately went into business.

Mayor Rossi had just removed $25,000 for *Gjøa* repair from the park's budget. Delegations went to see the Finance Committee and the mayor who was opposed to the committee and gave no encouragement. The case received considerable publicity and in the end the mayor reinstated the $25,000 in the budget.

The first aim of the foundation was to help pass the revised budget and to gain future influence during the visit of the Norwegian Royal Highnesses Crown Prince Olav and Crown Princess Märtha in 1939. At the gala dinner at St. Francis Hotel for some 300 guests, Acting Mayor Warren Shannon stated that the restoration of the *Gjøa* would immediately be undertaken by the City. Needless to say this announcement received strong applause. The board of the foundation was careful to point out that the credit was due to resolutions and other help from the other Scandinavian societies in the Bay Area, and also from the City's Park Commission.

The City came up with $12,500 in the 1939/40 budget and the foundation managed to raise a total of $3,300 by the end of 1939. It was the City's intention to supply the other $12,500 in the next year's budget. Due to the difficult financial situation imposed by the war this figure was reduced to $2,500. The 1939 survey by marine surveyors Pillsbury and Curtis showed that the *Gjøa* in spite of all the repair performed in 1932 was once again in a state of decay from rot, corrosion and termites. She was resting in a pillow of sand.

When work finally started in the spring of 1940, it soon proved that her condition was worse than expected, and that the money available would be insufficient. It was therefore decided that the first step would be to dismantle the standing rigging, the mast, spars and all deck equipment, and to build a temporary shelter over the ship. The hull was to be stripped down to sound material before restoration started.

The mast proved to be of no value and was given to the Foundation for making *Gjøa* models, as it had to be replaced. The Park Commission became worried about the amount of work that was necessary for the restoration and suggested that only a small portion of the ship be kept, probably the stem and the bowsprit. After considerable negotiation the foundation succeeded in convincing the City that the work should proceed with the original $12,500 set aside for the ship. These negotiations took place at the same time as the Nazi forces invaded Norway in April 1940, which created additional disturbance in the minds of Norwegians everywhere.

The Gjoa Foundation managed to save the ship from being abandoned by using a variety of clever proceedings and simply admitting that the work could take years. The Park Commission agreed to go along for the time being. The *Gjøa* was sitting nice and dry inside her new shed and work could continue with whatever funds would be available from the City and the Gjoa Foundation. This 1940 decision became another of the ship's many narrow escapes.

Work staging was built around the ship, and restoration work on the hull started in July. It was a convenient working place. The shed was built to incorporate all activities during the rebuilding period. A combined office-and-tool house and a steambox were constructed adjacent to the restoration area. The old enclosing fence was kept and the original mast with some of the rigging attached was stored inside the fence on

*Gjøa's first major repair and restoration were relatively superficial. Boards were put on to cover up bad spots, the worst parts were replaced and she was given a good coat of fine paint. Photo courtesy San Francisco Public Library History Room.*

the north side of the shed. The petroleum engine, anchors, windlass, pump gear, rigging parts and iron work were stored throughout the main building. New stem, sternpost, transom, frames and beams together with necessary fairing, ribbands and supports were fabricated and erected as part of the first reconstruction, after all the rotten parts of the ship were removed.

*Gjøa's deck gear was in relatively good condition up until the Second World War. View of her deck looking aft.*
*Photo courtesy San Francisco History Room, San Francisco Public Library.*

The repairs and reconstruction were set up in accordance with the regulations and instructions of the City, whereas all the plans were developed and furnished by the Technical Committee of the Gjoa Foundation, who also provided a very competent restoration foreman to supervise the work.

The restoration was an ambitious project. In Norway the *Fram* had been preserved some years before and was used as an example of the proper methods and goals for the future of the *Gjøa*. A plan and photograph list was developed together with additional plans and sketches furnished by the Gjoa Foundation to secure a correct rebuilding. It was also important to use timber that was as close to the original as possible even if standardized sizes had to be used. Redwood and Douglas Fir were the primary woods issued for the restoration. The deck planking was to be vertical grain Douglas Fir, seams properly prepared and caulked with two threads of oakum and payed with marine glue.

All spars and rigging were to be renewed, and the dolphin striker and other iron fittings were to be made. The deck fittings were to be restored. Main house, skylights, hatches, water closets, rudder and tiller, sidelight boards, etc., were all to be constructed as shown on drawings and photographs. One of the very few original items going back in was the original stern tube, while a new two-blade propeller was to be furnished and installed on a dummy shaft. Finally the original nameboards were to be reconditioned if available, otherwise two new boards were to be carved in accordance with sketches.

The foundation was determined to do a good restoration, but it would not leave much of the original *Gjøa* behind when it was finished.

The J. L. Stuart Corporation was hired to do the reconstruction, but soon those funds were exhausted and the work abandoned for some time while waiting for next year's budget. The $ 2,500 finally granted was too little to restart. The following year the United States had entered the war; the restoration was immediately affected. All work not connected with defense was postponed. The *Gjøa* was to be maintained in temporary housing for the time being and the foundation was assured by the Park Commission and the mayor that the ship would be fully restored later. During the war Rolf B. Schou and Jørgen Galbe, the new Consul General, joined the foundation.

In November of 1945 the foundation reminded the City about the *Gjøa* and received a prompt reply that the City would consider the ship in its 1947 budget. The foundation, however, felt that five years of postponement was enough and set about a new fundraising campaign. The City confirmed the original $12,500. The Foundation managed to raise $16,000, the Norwegian Government contributed $6,500, totaling $22,500, yielding $35,000 for completion of the restoration. A special committee of shipping people, marine surveyors and an architect were appointed to supervise the development and work on the ship.

By 1949, *Gjøa* was completely restored at a total cost of $34,800. The ceremony was held on May 14, 1949, to celebrate the task which took almost eleven years to complete. *Gjøa* was in full dress, looking new all over. The Norwegian Singing Society and the Normanna Glee Club sang from her deck, a tap was performed by military cadets and several speeches were delivered. Her site had been excavated and cleaned so she could more easily be seen. Even a new fence for $4,600 was put up around her. "We hope that in 1972 on the 100th year anniversary, both of Roald Amundsen's birth and of the original launching of the *Gjøa*, that those in charge of her welfare will acknowledge that what was done here in her 76th year really gave the *Gjøa* a continued lease on life," said Mr. Erik Krag of the Gjoa Foundation during a short address to Mayor Robinson and Mr. Teller, chairman of the City's Park Commission.

Another six years passed without much attention to maintenance, and the hostile environment of Ocean Beach in the northwestern corner of Golden Gate Park again took its toll on the newly varnished surfaces and wood of the *Gjøa*. Vandals had taken the ship into possession from time to time by breaking through the fence. They had smashed her deck hatches, cut her rigging and even experimented to see if the ship was flammable. The City repaired the fence, and the foundation gave $1,500 to have her painted.

"The ship should never be permitted to get into disrepair now that she has been so basically restored," wrote the Gjoa Foundation in 1955 in its first recorded meeting since 1949. In spite of that, it was obvious to people following the ship's situation closely that she was neglected by the Park Commission and once more starting to deteriorate.

In 1957 the newspapers suggested Norway as the future home for the *Gjøa*. Through the years after the war, members of the Fish Club had become more and more involved with the ship. As usual, the Club tried to establish and promote support of cultural matters in an informal way. On many occasions when visitors from Norway attended the Club and were sightseeing the City, *Gjøa* was "a must" and her situation was frequently discussed. Rolf B. Schou, the Gjoa Foundation chairman, confirmed publicly that he had received requests to return the ship to Nor-

*The ship came out of a ten-year restoration period in 1949 looking great. For a few years everything was fine.*

way. He had replied that, after all, the vessel belonged to San Francisco. It would be up to the City to make that decision.

Two years later an arsonist tried to set fire to *Gjøa* again. A bonfire was made under her bottom and burned a hole in her before it was reported and extinguished. One week later the same thing happened again at night. A policeman driving by smelled smoke and called the fire department, which quickly extinguished the blaze. The report showed that an arsonist had doused paper with igniting liquid and shoved it through the hole in her bottom caused by the previous fire, then set the paper afire.

It was only three months later, on February 1, 1960, that the ship experienced a new and predicted misfortune. The buffeting Pacific winds accomplished what Arctic blasts during the world's toughest sea passage couldn't do. The sturdy little *Gjøa* was dismasted. Her new mast broke in two and Amundsen's crow's nest was crushed against the railing of the ship, which also suffered some damage.

This misfortune was predicted by the foundation. In 1957 they forwarded a letter to the City that the mast should be strengthened. This was followed up by correspondence back and forth, but repairs never progressed beyond the planning stage. It was especially annoying for the foundation to learn that the park was not going to do anything with the broken mast, as plans were then under consideration to move the ship over to Aquatic Park in the near future. This answer was devastating as the Norwegian delegation of dignitaries to the Eighth Winter Olympics in Squaw Valley was expected in San Francisco in just a few days. They were followed by an armada of European journalists, who had scheduled the *Gjøa* as one of their main topics of interest while in San Francisco. As polar explorers and great sportsmen, Nansen and Amundsen had, indeed, nourished the growing interest for winter sports, which eventually found a modern summit in the Winter Olympics.

With permission from the City, the foundation took on a speedy repair of the ship, and the delegations to the Winter Olympics could inspect the *Gjøa* in fine shape when they arrived. The ship was still in as good a condition as could be expected under the circumstances, but it was realized that the situation would after some more years require new and costly restoration. The Park Commission, as mentioned, was not inclined to spend money on her as they contemplated moving her to a place in the lagoon at the foot of Polk Street where the new San Francisco Maritime Museum had been established.

Mr. Karl Kortum, Director of the Maritime Museum and the man behind this proposal, had visited and inspected the *Gjøa*. He prepared specifications of repairs he deemed necessary for the maintenance of the ship. His extensive suggestions were studied by the foundation and found to be precise and adequate. Cooperation between the foundation and San Francisco Maritime Museum resulted in a mutual approach to the City. It was realized that the moving of the *Gjøa* to Aquatic Park could take from three to seven years. The City's Bureau of Architecture prepared a 34-page specification for repairs and preservation of the *Gjøa* for the park department, based on Kortum's specifications. The foundation's policy was to start on the repairs instead of waiting for a future move of the ship.

Initial repairs and securing were done in 1961. For the time being it was considered sufficient, and she looked sound and good from the outside. Kortum removed several original items and had them trucked to the Maritime Museum and stored to save them from further deterioration. He replaced them with dummies. During the 1960's it became clear that the museum was not able to move the ship to a more suitable location.

In 1965 an NBC-TV representative launched the idea of transporting the *Gjøa* back to Norway by the United States Navy—"in due honor back to her home port." The foundation discussed the idea, contacted Kortum and the City and finally told NBC of the difficulties involved in moving her. This occasion shows that the board seriously looked into all new possibilities for future securing of the ship. In 1968 the ship received yet another facelift, including some repairs done prior to the official visit to San Francisco of His Majesty, King Olav of Norway.

The new problems with hippies, fires and frequent disorder at the site of the *Gjøa*, together with the everlasting natural deterioration must have been frustrating for the foundation. The Park Commission and the City government showed little interest in the *Gjøa*. The media over and over again defended the ship and criticized the City for its indifference. It was definitely not the little voluntary foundation's job to keep and save the ship for the City of San Francisco. It was meant to be a consultative and assisting body with expertise on this type of a vessel, stated the newspapers.

Quite naturally, the old idea of an alternative place for the *Gjøa* found nourishment. Mr. Kortum's plan to move her, which King Olav also found interesting, was work in the same direction. It continued to be quite clear that Golden Gate Park was the worst possible place for her to be.

Still, it came as a complete shock to Mayor Alioto when the Gjoa Foundation in 1970 told him that authorities in Norway had asked if the ship could be given back to its native country. The mayor, of Italian descent, pointed to the fact that the *Gjøa* was a landmark in San Francisco and of particular importance to the Norwegians. It had become a gathering place for Norwegian organizations of all types during national holidays like the 17th of May. The mayor insisted that all the Norwegian organizations in San Francisco should be asked for their opinion on the matter.

The organizations all came out in favor of moving the *Gjøa* back to Norway. A resolution in favor of an urgent restoration of the ship in Norway and keeping her on exhibit in the city of Oslo after the repairs was signed in July, 1971, by the head of twelve Norwegian American organizations in the Bay Area. It was also mentioned that this could be done in time for the ship's hundredth-year anniversary in 1972. When confronted with the result, Mayor Alioto agreed to help out.

Obviously the idea of sending *Gjøa* home did not originate in Norway. It was her closest friends, the people of Norwegian descent in the Bay Area who, in despair and distress over the City's lack of responsibility nourished the idea of a transfer back to her old homeland as a last solution. Even the Norwegian Maritime Museum of Oslo was skeptical when the letter arrived from San Francisco proposing to place her at Bygdøynes.

*Gjøa* was an artifact of world history. When her voyage through the Northwest Passage was repeated in 1969 by the hundred-thousand-ton steam tanker *Manhattan*, at a cost of 200 million dollars, people shook their heads in disbelief at such an enterprise at taxpayers' expense. When built in 1962, the *Manhattan* was the world's largest tanker. The ship needed extensive reinforcement of the hull, a new bow and special propellers to become an armored icebreaker solely for the enterprise. Even so, the *Manhattan* was stopped by the ice and had to turn around and make a detour through the Prince of Wales Strait and the Amundsen Gulf, following the path of the *Gjøa* to succeed.

Norwegian shipping people in San Francisco felt that the least they could do was to investigate the Oslo alternative for the *Gjøa*. When doing so, top officials of a major ship company in Oslo told Christian Blom right away that "*Gjøa* is going home!"

Then things happened quickly. The Norwegian shipping industry assured Blom that they would not only provide the transportation, but also pay for the complete restoration of the ship. The Norwegian Maritime Museum decided they would accept the ship and place the *Gjøa* outdoors, next to the *Fram* house.

The Gjøa Committee of Oslo, headed by shipowner Tom Wilhelmsen, was ready to take full responsibility as soon as the ship left San Francisco, while the Fish Club's Gjoa Committee in San Francisco would arrange for everything until she left on a freighter outward bound

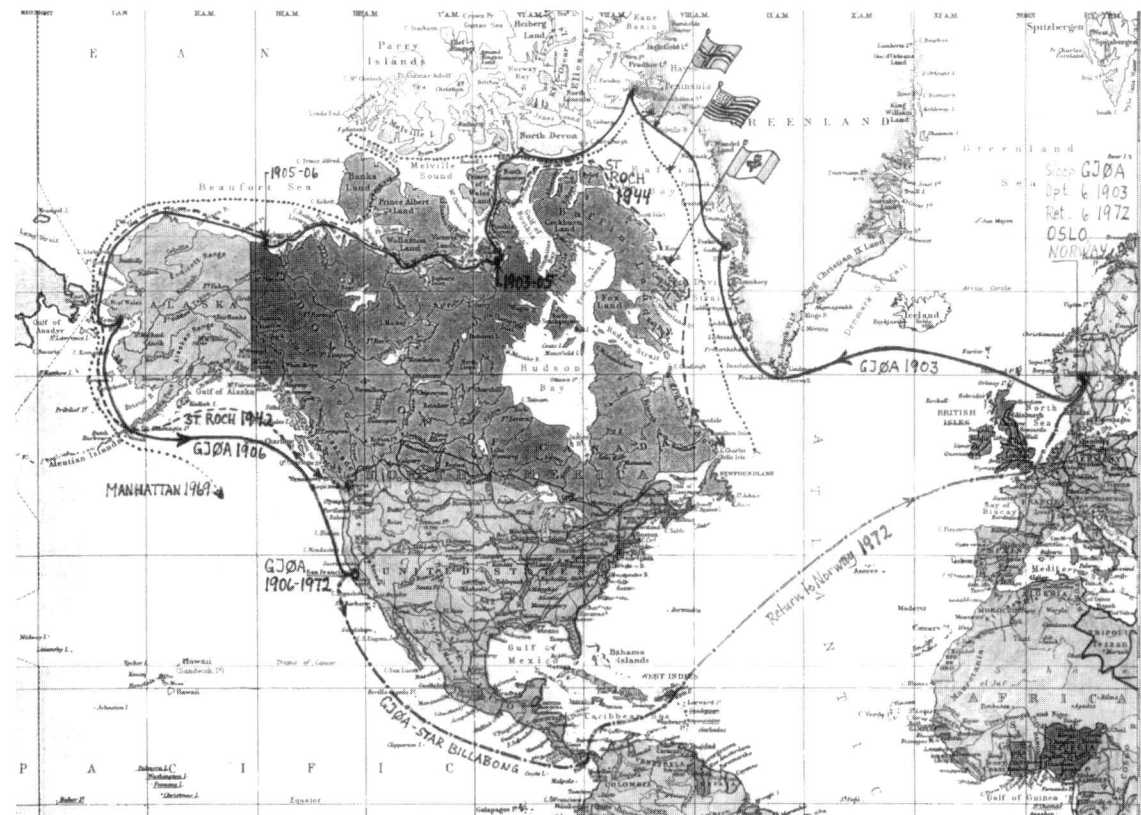

*Thirteen time-zones north of the Equator showing the voyage of the Gjøa, and of the American armored icebreaker* Manhattan *in 1969. The first ship, however, to follow the Gjøa through the passage was the Canadian St. Roch. She passed both ways during World War II.*

through the Golden Gate. The main task was to have the City give her back to the Norwegians. Until the legal ownership had been transferred, little could be done.

This plan triggered a series of articles in the San Francisco newspapers. They were not entirely in favor of keeping the ship. Retrospective articles and columns on the ship's situation over the years were printed. The City's neglect was never completely forgotten.

Over and over again during the prosperous post-war period, it was the Gjoa Foundation that inspected, reported, took action and repaired the *Gjøa*, while the City failed to allocate funds for the ship's upkeep. Young people crawled on board and broke the skylights, left beer cans, candles, textiles and trash on deck and opened the hatches.

In 1969 there was again an urgent need for repairs on the rigging. Riggers from the full-rigged ship *Balclutha* made new deadeyes and lanyards and rerigged her for a very favorable price. Skylights and hatches were repaired, rat-lines replaced and taffrail and fo'cs'le, where part of the bulwark had rotted, were repaired. The foundation paid the bills for this job as well as for occasional paint jobs on the ship.

After the City Board of Supervisors once more had turned down a maintenance and repair budget of $25,000 as well as a proposal for a new fence and floodlight to keep young people away from the ship, Consul General Finn Koren, Christian Blom and Rolf B. Schou suggested moving the ship to Oslo. A letter from Brynjulf Bull, the Mayor of Oslo, and Norwegian shipping executives helped in convincing the City that Norway was interested in bringing the *Gjøa* back to Oslo.

During 1971 the project created increasing activity in San Francisco. On September 13, Koren and Schou met with the Board of Supervisors and presented the case. After a short discussion a motion was made to grant the request, and it was unanimously approved to move the ship from its present site in Golden Gate Park in San Francisco to the Maritime

Museum in Oslo. The question was then how to move her.

Some odd suggestions surfaced concerning the implementation of the decision. Part of the Gjøa Committee in Oslo suggested that only the original part of the ship should be returned to Norway, which meant less than ten percent of the hull and also little of the rig and the rest of the equipment. As a joke it was suggested that the original parts could be shipped home by airmail.

Transportation to the ship was a problem because of all the overhead wires in the City. One possible way was to transfer her to a landing craft on the beach, take her out the same way she came in 1909, and later hoist her on to the ship. This alternative proved to be too complicated.

The plan finally chosen was to put a cradle under her and lift her out of the sand and onto a lowbed truck, take her down the Great Highway to Daly City, across the Peninsula and back up to San Francisco on the Bay side to avoid trolley wires and other powerlines en route to the pier. Even this travel involved removal of some overhead wires and had to be done at a particular time of day and with special permission and escort. The *Gjøa* was a rather large and clumsy article to move on land.

In March 1972, "red tape" in the City Attorney's office caused still another delay. Protesters showed up. Hippies joined in. A final approval was carefully discussed and recorded, and moved through the system under gentle pressure from all parties involved. It listed guidelines for the Gjoa Foundation to follow. Resolution No. 8976 of the Park Commission was finally issued on March 23, 1972 for the moving, transportation, insurance and responsibility, freeing the County and City of San Francisco from all and any claims. Even a complete cleaning up, redeveloping and nursing of the land where the *Gjøa* had been sitting for more than sixty years became the Fish Club's responsibility.

Such conditions might have concerned others, but for the Norwegian shipping community in San Francisco this was the green light. The Fish Club was on its home field. Shipping cargo was their profession and the *Gjøa* simply another special shipment. The difference was that this time they were shipping culture. It was an honor for everyone involved, every participant worked for free. The land move and cleanup was arranged by the Fish Club free of charge, as well as the transport and the ferrying in the Bay.

The motorship *Star Billabong* of Billabong Shipping Company in Bergen was selected for the voyage home. Their operating company was Star Shipping, and their San Francisco agents, Captain Ole Kalve and Captain Per Andreassen, were assigned to handle the transfer to the ship, loading and securing, while Per Høeg of Overseas Shipping administered loading in Golden Gate Park and the road transport. Rolf B. Schou had been the leader of the Gjoa Foundation for many years along with Erik Krag, and Schou supervised the whole enterprise. Consul General Finn Koren was helpful during the negotiations, and Christian Blom's good relations with Mayor Joseph Alioto were of great value. The common meeting place was the Fish Club. All the planning and organizing took place during the luncheons at Jack's. Per Høeg engaged Sheedy Trucking Company to do the work in the Golden Gate Park and get the *Gjøa* around the City and to the pier for shipment. Director Karl Kortum of San Francisco Maritime Museum moved the original parts out of the storage in the museum cellar. They were placed on board the *Gjøa* before she left.

The lifting of the *Gjøa* from her 1909 resting place and securing her in the cradle were done without problems. As predicted she was not too difficult to transport. The unit was loaded onto the lowbed truck, and Sheedy rolled her off with the police and a large escort including Pacific Gas & Electric workers to cut powerlines and connect them again when she had passed. Even a film team followed to record the event. She traveled around the peninsula by Colma and up to Overseas Shipping's Terminal on the bay side of the City. Ole Kalve reconfirmed measures and calculations and wired the data to his good friend Captain Øxnevad of the *Star Billabong* while the

*Gjøa left San Francisco 66 years after she arrived. The sloop was lifted on board a large ocean freighter. Finally she went through the Panama Canal, but not on her own keel as suggested before the Canal was built.*
*Photo by Karl Kortum, San Francisco Maritime Museum.*

ship was loading forestry products in Coos Bay, Oregon. Captain Andreassen was in Coos Bay and supervised the crew's welding of clamps onto the aft cargo hatch for the *Gjøa*'s rest during her long voyage home. Even the roughest Atlantic storm would not throw her overboard. While *Gjøa* was waiting at the pier, the whole Fish Club's team of "Tordenskjold Soldiers" lined up with paint brushes to do the final touch-up job on the *Gjøa*. She was going to look her best leaving San Francisco.

The *Star Billabong* was anchored in the stream. The loading was the hardest part. It was calculated down to inches, but to be sure Ole Kalve contacted the captain to advise him of the possible need to adjust the ballast. The *Gjøa* was taken out by a floating crane, lifted high and swung on board the 21,000-ton, high-riding freighter. She landed at her prepared place on the hatch. Within a short time the crew had secured her to the ship. Everyone involved in the shipment of the *Gjøa* was invited up to the captain's lounge for a reception, a short speech by shipowner Per Waaler, and a personal assurance from Captain Einar Øxnevad that "We will take good care of her!" Ole Kalve was the last man to leave the ship. He was back in his office at Star Shipping on California Street and watched as *Star Billabong* started her voyage home.

Later the Gjoa Committee in San Francisco gathered at Norway House for a farewell ceremony, while *Gjøa* herself was off at sea, high and dry on the aft cargo hatch of the *Star Billabong*. During the Amundsen celebrations in 1906 a member of the Norwegian Club suggested to his president that the *Gjøa* should be kept in San Francisco, and go home by the Panama Canal when, in the future, a canal was opened there. Could it have been P. R. Poulsson?

In Golden Gate Park the site was landscaped with shrubs and bushes planted inside the remaining fence, which still stands. So does the yellow-brown granite stone with the relief of

*On the hatch of the Star Billabong with the Gjøa well secured. From left Rolf B. Schou, Secretary-Treasurer of the Gjoa Foundation, Norwegian Consul General Finn Koren and Captain Einar Øxnevad with the bill of lading. Captain Ole Kalve, Star Shipping's operation manager is in the background in front of the propeller arch of the Gjøa.*
*Photo Karl Kortum, San Francisco Maritime Museum.*

# Gjøa, The Ship in the Park

her last captain, the Polar explorer Roald Amundsen. Few persons come to the site anymore to remember the *Gjøa*. But it still happens from time to time that people visiting the maritime museum ask for the way to the ship in the park, "What was the name again?"—*Gjøa*—"Oh, the Goha, I can't pronounce that!". They are surprised to learn she returned to Norway over twenty years ago.

The *Gjøa* came to San Francisco just after the big earthquake in 1906. For 66 years she remained in this part of the world. In those 66 years she became a distinct landmark of San Francisco, even older than the Palace of Fine Arts. It is not a surprise that visitors ask for her. Few ships have had more continuing interest from the Bay Area press over the years than this little herring sloop from Norway.

When *Gjøa* left San Francisco it was a day of mixed feelings for the City's inhabitants and the ship's greatest supporters. More than anything they wished her to stay. But at the same time they knew there was no other solution to her problems. San Francisco lost her first historic ship, but a small vessel had been saved and possibly functioned as an inspiration for other ship savers around the world.

Nansen's *Fram*, another famous polar vessel, was hauled ashore in Norway in 1930. But the Norwegians built a house around this much bigger ship and since then no rebuilding has been needed.

In 1972 San Francisco was still in the process of developing the world's largest collection of floating historic vessels. As this happened, San Francisco suddenly lost its first and oldest maritime relic. The *Gjøa* represented the foundation for the idea of saving old ships in San Francisco.

The *Gjøa* was saved and became a shrine before it became internationally common to collect and preserve historic ships. San Francisco has an exciting maritime history. It was for many years one of the greatest ports of the world and

*When Gjøa was secured in her new resting place at Bygdøynes in Oslo, a complete new restoration started. Photo Olaf T Engvig.*

for a long period also the ultimate port for sailors of all nations, either looking for gold, or just experiencing the great happiness of a sailor's life on the Barbary Coast. Gold Rush ships, left by their crew, sank at their moorings in the Bay. Even if badly damaged by teredo, remains of these ships are left under the City to this day waiting to be excavated. San Francisco has a potential in maritime and ship research like few other places. It is quite a tradition to keep.

The late Chief Curator Karl Kortum and his men have done an impressive job in establishing a fine collection of floating historic tonnage for the world to admire. It seems strange that the museum never got sufficient help from the City to add the *Gjøa* to the Aquatic Park collection; she was by far the smallest and least expensive ship to maintain. Lack of adequate support for sixty years made *Gjøa* synonymous with a bad conscience for the City. When serious attempts to save her occurred, they came almost too late.

*Gjøa*'s crossing to Norway was smooth sailing. Thirty days after she left San Francisco *Gjøa* was heading up the Oslofjord. Prior to *Star Billabong*'s arrival in San Francisco the freighter was scheduled for Rotterdam as her first European port of call. But the *Star Billabong* was Norwegian and her crew was from Norway. Star Shipping wanted to see the whole mission completed. A transfer in Rotterdam was out of the question. When steaming into the port of Oslo *Star Billabong* was flying the Norwegian flag for the occasion. She arrived on June 2, 1972, and her homecoming was proudly recorded. The *Gjøa* was taken to Bygdøynes by the Oslo harbor floating crane and placed on a concrete foundation next to the water. The Gjøa Committee in Oslo had managed to raise more than $100,000 in Norwegian *kroner* for the restoration and future maintenance of the *Gjøa*. On June 17, the very day 69 years after she left Oslo in a hurry, she was handed over to the Norwegian Maritime Museum.

Professional boatbuilders from Tørvikbygd in Hardanger, close to where the *Gjøa* was built, received the assignment to restore her hull and deck and make a new mast and yards. She looked good upon arrival, but when restoring started it was discovered that the whole ship was deteriorated. The best area proved to be part of the original ship, namely most of the keel, the transverse floors and a few of her bottom planks. From the bottom up she was renewed once more.

The Djupevåg family restored the ship beautifully during the summer and the fall of 1972 and 1973. In October of 1973 the ship was completely restored. In the spring of 1974 *Gjøa* was once again sparkling and ready to be rigged. She was even fitted out with a winter cover and is completely covered every fall. She has been rerigged every spring since 1975. Her winter dressing depicts her stay in Gjoa Haven at King William Island in the Arctic, 1903-1905.

The Norwegian Maritime Museum has used some of the ideas from Golden Gate Park. She still sits inside a tall fence and has not, until recently, been open to the general public. But contrary to her stay in San Francisco, she is well lighted and secure. People are not breaking through the fence to have parties on board anymore. Her bow is pointing out towards the water, even if the direction is not northwest. Close to the fence on the outside is a bust of her famous Captain Roald Amundsen on a more modest scale than the relief on the granite stone still to be found in Golden Gate Park. Underneath are two bronze plaques with summaries of her history including the years in San Francisco. One is in English and one in Norwegian.

The *Gjøa* has a fine location and can easily be spotted from the Oslo Harbor. It is a great addition to the great maritime collections at Bygdøy. However, the *Gjøa* is the only ship resting outside and still exposed to the wind and wet weather. Maintenance is observed much more closely than in Golden Gate Park, but a general knowledge of nature is enough to understand that she is slowly rotting away. That is just the nature of things.

The only way to save a wooden ship is to keep her inside a building. The Vikings built boathouses 1100 years ago, even so a wooden ship couldn't last forever and was broken up or placed in a burial mound to serve as the ship across to the other world. Thanks to this tradition we can display the beautiful Osebergship today even though the ship was hardly seaworthy when buried around 840 A.D.

Little *Gjøa* never got her boathouse. Not yet. She is still sitting outside. In her appearance of today she is a symbolic piece. From a distance she might be correct, the lines are beautiful. The *Gjøa* is a fine remainder of good and traditional Norwegian craftsmanship. But a closer look reveals that almost everything is different from the weather-beaten old ship that all the photos from 1910 so exactly depict. Photographs of the *Gjøa* in the park near Ocean Beach in San Francisco after her sailing days were over in July of 1909 show a ship with iron straps around her bow, and the gray and weather-worn hull and the extra three-inch oak planking Amundsen added outside her hull can easily be seen in stern view photos. After the land-hauling ceremonies in 1909 she was more or less left alone, and by 1940 she was ninety percent gone or more, and after yet another generation even less was left. Almost every item of the ship was crippled, stolen or deteriorated.

The *Gjøa* has a lesson to tell. We should start in time to save artifacts while they are still in restorable condition. Careful repairs and maintenance are possible if done properly. We are the ones responsible for saving history for the generations to come.

Only a culturally deprived society will leave little behind and provide the new generations with less ballast and a smaller platform to build their lives on. It is a good generation that saves for its children things to see and learn from, to make them feel important and proud of themselves and their ancestors' achievements. Since

*Rebuilding and rerigging of the Gjøa was a major ship construction project. When it was finished in 1974, she looked better than ever. Photo Olaf T. Engvig.*

the *Gjøa* was saved in 1909, several nations did well in preserving the last merchant sailing ships of the world. Today is the time to rescue the remaining steamships along with the last examples from World War II. So far San Francisco leads with the Liberty Ship *Jeremiah O'Brien*, the submarine *Pampanito* and seven other ships. This is the lesson the San Franciscans of today are teaching the world. They have a maritime collection for other cities to admire. But the San Franciscans had to learn it the hard way by observing the fate of the *Gjøa*.

Time changes, but the historic items preserved remain the same. The 1150 year old Oseberg viking ship is a good example. Transport memories are special. Ships, trains, cars and airplanes give a dimension to the past. Old times become very much alive on a ship propelled by wind, sails and muscle power or by steam, pistons and moving rods. Such ships are invaluable in spreading knowledge, history and understanding.

Of all the good deeds the Fish Club ever did through more than eighty years of service, the constructive work to save the historic ship *Gjøa* is by far the Club's greatest achievement. After newspapers, national television, the San Francisco Park Commission and a well established maritime museum failed, the Fish Club managed to rescue the *Gjøa* from the sand at Ocean Beach.

*The location where San Francisco's first historic ship spent more than sixty years. The place is as it was after Gjøa left in 1972. The old Dutch Windmill is in place. The Roald Amundsen monument is resting where it was erected and so is the fence; only the ship is missing. It is almost as if the City is waiting for Gjøa to return. Photo Olaf T. Engvig.*

# Gjøa, The Ship in the Park

*In 1995 Gjøa appears to be in good condition even though she still is sitting outside. Maintenance and protective cover up over the winter helps much in keeping the old ship sound.
Photo Olaf T. Engvig.*

CHAPTER IX

# The Windjammer

Christian Radich, the ship from the movie *The Windjammer*, is still remembered by thousands of Americans who went to see the motion picture. When she shows up in ports along the East Coast of the United States, the ship is always identified as "the movie ship."

Christian Radich was a star long before the film, but it was *The Windjammer* that earned her worldwide fame and distinction as a famous ship. She never got the Oscar, probably because the Academy would believe it to be somewhat peculiar to present the Oscar to a sailing vessel, even if she is quite a lady and did give a most outstanding performance.

The Windjammer *movie showing at the Chinese Theater, Hollywood, in August of 1958. Christian Radich finally sailed to California in 1979, arriving 22 years after the shooting of the film.    Photo Olaf T. Engvig.*

In the late 1950's Hollywood filmmakers were experimenting with new film techniques to be ahead of the rapid TV development. One of the most advanced was the Cinemiracle, a monstrous system with three cameras and six Hi-Fi sound channels. To present this system's superiority, a sailing vessel from the past was selected. Hollywood went to Norway and chartered *Christian Radich* for a six-month film cruise. The filmmakers managed to produce an extraordinary show even if the story was rather vague. It became a film to remember

*Sail Training ship* Christian Radich *on her longest voyage ever, inward bound through the Golden Gate.*

because of the variety of its venues, along with the format, color, sounds, and music. The beauty of snow-covered mountains, green islands, beautiful girls, blue seas, and white sails, along with eighty-five very young Norwegian cadets, full of life and discovering the world, made this film a legend.

The fact that the cadets were between fifteen and eighteen years of age and trained for the merchant marine makes the *Christian Radich* different. Most sail training ships train cadets for the navy. These cadets are older and appear much more grown up than the Norwegian boys, some of whom looked like kids. People often wondered how these young lads were able to handle a tall ship. *Christian Radich* has a reputation as a swift vessel under sail. This is due not only to the ship itself, her fine lines, her master, officers and crew, but also to the ability of the ship's cadets to work sail under all conditions. The ship has won many great international races.

In 1979 *Christian Radich* added another accomplishment to her fine list of achievements when she sailed in past the Golden Gate and entered San Francisco Bay. She was on the West Coast for the first time and further away from home than ever before. As for many a fine windjammer in the good old days of sail, San Francisco was the final destination on the outbound voyage.

Everyone on board was looking forward to this visit in San Francisco. The cadets had been on board several months and had called at London, Tenerife, Barbados, St. Thomas, the Panama Canal, Acapulco and Los Angeles before heading north for the City by the Bay.

This sailing endeavor had been planned for years and was a joint venture of the the Norwegian Export and Trade Council, a number of major Norwegian companies including SAS, the ship's owners and education authorities in Norway. The visit had been cleared with the United States federal authorities and the Royal Norwegian Ministry of Foreign Affairs through the Embassy in Washington, DC. In San Francisco the Consulate General was the host for the ship.

*Christian Radich* is a school for seamen, to a large extent paid for by the Norwegian Government. The ship belongs to Østlandets Skoleskip in Oslo. It is Norway's oldest sail training association. *Christian Radich* is manned by seven officers, ten petty officers and able seamen and some 88 cadets. They were close to the end of their training period when the ship reached San Francisco. By then they were well experienced in setting and shortening sails and performing all kinds of traditional shipwork.

The Consul General informed amongst others the Fish Club and asked their Rex Sole what could be done to make the stay in San Francisco a pleasant and exciting one for the ship's officers, crew and cadets. In a short answer to Mr. Prøitz, Rex Sole wrote, "I acknowledge with pleasure your letter of March 15th (1979) and will enjoy being part of the Honorary Advisory Council. You can count on me and my company to do everything possible to make the visit of the *Christian Radich* a real success."

On this particular occasion the Fish Club members and associates even took an active part in the celebration and entertainment during the ship's stay in Los Angeles prior to her arrival in San Francisco.

Long before *Christian Radich* had left Oslo, San Francisco had established an Honorary Advisory Council consisting of Herbert Bals, Iver Lyche, Jeffery W. Meyer, Warren Titus and Christian Blom to assist the Consul General and the Norwegian Consulate in making arrangements for the ship's visit in San Francisco. Again it was the people getting together for the Thursday luncheon at Jack's that rolled up their sleeves. They managed to involve local organizations and clubs to host and assist the cadets, while also attending to the fundraising needed for the event. The Seamen's Church handled the cash and would receive whatever was left over.

In less than one hour, and after several calls had been made, all funds needed for bus transport for a week for the entire crew of 105 persons were in hand. None of those solicited declined to assist the enterprise. Each cadet was given ten dollars for "pocket money," and another five dollars for lunch . The funds paid for a party the cadets themselves arranged on board, including pizza, soft drinks, disco-music and decorations. The funds were also sufficient to purchase tickets to a rock concert and a lunch and dinner at Norway House so the galley staff also could have a day off. Telephones and three color TVs on board were also provided. As in the good old days, the captain went ashore and lived in a hotel. A hotel room for the captain and his wife was provided. In the end a goodly amount of the funds was left for the Seamen's Church.

Consul General Per C. Prøitz was impressed with the efficiency and the help he received from the committee behind the event. For the shipping members of the Fish Club, the *Christian Radich* was just another ship, except that this time she was a famous old full-rigged lady, and she would have everything for free.

Vice Admiral J. S. Gracey of the Twelfth U.S. Coast Guard District advised in all the necessities, while Overseas Shipping and their business associates handled the arrival and departure, and cooperated closely with the harbor authorities and others for pilot, tug, mooring space and water, as well as fireboat and escorts. All port dues, pilot fees, tug and line fees were waived. U.S. Custom and Immigration Services helped the ship similarly and made the Consul General's task easy.

The Consul General was assisted by a working committee consisting of Per Høeg, Hans Berge, Ole Kalve, Arne Borgersen, Pastor J.

*Captain and pilot discussing the harbor approach with 14 square sails still standing and the ship propelled by wind alone.*

F. Knudsen, John Pedersen, Rolf Ruud, James Knudsen, Alex Vanderlinden, Vice Consul Enok Nygaard and Lisbeth Smestad from the Consulate. This committee assisted the Consulate in a wide range of efforts from mini-cruises and promotion on board the ship to the welfare of and service to the seamen sailing her.

The yacht clubs in the San Francisco Bay Area were advised of the ship's arrival and encouraged to form a flotilla of boats to accompany the *Christian Radich* from where she picked up her pilot, under the Gate and to her berth at

Pier 45. They responded positively and asked their members to join the escort. The powerboats were to be out in the ship channel and the smaller craft were to intercept her further in. She was scheduled to arrive under the Golden Gate Bridge at approximately 9:15 am on November 24, 1979. The Coast Guard and the City of San Francisco provided the heavier tonnage for the official welcome.

When the *Christian Radich* was secured alongside, Commander Jan Fjeld-Hansen was greeted by the Deputy Chief of Protocol for the City of San Francisco, the Port Director, the Director of Customs, the Chief of the Fire Department, the Commanding Officer of the Naval Support Activity (US Navy), and the Norwegian Consul General. The guests were invited on board and were served refreshments in the captain's quarters. A few short speeches were exchanged.

The week between November 24, and December 1, 1979 was proclaimed *Christian Radich* Week in San Francisco. The ship's visit became a special event. Young Norwegian cadets in their navy-blue uniforms strolled around Fish-

*Cadets on shore leave in San Francisco.*

erman's Wharf discovering whatever was left of this famous old sailor's town on the West Coast of the United States.

During the week residents of San Francisco had several opportunities to get a closer look at the *Christian Radich* through on-board visits, as well as seeing her with sail set in the Bay and at the Golden Gate. The young cadets also learned a lot. The Fisherman's Wharf pier was a strategic position for the crew to experience San Francisco on ordinary shore leave. It was a goal that each of the boys get the most out of their stay. There always had to be some boys on board as watchmen, for preparation of meals and other duties, but the ship's work was rotated so everyone could go ashore. The cadets found San Francisco friendly, fascinating and colorful.

Possibly they experienced some of the same feelings as many young sailors in the old days felt when their ships took them to San Francisco. The cadets fell in love with this City just as their predecessors did. In the old days, many seamen jumped ship. Young deckhand P. R. Poulsson of the great four-mast bark *Breidablik* of Drammen came to San Francisco in 1894 on a long voyage around Cape Horn from Scotland. The ship stayed in port for 41 days. *Breidablik* returned to England without P. R. Poulsson, and on the next voyage out she foundered on the coast of east Africa. Three of her crew drowned. As we know, the young deckhand left behind became a full-fledged San Franciscan, and the father of the Fish Club.

The cadets of the *Christian Radich*, however, didn't jump ship; they were scheduled to be home with their families before Christmas. The youngsters had lots of fun. They went sightseeing and shopping, participated in a church parade and a service in the Seamen's Church. The young sailors were taken to Muir Woods, played soccer games, and attended a dance at a local high school. They were hosted by Norway House and were given a nice reception at the Norwegian Club. The cadets dropped in at the Seamen's Church just like full-fledged sailors, and they discovered the City on their own.

Being ambassadors ashore, promoting Norwegian products on board, guiding people around the ship, showing skill and seamen's work, conversing with visitors and explaining

*The* Christian Radich *on a day cruise off the Marin Headlands.*

different parts of the ship and rigging were all part of the cadets' education on this particular voyage of the *Christian Radich*.

The Consulate General and the Norwegian American Chamber of Commerce coordinated a mini-cruise on the Bay and outside the Gate for all the participants. American and Scandinavian visitors were impressed with the cadets' performance as they went aloft and set square sail to give the guests a little personal experience of sailing life on a windjammer. A sailor's supper party on deck was arranged by members of the Norwegian Food Industry. SAS hosted a dinner party. On the last night, while Captain Fjeld-Hansen was giving his farewell party, the cadets were invited to a Johnny Cash concert. Many of them got to meet the singer and talk to him.

On December 1, the *Christian Radich* sailed for San Diego, saying goodby at the Gate to her escort of yachts and a Coast Guard vessel. Five days later, Commander T. A. Goodall from the Navy's Sealift Command Office in Long Beach personally escorted the officers and cadets onto the SAS jumbo jet homeward bound for Oslo from the Los Angeles International Airport. He provided each one with the latest press releases for their scrapbooks, promising Captain Fjeld-Hansen to keep a close watch on his ship at the U.S. Naval Station in San Diego. The old lady was left behind to celebrate Christmas with the Americans.

Commander Goodall conveyed a very complimentary letter to the Norwegian Embassy in Washington, DC, recognizing the captain, officers, petty officers and cadets of the *Christian Radich* for their good seamanship and a job well done in representing their nation.

The *Christian Radich* has a rather remarkable history. This sail training ship was built by Framnæs Mek. Værksted, Sandefjord, Norway in 1937. She is a three-masted, full-rigged ship of 676 gross tons, 205 feet long, 36 feet beam and 15 feet draft; she carries 1330 square meters of sail, her mainmast head is 128 feet above the sea. Maximum speed with sail alone is fourteen knots. During the 1979 voyage she had an auxiliary GM diesel

SHIPPING AND CULTURE

The Christian Radich *is one of the world's most famous wind ships still in operation on the high seas. Only in drydock, as here in East Boston, is it possible to see the lines that make her sail so well. Photo Olaf T. Engvig.*

## The Windjammer

The windjammer is made to cooperate with nature, in respect of the environment.
She will sail the oceans by wind alone, managed by lines and tackles
operated by the muscles of able men.
Photo Olaf T. Engvig

engine of 650 HP, which gave her a speed of nine knots. She is a "square-rigger" and "fully rigged," meaning she has square sails suspended horizontally from five yards on each of the three masts.

Christiania Schoolship Association, to which the *Christian Radich* belongs, started back in 1877 when a number of dignitaries in Christiania decided to buy the old Maine-built ship *Star of Empire,* then named *Lady Gray.* She was renamed *Christiania* and became a stationary sail-training vessel in Christiania each summer until 1902. She was relieved by the sailing brig *Statsraad Ericksen.* This ship provided sail training for merchant marine cadets until the *Christian Radich* started her career in 1938. During the years since the first ten cadets embarked on the *Christiania* in 1881, approximately 11,000 cadets have been given basic training in seamanship on board these three sailing ships.

*Christian Radich's* history makes her a great ship. She has become known as an outstanding sailing vessel, distinguishing herself in many of the Sail Training Association's international races over the years, often winning the tall ships class.

Her career did not start well. After a visit to New York and the World Fair in 1939, she came home to Norway as World War II broke out. Before a new season started, Norway was invaded. The Germans took this new ship into their possession. It is fair to say that she was not treated well. During a drydocking in Kiel towards the end of the war, the dock was heavily damaged in an allied air raid and capsized with the *Christian Radich* inside. The ship suffered considerable damage to her hull, deck, superstructure and rig. After the war, research started in Norway to try to locate her.

She was found submerged inside the crumbling dock in Kiel Harbor; her topgallant spars and some yardarms were all that was visible. It was doubtful whether she would ever sail again. The ship was salvaged and towed to Norway to the yard that built her. Needless to say, the windjammer looked terrible, but the owner, the yard and the people of Norway wanted to repair her. Shortages of almost every item of shipbuilding and repair materials made restoration of the *Christian Radich* lengthy and difficult. Not until 1947 was she ready to take on her first contingent of post-war cadets. This first voyage was to Lisboa, Funchal, Ponta Delgada and Aberdeen. A film team followed and shot the motion picture *Vi seiler.* The film was shown in cinemas all over Norway during the following years.

The late 40's and the 50's were booming years for Norwegian shipping. Ships were being built for Norwegian shipowners in large numbers, and the demand for seamen was almost unlimited. Many young Norwegians went to sea to earn good money and see the world. Training of cadets accelerated. Intensive courses of two months became common, and even during the winter young boys received training. Cadets and teachers struggled through the winters in a cold ship with frost and condensation inside the hull. Epidemics of flu and cold raged. The cadets' only longing was for the day they could leave for the tropics. The ship was built for summer expeditions and was not suited for use during the cold Norwegian winter. Everyone suffered. *Christian Radich* took a lot of strain, and by 1954 she looked tired.

Mariners have always competed. It was prestigious to be on a fast ship and fly away from slower sailing vessels. In port, rivalry among ships could trigger severe fistfights, or sophisticated ways of pinching something off a nearby ship. During the days of sail, competition in rowing or sailing small craft was common. Today it is football and other shore activities. The British formalized traditional sailing ship rivalry when a committee called "the Sail Training Association" (STA) in 1955 invited the last remaining tall ships in Europe to a formal race. The following year the race was run; it was between Torbay and Lisboa. An impressive armada from eleven nations participated. *Christian Radich* and *Sørlandet* represented Norway. This first post-war competition among square-riggers can, in many ways, be seen as the link back to the informal but still demanding races with cargos of tea and other products, that were concluded with the famous grain races during the inter-war period.

The international Tall Ships Race developed and has been the tradition ever since. In this very first tall ship race, *Christian Radich* sailed a fine race and won.

She became famous. Tall ships experts from several maritime nations marveled at how the little Norwegian full-rigged ship with very young cadets could leave behind bigger and bolder ships. Even the Americans were impressed. Hollywood became interested. In December of 1956 *Christian Radich* left Oslo on a six-month charter for America and a film contract. Among the sponsors were Norwegian shipping interests. For a whole generation of people, the motion picture *The Windjammer* became a synonym with the *Christian Radich*.

With the cameras whirring, the ship left Oslo right before Christmas 1956 for Madeira Islands in the Atlantic and crazy sledge rides down steep pebblestone roads, then on into the West Indies with calypso and limbo dances and beautiful girls for all the boys, and finally on to New York. The rendezvous with the world metropolis became an orgy in light, color and sound. There was even Grieg's Piano Concerto in A-minor on the pier next to the ship with the Boston Pops Orchestra and Arthur Fiedler and the young cadet Sven Erik Libæk as solo pianist, accompanied by pictures of the snow-covered mountain ranges, valleys and fjords of Norway.

It was culture on all levels and for every taste, a film that had everything. The climax was a joint exercise with a U.S. Task Force with carriers and air support roaring by. In the middle was the *Christian Radich* with all sail set and at full speed heading right at you—into the theater—a great bow wave being thrown up straight towards your face. If you were eight or eighty you would remember that sequence. It was the ultimate of thrills and action in those days.

The motion picture was shown at Hollywood's Chinese Theater well into the summer of 1958. In all the history of sail no single recording of a sailing ship has been given more attention as ultimate film entertainment. Landlubbers with no relation to the sea remember *The Windjammer*, as does everyone else old enough in the late 1950's to have seen the movie. Since then she has always been "the ship from the movie."

This was excellent publicity for Norway, and for the next few years the ship was a hit. The next summer she sailed to Las Palmas, with a visit of condolence to Hamburg for the loss of the *Pamir*. During the filming, *Christian Radich* had met with the large German cargo-carrying sail training vessel *Pamir* in mid-Atlantic, when both were outbound. The two ships sailed together for a while, exchanging regards. *Pamir* was on her way to Montevideo, Argentina to pick up cargo. She never came home to Europe. On her return voyage in 1957 she was lost in a hurricane southwest of the Azores. Only six of 86 cadets, officers and men survived. The *Pamir* disaster was the end of cargo-carrying windjammers as sail training ships. Too many tragedies with sail training cargo vessels had occurred.

In 1960 Oslo was host for Operation Sail or "Op-Sail," and the race went from Færder to Ostende. Because *Christian Radich* was a fast ship and home ported in the host city, she carried all the trophies for the race. She made an excellent start, and sailed ahead of everyone. Her captain chose a more northernly course. Unfortunately, calm weather struck the North Sea and the time limit was approaching with little progress for any of the tall ships. Then a wind arose and all competitors swiftly finished, apart from *Christian Radich*. She struck headwinds and was tacking back and forth in the North Sea, having a hard time getting into port for the award ceremony; the moral being, of course, that everyone has a chance against wind and weather.

During the meeting in Oslo the idea was launched to have an Op-Sail race across the Atlantic for the 1964 World Exposition in New York. The STA supported the plan, and the first Trans-Atlantic Tall Ship Race from Lisboa to Bermuda was born. Norway was able to send all her tall ships to this race. It was the first and the last time the nation managed to present the *Statsraad Lehmkuhl*, the *Christian Radich* and the *Sørlandet* in the same race. Together they were

USCG Eagle *and* Christian Radich *in a close call, shortly after the start of the Trans-Atlantic race on the last lap of the voyage home from San Francisco. Photo Olaf T. Engvig.*

manned by 327 merchant marine cadets. As we know, *Christian Radich* was the winner. The parade in New York became a great gathering of sail training ships. It was particularly noticed that the small nation of Norway was presenting three ships full of young boys. *Christian Radich* then repeated her grand maiden voyage of 1939. She sailed to Montreal and the St. Lawrence Seaway, becoming that summer's main event in cities like Milwaukee, Detroit, Cleveland, Alphena, Toronto and Chicago where thousands of people waited in line for hours to get on board the "Windjammer" herself.

Despite all the fame and glory abroad, for many years during the late 60's and the 70's the owners of these fine vessels struggled to make them survive as schools for young boys to be trained as sailors. The argument about the relevance of training in sail for the work in modern ships never ended, even with pedagogical specialists and psychologists confirming that sail training is a good basic training for life at sea, as it is for life on shore. The proud sailing ships and their great supporters were fighting a losing battle against bureaucracy. The government grants for such education declined steadily and *Statsraad Lehmkuhl* and the *Sørlandet* were finally retired as cadet training ships and sold. The fight for the *Christian Radich* went on. Actors from the Windjammer movie and other celebrities volunteered support for the ship.

In a last ditch effort to keep this classic Norwegian cadet ship sailing, the ship's board of directors joined the Norwegian Export Council in an attempt to use the ship as an ambassador for Norwegian trade and export products. Scandinavian Airlines, Norwegian sardines. Jarlsberg and Kavli cheese, Helly Hansen products and Unitor Ships' Service would all be presented on board the *Christian Radich* on short harbor or coastal cruises for specially invited guests. Commercial Attaché Bjørn Kvisgaard of the Norwegian

Export Council was the architect behind this joint venture, together with President Hakon Lunde and Director Øivind Schau of the ship's board. Scandinavian Airlines was the major contributor. This novel initiative is what drove the cruise across the oceans to the Pacific and San Francisco. The big question was whether this sales enterprise could be combined with proper education of merchant marine men.

*Christian Radich's* expedition to the Pacific Ocean and the western United States was the longest voyage any Norwegian sail training ship had ever made. The ship covered nearly 20,000 nautical miles on her voyage to the other side of the world and back. This voyage started from Oslo, Norway in August 1979, and she arrived in San Francisco on November 24. She used her auxiliary engine part of the time and sailed through the Panama Canal on the way.

Her crew, with Christmas presents from San Francisco, was flown home on Scandinavian Airlines and enjoyed a nice Christmas with families and friends. They returned to California in January 1980 to man the ship together with new cadets.

On the homeward voyage from San Diego the ship called at Acapulco, the Panama Canal, the Caribbean Islands and several cities on the east coast before arriving in Boston, the last port of call in the United States. She was drydocked in East Boston before joining the grand parade that commemorated the 350-year anniversary of the city of Boston under the motto "The Tall Ships Are Back," together with an armada of other sailing vessels.

The start of the 1980 Trans-Atlantic Tall Ships Race to Kristiansand, Norway followed immediately after a week of celebration. For the *Christian Radich* it was the last lap of the homeward voyage from California. For the first time STA had decided to plot the race in the north Atlantic from Cape Race to Rockall, the favorite path of low pressures blowing across the Atlantic. They could not afford another race canceled or aborted due to lack of wind. *Christian Radich* had scored well in earlier light weather races. Many competitors came to think of her as a fast ship in light wind. Experienced mariners knew that this time the wind would show up, and they expected that the fairly small Norwegian would not do well when the ocean started roaring.

When the boys came on board in San Diego they were told that three things were very important. They would receive a maritime education, they would act as ambassadors and help promote Norway, and they were to win the race. Much had happened since San Diego. They had finished their exams. The cadets had shown that they could take orders, work hard and pull together. In their blue uniforms and with their exemplary behavior, they had made many friends and charmed foreigners. Finally, *Christian Radich* had the opportunity to show that the smallest ship of the pack still was the fastest even in strong wind, when bigger ships with a longer waterline according to physical laws could maintain a far higher top speed.

One member of the Fish Club, the author, signed on the *Christian Radich* in Boston for this trans-Atlantic race. The following is from his diary account of the voyage.

> The whole north Atlantic Ocean lies ahead, and we are 104 men on board a small sailing vessel with no way to escape. We have one tap for water, guarded by the watch on duty and only for drinking, cooking and shaving. For all other needs from shower to laundry, seawater would do. Only the wind will help us across. Optimists predict reaching the North Sea by July 1.
>
> After the start from Boston on June 4, the *Christian Radich,* with all her yards braced on the wall, picked up an eight-knot speed. The *Eagle, Guayas* and *Creole* were left behind and disappeared under the horizon. *Gorch Fock* was out of sight on a more northern course. Only *Danmark* followed behind, way to the south. When she was out of sight, it was not expected that any of the ships would see each other until in the port of Kristiansand.

The ocean is so big, the courses and speeds so different.

Before the end of the day we stopped. Completely. No wind. Sails clapping against masts and rigging as she rocked in the sea. Nothing much happened the next day apart from a couple of heavy squalls. They were pitch black and the cadets took in all the upper sails. But little wind showed up, only pouring rain. It happened over and again. Finally the old mate, with 23 years on the ship, got tired of the pointless exercise; no cadets were sent aloft. Of course, that was the one big squall absolutely full of wind. Before any one really knew, the *Christian Radich* heeled over and took off like an arrow. On a flat ocean she plowed cascades of white water from her bow and left it way down on the lee side. With royals on top the log showed close to fourteen knots. She had never in her 42 years been reported doing that much. The two old mates started joking. The masts were going to be replaced when she got home. Why not give them the final test, help the shipyard, and cut costs of removing the old ones?

Shortly after, the first big low pressure came up from behind. The ship got a fine push. She moved fast, very fast. The old watch record of 44 miles in four hours, made before World War II, was suddenly within reach. She did 12 knots then, should she perform better than in her youth? The answer came within the watch. She did 46, the next watch 47, another 46, then 47. She finally closed off the day doing 48 nautical miles in four hours, or a nice 12-knot average. In the blackest night the cadets were sent aloft. Royals were furled at midnight. At 12 o'clock the next day she had done 275 miles through the sea. With the full force of the Gulf Current pushing from behind, the ship had made close to 330 nautical miles towards Europe.

Captain Fjeld-Hansen finally decided it was time to leave the deck. He gave his mates the order to contact him before taking in any sails. Then he went below. The experienced mates knew they did not want to wake up their captain for no reason, so they held on. The helmsman was ordered to be alert and stay on course. She had never sailed like this before. It was just as if she never had been challenged. And the weather continued with good and steady wind from behind. Still the *Christian Radich* with her short waterline, compared to the *Gorch Fock*, never had a hope of reaching the top speed of this German. It passed the *Christian Radich* far to the north and on a slightly shorter course. At one point she was 400 miles ahead. If she continued, even fighting the handicap of the smaller *Christian Radich*, she would clearly be the winner of the race.

The third and largest low pressure in a row was closing in. *Guayas* withdrew from the race. *Danmark* had rig damage and was sent hundreds of miles off course. She left the race and headed for the Channel. *Creole* had broken a mast. A couple of the smaller vessels did not report. People ashore started worrying. The *Christian Radich* was sailing steadily, close to a 12 knot average, and continued to show 14 knots in the fastest sprints even when more and more sails were taken in. Finally she was flying on mainsail, foresail and bare masts, still logging 12. The *Eagle* had withdrawn from the race early due to other assignments.

The sea started to look ugly. Huge masses of water towered up from behind. The *Christian Radich* was running downhill, speeding across a short plain, up and over the next hill, surfing into the valley of the wave. She was sailing magnificently even if the storm was furious. No wonder ships behind reported trouble.

The wind indicator topped 64 knots relative wind, she did 11 and was sailing well. The air was full of water. The top of each wave was blown off. Visibility was only a few hundred yards. The big German was the only tall ship left in the race, fighting the *Christian Radich*. Being to the north she got on the wrong side of the pressure center and suffered head winds. She had to tack. By the next day she had lost 500 miles to the *Christian Radich*, which was standing into the North Sea as the very first ship in the race.

*Christian Radich* then got a head wind and had to tack past the Frigg oilfield, while the later contenders picked up a new breeze at Shetland and headed straight for the finish. The race's last position report showed that the German had a 45 mile lead and was further out, but the wind was falling off. *Christian Radich* sailed up close to the Norwegian coast and picked up the summer breeze and the coastal current going around the Lindesnes. The Germans understood that the *Christian Radich* now could sail faster.

It was very early morning and quite foggy at the finish line outside Oksøy Fyr. Suddenly the VHF-radio of the *Christian Radich* picked up the well-known voice of *Gorch Fock's* radio operator as they passed the finish line, calling Kristiansand Harbor and reporting, immediately continuing: "Where is *Christian Radich* ... we can't see the *Christian Radich*, and, after a short pause, a trembling voice, 'Is she in port?' The answer was no. 'Are we first then?'" the operator shouted into the microphone. A short time later the *Christian Radich* passed the finish line. Everyone was on lookout; the *Gorch Fock* was out there somewhere in the haze.

The 1980 Boston-to-Kristiansand race between the *Gorch Fock* and the *Christian Radich* is written into the history of sail as one of the great races between famous windjammers. It had all the ingredients of outstanding seamanship and sailing performance. It resembled some of the greatest races between famous ships back in the days of sail. After a continuous battle with the elements across a whole ocean and 3300 nautical miles, the two ships were next to each other across the finishing line.

Due to her smaller size and shorter waterline the *Christian Radich* won over *Gorch Fock*. with almost 24 hours. Once and for all she proved that she is a good sailer in all weather.

The crossing from Boston to Kristiansand took fewer than eighteen days, which is an outstanding achievement. It is said that only once in the history of sail has a ship made the same passage in less time. That was long ago.

Before this voyage, the *Christian Radich's* record speed for a watch was 11 knots. On this incident, she broke that record 19 times. Half of the passage she did more than 200 miles a day, and her average speed for the whole run was eight knots. That is very good, bearing in mind that she was sitting almost still for the best part of two days. The cadets longing for a mid-summer's night in Norway got their wishes fulfilled. The round trip from Oslo to San Francisco and back was completed in a little over ten months.

The *Christian Radich* was the last windjammer built in Norway. It is fair to say that the constructor of the ship designed a ship that today is among the most beautiful and famous wind ships left on the oceans of the world. Over the years she has been this seafaring nation's greatest maritime representative abroad, a fine ambassador, and excellent training for young Norwegains. This ship's adventures have been many and outstanding. Former cadets look upon their days on the *Christian Radich* with pleasure and appreciation, knowing the experience has been fundamental to their development.

Few memories of the past stimulate the fantasy more than the old-time sailing ship. They connected the continents when there was no other way. Today they keep our own age connected to the past. The symbolic value becomes

## SHIPPING AND CULTURE

*Under a full storm in mid ocean she reefs down to a minimum of sails;
even then she continues to fly away at speeds exceeding twelve knots.
Photo Olaf T. Engvig*

## The Windjammer

The sea becomes ugly as waves grow to 25 feet or more and keep coming on deck.
However, the Christian Radich continues racing.
Photo Olaf T. Engvig

*The teenagers who sailed the* Christian Radich *to victory in the most demanding STA race ever, lining up for a grand reception by the Mayor of Oslo in the City Hall, immediately after the ship's safe return from her epic voyage to San Francisco. Photo Olaf T. Engvig*

greater because there are so few sailing vessels left that still can perform in a race. The *Christian Radich* carries on a classic tradition. In Norway it can be linked to the early days when sailing vessels were a necessity for people living on a long and rugged coast. They also were the means of transport for the first generations of settlers from Norway to the United States. Last but not least, the *Christian Radich* is a proud memory of a time when hundreds Norwegian merchant square-riggers sailed all the seven seas.

Going to or from America on a windjammer driven across the ocean by wind alone is a privilege few modern men have experienced. Those who have will never forget it.

The *Christian Radich* has not been involved in new enterprises like the San Francisco voyage of 1979-80. But she is still in full operation as a cadet ship, for both boys and girls. The Fish Club of San Francisco is one of many organizations which has helped the *Christian Radich* survive, and survive she has through narrow escapes in war, at sea and in government offices ashore.

CHAPTER X

# Royal Visits

There are many ways in which to make friends. One of the more obscure is to knock down a royal person with an oar. After graduation in Norway, Christian Blom went to England for a business education at Oxford. He attended St. Catherine's. As a good Norwegian, he knew how to row and was soon on St. Catherine's Eight together with a couple of Americans and a British coxswain. The competition among the different colleges at Oxford was fierce, the river rather narrow, and to be the better boat, the boat behind had to row up to the boat ahead and "bop it." During one of the traditional river battles, St. Catherine's boat overtook Balliol, another Oxford team. In the heat of the battle Christian Blom struck no. 6 in the Balliol boat with his oar, only then realizing it was the Crown Prince of his native country. There were few Norwegians attending Oxford and young Blom went over to apologize for his rude behavior.

Blom's family had a summer cottage at Vikane not far from Bloksberg, the royal family's summer home on the island of Hankø. During a masque ball at Hankø, young Christian met a beautiful girl that made his heart beat. He danced with her the whole evening, but before the masks came off, she disappeared. He searched high and low trying to find out who she might be, but in vain. She had vanished completely, just as in the fairy tale. The heartbroken teenager started investigating and learned that her name was Lissi. She was the fourteen-year-old sister of Astri Berg, who was married to Captain Emil Nicolaysen, King Haakon's Aide-de-camp. Astri Nicolaysen was a close friend of Princess Märtha of Sweden, who was to be married to the Crown Prince of Norway. Young Blom had lost his heart to the Cinderella of Hankø. They met again. At another party given by Lissi's father, Dr. Berg, the Crown Prince attended. The two former Oxford students became friends.

Christian Blom left for the west coast of the United States shortly after, but could not forget his masque ball princess. In 1932 he married Elisabeth (Lissi) Berg in Los Angeles, California. Crown Prince Olav had married his Princess three years before. As a result of these interfamiliar acquaintances, a lifelong friendship began to develop between the Bloms and the Royal Couple. When the Crown Prince and Princess came to the United States in 1939 they found old friends in San Francisco, and were pleased to learn that the Bloms had moved into the Fairmont Hotel to be close by during the Royal visit.

On their first visit to the America, His Royal Highness Crown Prince Olav and Her Royal Highness Crown Princess Märtha arrived in San Francisco on the early morning of Norway's Independence Day, May 17, 1939. The seventy-day-tour through the United States was their first long journey away from official obligations in Norway and their three children: Princesses Ragnhild and Astrid and the little Prince Harald, only two years old at that time.

The tour started in New York with the arrival of Their Highnesses on board the *S/S Oslofjord* on April 27th. The Royal Couple went to Michigan, Illinois, Wisconsin, Minnesota, Iowa, Missouri and Kansas, on to Williams in Arizona, with a side trip by bus to the Grand Canyon and the El Tovar Hotel, the next day to Boulder Dam. From Kingman, Arizona, Their Highnesses traveled on to Los Angeles, San Pedro and San Diego. The schedule was to be in San Francisco for the 17th of May Celebration. The express night train arrived in San Francisco that morning and the Royal Couple was met at the station by a welcoming committee, headed by Consul General Sigurd Steckmest, his young daughter with flowers, a brass band playing, and many cordial handshakes of welcome. They were soon escorted to the Fairmont Hotel where Their Highnesses had a suite with the most superb view of San Francisco, the Bay and its new bridges, and the Exposition site at Treasure Island.

After a private luncheon held by the welcoming committee and a press conference at the hotel, the Royal Couple went on a tour of the City. It included Mission Dolores with a visit inside the old church with the soft light, a reminder of medieval churches in the Old World. Across the street was the Scandinavian Lutheran Church at 19th and Dolores Streets. The church was jammed with people, as the Royal Couple entered. The pastor proudly told of the happiness everyone felt having them there. His Royal Highness Crown Prince Olav made a short speech about tradition and historic ties. He emphasized the importance of the church in nurturing and keeping the Norwegian spirit and tradition alive all over America.

The tour continued on to Twin Peaks for a view of the City with its skyscrapers, large business district, and all the neatly kept Victorian houses that are such a distinct landmark of San Francisco. The Royal Couple got a taste of the steep hills. They saw Chinatown, which was said to be the largest Chinese township in the Western World. Even a fishing harbor, so Italian that it could be mistaken for a Mediterranean fishing port, was part of their experience of San Francisco.

In Golden Gate Park near Ocean Beach was the site of the Norwegian relic *par excellence* in San Francisco, the sloop *Gjøa*, with a proud profile of her skipper, explorer Captain Roald Amundsen on the granite stone in front of the ship. As one would expect, many Norwegians were gathered at this spot. Their Highnesses were told that it was a tradition for Norwegians to gather at the *Gjøa*. The sloop did not look too bad, but when the Crown Prince wanted to go on board he was warned not to. *Gjøa* was not safe any more, but the City had finally promised to do

*In 1939 HRH Crown Prince Olav and HRH Crown Princess Märtha became the first Norwegian royalties ever to visit the United States of America. This signed portrait picture was given to the Norway House after the visit in 1942.*

something for the ship. The Gjoa Foundation, then a new organization, gave an orientation. Their goal was to assist the City and get the ship under a roof and inside a structure. The foundation hoped to create a polar museum around the ship, with the *Gjøa* as its centerpiece.

After a stop at the hotel the party drove out to Treasure Island and the 17th of May banquet at the California Hall where 700 people were gathered. On the gallery between the large Norwegian and American flags was the California flag. California's governor, an elegant gentleman of Scandinavian descent, was seated between the Royal Couple at the head table. In his speech the governor praised the Norwegian contribution to California, and Crown Prince Olav answered by giving thanks to California for treating them so well.

After the banquet, Crown Prince Olav and Crown Princess Märtha were taken on a tour of the Exposition while the California Hall was made ready for the 17th of May entertainment. The Exhibition reminded them of a scene from Arabian Nights with trickling fountains illuminated in various colors, all kinds of flowers and trees lighted under a clear dark night sky. The Royal Couple commented on the architectural composition, cultivated and exquisite in form. The impression was that the architects behind the structures had struck a fine balance of modern lines and respect for tradition. They found the site to be extremely well arranged.

Some 1500 persons gathered inside the great Hall for the grand party. Music was provided by the famous Norwegian Singing Societies and the singer August Werner. The Crown Prince gave the main speech of the day. He emphasized the strength of having a particular togetherness day for a people so scattered around the globe as the Norwegians, to unite people living under different conditions, without a division in party or class: a day of tradition, and to remember those who have passed and those who will follow. Only persons true to their origin and with respect for their parents can become good sons and daughters and be good citizens in a new country. "That is just what I have experienced today," said the Crown Prince.

"Norwegians coming to America cultivated the new land, manned American ships, became fishermen of the Pacific. They left strong impressions in industry and in cultural life. They built churches, schools and even universities. They created a press and a rich literary legacy and became important contributors in science and art. They also became leaders in politics and governors of states. The Norwegian immigrants were good citizens and faithful inhabitants of their new homeland that gave them a good opportunity. But they didn't forget their old country. For all this Norway is grateful...The storm that today is raging in the world unites the USA and Norway as never before. The spirit of the 4th of July created a new spirit at Eidsvoll. That's why the message May the 17th is bringing is aiming towards all of us in the USA as in Norway and fastens the ties between us," finished Crown Prince Olav. The speech was met with a long standing ovation, finally ending when everyone started singing the Norwegian National Anthem. When the Crown Prince Couple left, they were cheered with loud shouts of "HURRAH!"

The next day the Royal Couple concentrated on seeing the different parts of the Exposition. His Royal Highness was in uniform and was received with full military honor. The tour around the different displays and pavilions included a special visit to the Danish and the Swedish pavilions, while Christian Blom in striped trousers and top hat tried feverishly to mop up the floors of the Ski Lodge. Someone had forgotten to turn off the sprinklers watering the grass roof and water had escaped and soaked the outside lawn. An inspector of the lodge had trotted all over and later gone inside with muddy shoes. The Royal Couple ended up in the Norwegian Ski Lodge in due time trailed by photographers and news reporters.

The story told is that the Crown Prince managed to slip away to the kitchen for a glass of water. Only a waiter was in there and recalls this young military guy to whom he gave water: "He asked permission to sit down, and sat down by the stove on the box for firewood and started asking about my family and other things. We had a nice little chat while I attended my business. I took him to be a soldier in the Royal Escort. His English was excellent. Then a distinguished man came in and said: 'Your Highness, there you are. I see you have found something to drink. People are wondering where you went.' The Crown Prince handed back the glass and said 'thank you' with a bow. I couldn't dream he was the Crown Prince of Norway, he was so nice and friendly."

The luncheon was given by the Exposition at the Yerba Buena Club for 200 special guests. Going home from the Exposition, the Royal Couple went across the bridge to see Oakland and Berkeley and to pay a short visit to the UC Berkeley campus and look at the Sather Tower. In San Francisco the Commander of the 9th Army Corps, General A. J. Bowley, and his wife gave a reception for Their Highnesses in the park-like environment at Fort Mason.

The evening dinner was hosted by the City and its Chamber of Commerce at the St. Francis Hotel. The room's setting was that of a European chateau. Well-known Norwegian-Americans, city authorities and foreign attaches were present.

This dinner was directed by a somewhat cheeky toastmaster. He gave a toast suggesting that the wine was as smooth as cod liver oil and lauded Norwegian shipping, saying the country's achievements in this area certainly made them the leading nation in their part of the world.

The toastmaster recounted that the representative body of 150 in the Norwegian *Storting* had a salary of only three dollars a day, producing short and easy-to-interpret laws. To be governed so well for such a low price must be a privilege and an honor. "That's what we really need here in California," he added, and turning towards Crown Prince Olav, he asked politely on behalf of all Californians if His Royal Highness could stay for a while and teach the Americans how to govern. And he suggested that the Crown Prince could augment his remuneration by taking a job on the side as a movie star in Hollywood. The request for the Royal Couple to remain in San Francisco elicited great cheers. The tone was set, and when Mayor Shannon in his speech assured his audience that the City now would go ahead and restore the *Gjøa*, the Norwegian spirit rose even more. Thomas J. Watson of the International Chamber of Commerce also spoke on the shipping industry's great success.

In his answer, the Crown Prince first politely regretted he could not accept the request to become a Californian, due to constitutional laws of his home country. He then talked about his nation's trade deficit with the United States. "Norway's large, speedy and modern merchant marine is not only the nation's pride, it is also a necessity," said Crown Prince Olav. "We buy much more than we export to the US, and need the strong currency the shipping produces to pay for the balance. In good and in bad times the Norwegian merchant marine has sailed the high seas without support from the state. This particular area has seen an enormous expansion. More

*A pack of six-meters of the Olympic class of which Crown Prince Olav was an Olympic Champion. Photo courtesy St. Francis Yacht Club.*

and more shipping-related people from Norway settle here. My only wish now is that more and more Californians will come and see us in Norway. They are all heartily welcome," said Crown Prince Olav.

The following day the Crown Prince went sailing on the Bay in a six-meter sailboat similar to *Norna VI*, his boat at home. Crown Prince Olav skippered the *St. Francis* in competition with some of the St. Francis Yacht Club's most able yachtsmen in the other sixes: the *Strider* (ex *Lulu*), *Corinthian V* (ex *Light Scout*) and the *Saga* over a seven-mile course off the St. Francis Yacht Club, in good sailing conditions and a very fresh breeze from the west. The newspapers were all there and reported:

San Francisco Bay yachtsmen yesterday met a Norwegian sailorman. He liked them. They liked him. In a 7-mile race in good wind a 6-meter combat took place off the Marina Shore. His Royal Highness not only took the *St. Francis* across the starting line in front, he led at every mark in the race, until the run home from Crissy Field buoy when a recalcitrant spinnaker refused to lift. He lost by a spare ten seconds to Stanley Barrows in the *Strider* after a lead of more than a minute a beat to windward.

Members of the Crown Prince's crew were sorry about the spinnaker, but proud of the clever start and his leading at all five buoys. They presented the verbal accolade, "He really can sail a Six!" The sailing event was followed by a luncheon at the club. Several of the club members had sailed in Europe and some even at Hankø. The Crown Prince's sailing skill was well known to them. After all, he won an Olympic Gold medal in the six-meter class for sailboats during the 1928 Olympic Games. When Crown Prince

*Crown Prince Olav in the* St. Francis *is leading the race off Crissy Field during the friendly competition in the Bay in 1939. Photo courtesy The Royal Palace.*

Olav was about to leave, the yachtsmen started singing "He's a jolly good fellow."

The Crown Princess joined her Prince at the yacht club for an automotive excursion across the Golden Gate Bridge and to other points of interest. Their Royal Highnesses left that afternoon from Oakland by Southern Pacific Railway for Portland, Oregon.

The San Francisco stop was considered one of the great highlights of the visit of Crown Prince Olav and Crown Princess Märtha's grand tour of America that started on April 27, and

*Crown Prince Olav's Racing Pennant presented by His Royal Highness to the St. Francis Yacht Club on May 19, 1939.
Photo Olaf T. Engvig by courtesy St. Francis Yacht Club.*

ended on July 6, 1939, when the Royal Couple sailed home to Norway from New York on S/S *Stavangerfjord*.

The tour of America was also a lecturing journey for Their Royal Highnesses. In San Francisco as in many other places speeches were given on topics of mutual Norwegian-American interest. On several occasions during the visit to San Francisco the newspapers took pictures and interviewed the Royal Couple. The papers described their program as strenuous. They gave the Royalties fine press and had space also for friendly remarks. The media showed great concern for the Crown Princess' scant time to go shopping for the children. As a whole the visit proved to be valuable in promoting Norway. Norwegian-Americans all over the country turned out to see and cheer the royal visitors from their native land.

Just months after Their Royal Highnesses arrived back in Norway, the world was thrown into turmoil by Hitler's invasion of Poland and the declaration of war in Europe. As in World War I, Norway tried to remain neutral and for some time seemed successful. Norwegian merchant ships were sunk by the Germans, and the country was forced to act on a few incidents of neutrality disputes. The American merchant ship *City of Flint*, taken as a prize by the Germans, was liberated in Haugesund and her German prize crew detained in Norway. The "Altmark Case" in Jøssingfjord also aroused prompt international discussion. Some were blaming Norway for not protecting her neutrality, saying such action could be used as an excuse for an assault on Norway. Today we know that Hitler's intention long before this was to occupy Norway for strategic reasons and to secure access to raw material for the German war industry.

The invasion of Norway on April 9, 1940, came as a shock to many Norwegians, partially because the government refused to believe intelligence reports indicating that an attack was being launched. They relied on a strong belief that the country could stay neutral. Norway experienced something similar to what the United States learned in the surprise attack on Pearl Harbor.

Reality reached Oslo when a small patrol boat, the converted whale-catcher *Pol 3*, charged the German naval force at the entrance to the Oslofjord. Her skipper was killed. The invasion of Oslo was further interrupted by the stopping and sinking of the main German ship the *Blücher* in the narrows by the Oscarsborg Fortress later the same morning. It gave the President of the *Storting* the few hours needed to improvise an escape for the King and the Royal family, to gather the important people needed for Norway to constitutionally function, to secure important documents and to move the gold reserve out of Oslo. It was hastily loaded up in a long convoy of trucks and taken north into the country. The President of the *Storting*, C. J. Hambro, and his men did an excellent job in providing for the formal bodies needed to set up parliamentary meetings and govern the country together with the King in various places inland, while German airplanes tried to locate and bomb them. King Haakon's and Norway's "no" to the Germans was loud and clear. Unlike other nations occupied by Hitler's forces, Norway withdrew without surrender, leaving the stage to the intruders and their puppet, which never had more than a fraction of support from the Norwegian people. Their leader, *Nasjonal Samlings*-führer Vidkun Quisling, tried to recall the mobilization order and wired Norwegian diplomatic missions abroad without success. In San Francisco, Consul General Sigurd Steckmest received a telegram on April 10, 1940, with a demand of obedience to Quisling. He immediately notified Ambassador Wilhelm von Munthe af Morgenstierne in Washington DC by telegram and learned that Washington and New York had received similar telegrams. The Ambassador advised "no answer," and sent the embassy in Stockholm a telegram of full support for Foreign Minister Halfdan Koth.

The large Norwegian merchant marine fleet received orders to proceed to the nearest neutral wegian monarch to visit the American continent, even though Norway had been a kingdom for more than 1100 years.

Prior to this visit, Christian Blom, Rex Sole of the Fish Club, wrote a letter to the members of the Club that begins:

> On April 30, 1968, H. M. King Olav V of Norway will be coming to San Francisco with a contingent from the Norwegian Government, Norwegian Embassy, and also a delegation representing Norwegian industry, shipping and travel. The business delegation, however, does not accompany His Majesty and does not participate in the official part of the King's visit.

The letter requested that the Fish Club members host the business delegation. King Olav came to the United States on a sixteen-day tour by invitation of President Lyndon B. Johnson, who had visited Norway as vice president some years before. The King arrived in New York and then continued on to Virginia for the night before meeting with the President at the White House.

The next morning King Olav arrived in Washington, and was greeted with full military honors at the White House and welcomed by President Johnson, Mrs. Johnson and Secretary of State Dean Rusk as "an old friend of this country." The Navy band played the national anthems of the two countries while a battery of howitzers fired a 21-gun salute in his honor. In his welcome speech President Johnson noted that there were more than three million Norwegians and people of Norwegian descent in the United States. The press noted that King Olav V was a reigning, but not ruling, constitutional monarch.

In his dinner toast, President Johnson called the King "the rarest of all distinguished visitors to this house—a man who is non-political by law." King Olav in his toast told President Johnson that the Norwegian people expressed "relief and pleasure" at news of the initial negotiations for peace in Vietnam," and he added that he spoke for all of his countrymen in expressing "the

*On the South Lawn of the White House, before undertaking the official tour of the United States in 1968 that ended in San Francisco, the King of Norway salutes his hosts. To the right, Secretary of State Dean Rusk. To the left, Norway's Minister of Trade Kåre Willoch. Photo US Army, by courtesy The Royal Palace Library.*

fervent hope these negotiations may be attended with success and lead to peaceful settlement."

King Olav traveled on to visit Cape Kennedy, Houston, Los Angeles and San Francisco, where the official part of the tour ended. There the *Examiner* offered a whole front page on May 1, 1968, with a portrait picture of the King of Norway, and VELKOMMEN DERES MAJESTET in royal blue capital letters on top. The saluting was done in a spectacular regal manner. San Francisco's Mayor Joseph Alioto himself was said to have been its architect. According to the paper, the mayor showed his "unique ability to bring color and drama to the ceremonial functions of his office." Magically he had the majestic rotunda of the City Hall transformed into a banquet hall bedecked with flags. Red carpets ran for the entire length of the grand staircase. King Olav and his official party came down the stairs after a visit to the mayor's office. The King took his seat at the head table together with Mayor Alioto and his wife and His Majesty's entourage.

The table was set with gold service from the St. Francis Hotel. The white tablecloths were draped over with red and blue cloth, and flower arrangements were in red, white and blue. Heraldic banners hanging all around the rotunda gave the City Hall the appearance of an old European castle.

Two-hundred-fifty city officials, dignitaries and members of the Norwegian American colony toasted His Majesty King Olav V of Norway on his first official visit to San Francisco. The King in responding to the mayor's toast acknowledged the warm and sincere feelings he and his countrymen had for "this beautiful City."

The hostesses were in either red, white or blue outfits and wore miniature flags. At each table was a centerpiece cluster of red and white carnations surrounding a world globe with small national flags placed in Oslo and San Francisco on each side of the globe. The superb luncheon came from the kitchen of the St. Francis Hotel. The municipal band played background music.

*King Olav V arrives at the City Hall for talks with Mayor Joseph Alioto and a royal luncheon in the rotunda.* Photo San Francisco Chronicle.

*In San Francisco the great City Hall was the site of the reception for the official visit of His Majesty King Olav V of Norway. Photo Olaf T. Engvig.*

today part of San Francisco's history, but it is hardly forgotten by anyone who had the privilege to attend this unusual occasion. The spacious rotunda has frequently been used for floral displays and ceremonies while receptions for reigning monarchs remain among the rarest events.

The City Hall was dedicated in 1915, and is considered one of the finest examples of French Renaissance architecture in America. The lofty dome rises more than 307 feet from the ground and is 13 feet higher than the Capitol in Washington, DC. San Francisco's old City Hall was totally destroyed during the 1906 earthquake and fire. The new City Hall did, however, suffer severe damage in the 1989 earthquake. It is scheduled to be completely retrofitted and repaired before the turn of the century.

Potted shrubs, olive trees and other greens from the Golden Gate Park lined the rotunda and the corridors.

It was the first time the City Hall had served as a banquet hall for a King. In effect, Mayor Alioto tossed a noontime ball in honor of the Norwegian Monarch's first visit to San Francisco since the years of World War II. It was part of a plan to bring City Hall more into the City's ceremonial public life. In that respect he did well. Europeans, being familiar with using their City's "grand living room" for special occasions, found this quite natural. Why hire a hotel when the people have their own guildhall to attend to high official visitors, even if they are left with a lot of dirty dishes? Mayor Alioto's experiment and the 1968 Royal Banquet at the City Hall is

The City Hall banquet was the grand finale of His Majesty's 23-hour visit to San Francisco and the end of the King's official visit to

*King Olav took time off to greet and chat with the crew of the motor vessel Traviata before the luncheon on board the ship. Photo courtesy San Francisco Chronicle.*

163

the United States in 1968. This brief visit to San Francisco started at 4 p.m. the day before when the King landed at the airport in an Air Force jet and was greeted warmly by Major Joseph Alioto, the acting consul general and the local committee including old friends. King Olav stayed at the Fairmont Hotel and attended a reception with nearly 400 persons. Later the same day a formal dinner in the King's honor was given by members of the World Affairs Council at the Pacific Union Club, and attended by about ninety persons. At this exquisite dinner, King Olav was presented with the Order of Maritime Merit and its highest rank, that of Grand Commander.

At the same time another dinner was given by the Fish Club at the St. Francis Yacht Club for some 200 persons, honoring the representatives of the Norwegian trade delegation traveling along with the King and working with contacts and partners on the way. Their mission was to improve business and trade relations with the United States. In 1968 Norwegian ships still made more calls in the Bay Area than ships from any other foreign nation. But the trade mission was also interested in new markets as well.

The morning before the reception at the City Hall, His Majesty went on a motor tour around the City with a grand police escort to help keep a tight schedule. The King visited Fisherman's Wharf, Ghirardelli Square, the Marina and the yacht harbor, the Palace of Fine Art, the Legion of Honor, Seal Rock, the *Gjøa* and back through the Golden Gate Park to the Norwegian Seamen's Church on Hyde Street in less than one hour, skipping the new sightseeing hotspot, Haight Ashbury and the cradle of the world's hippie movement and young "flower-power" in 1968.

For nearly an hour he stayed at the Church, greeting children, shaking hands and talking to seamen and members of the Norwegian colony. King Olav was famous for remembering people. Suddenly his blue eyes looked at one man in the line, and looking a little surprised the King said, "I remember you. You were in the same class as my son Harald." That was many years ago, the man could not have been more than a boy then.

From the Church, King Olav moved on to the liner M/S *Traviata* at Pier 26 for a mid-morning champagne reception hosted by Christian Blom. Newspapers noticed that the dignitaries waited while the King shook hands with the crew, chatting a little with some of them and laughing cordially.

His Majesty was introduced to distinguished guests including federal and state officials involved in shipping and other endeavors between Norway and the United States, and conversed with members of the local shipping community. The King was supportive of the plan of Karl Kortum, director of the maritime museum, to move Amundsen's polar ship *Gjøa* from Ocean Beach to Aquatic Park. "It would be logical to move the ship to a location where more seafaring people congregate," the King told Kortum and Mr. Rolf Schou, head of the Gjoa Foundation. His Majesty left the ship in time to visit Mayor Alioto at his office in City Hall before the grand reception described above.

The King then continued on an unofficial visit to Seattle before stopping in several places in the midwest, including Minneapolis, Minnesota and Fargo, North Dakota. At the dinner in Seattle, it was noticed that the King's only decoration was a gold pin in his lapel, a miniature of the Legion of Merit presented to His Royal Highness, the Crown Prince, right after World War II by President Harry Truman.

Many Norwegian immigrants that came to America during the last century settled as farmers in the Midwest, inspired by the Homestead Act of 1862. Others settled in the Pacific Northwest working in the fisheries and forestry, with Seattle as its center. A second migration has taken place this century within the United States as descendants of the first settlers moved to the cities and to the West Coast together with new immigrants from Norway.

Seven years passed, and His Majesty once again returned to the United States. During October of 1975, a grand celebration of the Norwegian-American Sesquicentennial Jubilee took place. It was 150 years since the very first organized immigration from Norway to the United States arrived in their new homeland on the sloop *Restauration*.

King Olav stayed in the United States for 25 days, visiting different parts of the nation and seeing Norwegians and people of Norwegian descent from coast to coast. When the visit was planned, the King personally insisted that a visit to San Francisco be included in the itinerary. King Olav later stated himself that he had happy memories from previous visits "to this beautiful City" in 1939, 1942 and 1968. Again Mayor Joseph Alioto was at the airport to meet him, as did Christian Blom, the chairman of the Sesquicentennial Committee of San Francisco.

The visit to the Bay Area and later to Monterey was planned with a minimum of formal occasions in order to give His Majesty some rest and privacy after sixteen days of touring the United States and before the final days in Alaska and the trip home. A grand dinner for His Majesty on board the new Norwegian cruise ship *Royal Viking Sky* at Pier 35 was to be the highlight of his stay in San Francisco. The ship was then a new first class cruise ship with owners' representation in San Francisco.

The King was accommodated by another member of the Fish Club, Iver Lyche, President of the prestigious Burlingame Country Club in Hillsborough, south of the City. His Majesty went directly from the airport to the country club after the formal introductions at the airport. Consul General Per C. Prøitz accompanied the King to the former Crocker family estate, where Iver Lyche and the manager of the club waited. King Olav enjoyed a cocktail and a private dinner with friends, hosted by Mr. Lyche.

The next morning His Majesty went sailing with members from the St. Francis Yacht Club. Prior to that, some old American friends from the days when King Olav as Crown Prince participated in international competitions hosted a private cruise on the Bay aboard the S/Y *Cordonazo*. The party sailed to a little inlet near Angel Island, where they anchored and had a picnic luncheon on board, before the King embarked in the St. Francis Syndicate's *St. Francis VI* to skipper this newly constructed six-meter on the Bay. The owners were, of course, eager to hear this able yachtsman's comments on their latest creation.

The crossing went from Angel Island to the St. Francis Yacht Club. The 72-year-old Monarch had ordered good foul weather gear, and to the younger crewmen's delight he handled the six-meter sailboat with grace and great skill. A powerboat full of Secret Service members and rescuers in wet suits tailed the Royal Helmsman like a shadow. This support was provided in case something unexpected should happen, such as His Majesty's falling overboard. The worried followers were very happy when His Majesty called it a day.

Through a long life of yachting King Olav has sampled many fine sailing craft and some of the most celebrated yachting areas in the world. The boat *St. Francis VI* was an all new six-meter built by a consortium in San Francisco. The designer was Gary Mull. He sailed along as mate, together with one world champion and one Olympic winner as crew members. His Majesty truly enjoyed the boat's performance.

Some twenty-four hours before His Majesty's San Francisco visit, an

# SHIPPING AND CULTURE

Club to change from raingear to black tie before heading for the luxurious cruise ship. The ship was decorated with festooned lights from stem to stern for the Sesquicentennial Jubilee dinner in the King's honor, which was attended by the Norwegian ambassador to the United States, Søren Christian Sommerfelt and the rest of the King's entourage. Christian Blom welcomed His Majesty at the dockside.

The captain accompanied His Majesty on board, where the King was introduced to representatives of the Royal Viking Line. Mr. Blom was in charge of the dinner and managed to engage Mayor Alioto in some fun about Norwe-

*His Majesty's sailing adventure in San Francisco Bay. Photos by courtesy Stein Fjesme, Adresseavisen.*
- S/Y Cordonazo *with King Olav on board passing Alcatraz Island (previous page).*
- *His Majesty skippering the* St. Francis VI *heading for the Golden Gate to a rendezvous with the cruise ship* Royal Viking Sky *(above).*
- *King Olav, still in the boat, is sharing his experience with people on deck and alongside. His Majesty was well known in the yachting world for his great sailing knowledge and skill (below).*

entirely unexpected problem arose. The *Royal Viking Sky* was arrested in Los Angeles after narcotics were discovered on board. Christian Blom was notified. He telephoned the Director of Customs in Los Angeles, who had been invited to the gala on board the ship in San Francisco and Blom told him that he would have to cancel his flight tickets and return his wife's new dress, and that, alas, her hair styling may have been in vain because the dinner for the King of Norway they had long planned to give aboard the ship in San Francisco was in jeopardy: "Your own people down in Los Angeles have arrested the ship. How can we arrange a party here when you keep the ship there?" said Christian Blom. Shortly afterwards the ship was released and the captain was ordered to proceed to San Francisco at maximum speed. He did, and managed to berth at Pier 35 just before King Olav sailed by on his final crossing to the St. Francis Yacht Club. The King returned to the Burlingame Country gians and Italians. Blom reminded Alioto that the Viking Leif Erikson was the first to discover America, and he even started out from Trondheim, also the home port of this fine ship. He came to America centuries before the Italian Christopher Columbus who tried to take all the credit. Joseph Alioto in his answer said he was getting used to Norwegians always getting ahead. "Look what you did in recent years," Alioto continued, "the Italians founded and built the greatest bank in this country, the Bank of America. And guess who is sitting at the top of that bank?" asked Mayor Alioto. "He is a Norwegian and he is sitting over there," said Alioto and pointed straight at President and CEO A. W. Clausen. After dinner the party continued with coffee in the lounge and dancing till midnight.

The following morning King Olav visited the Norwegian Seamen's Church and met the congregation and sailors in port. His Majesty greeted them and received a model of the first immigration sloop *Restauration*. He was met at the Church by Christian Blom, President of the Church, Ole Kalve, Pastor Ole E. Holck and Consul General Per C. Prøitz.

His Majesty continued on to Norway House, which the King had visited as Crown Prince back in 1942. The King was received by members of the board including Vice Consul Torvald Rafoss, Trygve Knudsen, Trygve Morkemo and Hans Berge. He met Norwegian seamen and people from the maritime community of the Bay Area including war sailors. His Majesty was presented with a life membership in the Far West Skiing and US Ski Association in recognition of the King's skiing achievements. In his young days Crown Prince Olav participated in the national ski championships and jumped in the Holmenkollen Ski Arena in Oslo.

The King moved on to the St. Francis Yacht Club for a luncheon with friends. About an hour and a half later, King Olav left together with Christian Blom for the airport. The Royal Entourage followed in separate cars for the flight to Los Angeles and the next part of the Jubilee. The King stayed in Los Angeles less than 24 hours and arrived in Monterey on Friday afternoon for rest and recreation. His Majesty's stay in Monterey was, as at the Burlingame Country Club, all arranged by Mr. Iver Lyche. It included Friday evening, the whole of Saturday and Sunday until the afternoon.

It had been an especially exhausting tour for King Olav. His Majesty's private secretary, Mr. Vincent Bommen, became ill in Chicago and was hospitalized. The Director of Press and Information of the Norwegian Ministry of Foreign Affairs, Mr. Jerving, was also hospitalized. Both left His Majesty's entourage. A.D.C. Major Magne Hagen and other members of the entourage had to take on additional duties. The 72-year-old Monarch himself, however, did very well throughout the breathtaking tour of the American continent.

In Monterey Mr. Iver Lyche had borrowed a house from his good friend Gilbert Mackay. It was located in beautiful surroundings overlooking the golf course at Pebble Beach. His Majesty arrived from Los Angeles for a quiet dinner with only the ambassador and Mrs. and Mr. Lyche, at Del Monte Lodge in Pebble Beach.

The following day was entirely at the disposal of His Majesty. The weather was marvelous and the King relaxed on the terrace of the Cypress Point Country Club as a guest of the Lyches. California displayed its gorgeous late October, with pleasant temperatures, gentle winds and a calm sea. The view from the clubhouse was superb, overlooking the private golf club of Cypress Point, with the beaches and the ocean behind, a delightful sight in a perfect setting. The King had a fantastic lunch. It was followed by a limousine cruise along the "17-mile drive." The evening was spent at the house with a barbecue dinner. An all-girls choir from a nearby high school had been invited to sing American songs for His Majesty. On Sunday after lunch the King and his party departed from Monterey Airport in a private plane for a three-day visit to Alaska. This part of the tour included a one-day trip to Prudhoe Bay to inspect the oil installations, before returning home to Norway.

*Prince Harald attended primary school in America in 1944 and 1945. The eight-year-old Prince in front to the left with his classmates and teacher. Courtesy of the San Francisco Chronicle Library.*

The 1975 visit was King Olav's last visit to California and San Francisco.

During World War II Prince Harald lived near Bethesda, Maryland, with Crown Princess Märtha, his mother, and the Princesses Ragnhild and Astrid. The Prince attended the first grades of primary school there. He became Crown Prince in 1957 and King in 1991, and has been back in his "second home country" several times. On November 25, 1963, Crown Prince Harald was in full uniform, attending the funeral of President John F. Kennedy. Shortly after this formal occasion, the Crown Prince returned to the United States.

In January 1964 Crown Prince Harald came to the West Coast. He spent one day in San Francisco escorted by the Norwegian Ambassador, Hans Engen. Consul General Carl O. Jørgensen was the host in the City by the Bay. The 26-year-old Crown Prince was still unmarried and one of the most eligible young men in Europe. The best part of the *Chronicle*'s coverage of the visit was the happy reunion with his old second-grade teacher Priscilla Ruggles, at that time working at the Mountain View School in Martinez. She had been teaching the young prince and other second-graders at Whitehall Country School in Bethesda, Maryland during World War II. The *Chronicle* reported:

> The Crown Prince, who had been affable but reserved, showed signs of real animation as Miss Ruggles came down the receiving line. He greeted her warmly and engaged her in lively conversation. It was a mutual moment of delight and remembrance of days when she was teaching the young Prince arithmetic and other second-grade topics. For Miss Ruggles the Crown Prince's first visit to the Bay Area gave her the opportunity to see the tall, blond young Crown Prince who had brought so much excitement into her classroom many years ago back on the East Coast.
>
> "I particularly remember Prince Harald's arrival in my classroom on the first day of school," Miss Rruggles reminisced. "He walked up to my desk, bowed low and with a blue-eyed smile presented me with a red rose." His graciousness and charm remained constant throughout the school year. The future Crown Prince was a lively, curious little boy whose adventurous spirit kept his teachers and the ever-present FBI agent alert. Upon one occasion he climbed to the top of a tall apple tree, only to discover that he could not get down again. When asked why he had climbed up so high if he couldn't descend, he called down cheerily, "How did I know I couldn't get down until I got up here?" Although Harald, who spoke perfect English, was a popular and democratic member of the class, he never forgot his royal position. When his

schoolmates chose him to play the prince in their production of Cinderella, he was highly flattered, but added. "Of course, I am a prince." His parents often visited the school. Once Crown Prince Olav sat for half an hour in a tiny classroom chair to observe his son's performance in an arithmetic class.

Prince Harald's happy years in an American school ended in 1945 when the royal family returned to Norway. Every schoolteacher follows the progress of some of their former students with special interest. Priscilla Ruggles is a rare American teacher, seeing one of her students grow up to become head of an European country. When her first-graders in Martinez were told the story, Priscilla Ruggles says, "I don't think they really believe it's a true story. It all seems like a fairy tale."

In 1985, Norway launched its "Year of Export" and kicked it off in January with a visit of Crown Prince Harald to California. Tandberg Data's head office in Oslo had established a subsidiary in Anaheim which the Crown Prince was asked to open.

Crown Prince Harald's new visit to San Francisco started with sightseeing of the City and the maritime museum. The party traveled north across the Golden Gate Bridge to Sausalito and through Marin County to Napa Valley, where His Royal Highness made stops at Mondavi in Rutherford and Domaine Chandon at Yountville.

The Crown Prince stayed at the Huntington Hotel and had dinner at the St. Francis Yacht Club with the Norwegian American Trade Mission and the Business Forum as hosts. In his speech Crown Prince Harald first mentioned the close ties between the two countries, leading to confidence and friendship. His Royal Highness emphasized the peace and freedom Norway has had since the establishment of NATO, and continued by declaring that a cornerstone of Norwegian foreign policy is the relationship to the United States, which also makes a base for economic cooperation. Even though the trade with the United States is modest, Norway depends heavily on foreign trade. Crown Prince Harald described Norway's exports as unusual in that only one third comes from traditional sources, while one third comes from oil and gas, and the last third from services, where the shipping industry is significant. The Crown Prince mentioned shipping, and that the United States is the world's largest user of shipping services. Forty percent of the Norwegian merchant fleet is engaged in transport to and from the United States. A considerable part of United States' foreign trade is transported on Norwegian ships. Crown Prince Harald concluded his speach with a few words about recovery of the world economy and the importance of facing the years to come with optimism even with a high unemployment in most western countries. "It seems to be a very difficult task to fight," Crown Prince Harald concluded at the St. Francis Yacht Club dinner in 1985.

The next morning His Royal Highness left San Francisco and proceeded to Stanford University for a tour of the campus aided by Provost James Rosse. They visited the Center for Integrated Systems and Stanford Stadium.

Luncheon was given at Masstor Systems, after which Director Erik Salbu conducted a tour of the premises. Crown Prince Harald continued on to nearby Apple Computer where his host was John Sculley, President and Chief Executive Officer. The Crown Prince was taken on a tour of the facility. In the afternoon the Crown Prince left Silicon Valley from San Jose Airport and flew to Los Angeles for the opening ceremony of Tandberg Data's new computer products facility in Anaheim.

This event was broadcast live to Norway via satellite. The Tandberg's Anaheim manufacturing plant, a Norwegian-owned company, occupied a 32,000 square-foot building in Orange County. The California company decided that an appropriate commemorative gift for the Crown Prince was a remote-controlled sailboat, knowing His Royal Highness' love for sailing.

Crown Prince Harald stayed at the Hotel Meridien in Newport Beach, which prepared for the challenge of hosting a real prince by sending parts of the staff to a course to learn rules of protocol.

The Crown Prince had official matters to attend to following the ribbon-cutting occasion at Tandberg. He met with several of California's business and political leaders at a luncheon to promote Norwegian export.

The Fish Club was sorry, of course, that this devoted yachtsman left California with only a remote-control boat and did not get the opportunity to sail the Bay as his father had done twice when visiting this part of the world. But for the experienced yachtsman, a look at the Bay driving across the Golden Gate Bridge must have convinced him that this was a challenging place to practice yachting skills against sea, wind and current.

Only three years passed before Crown Prince Harald was back in San Francisco. The goal was set; he was "to go sailing." In Kiel, Germany in 1987, His Royal Highness became the winner and the world champion of the one-ton sailboat. It including an offshore race up to the coast of Sweden and back, which the Crown Prince and his crew did in 56 hours. It was as the reigning World Champion in the one-ton sailboat class that His Royal Highness returned to San Francisco in August of 1988.

This time the Crown Prince arrived as a sports competitor. His intention was to keep a low profile, get enough rest, concentrate on the sporting event, and defend the championship against an armada of 28 one-ton boats from all over the world. He would participate both in the shorter competitions on the Bay and in the longer offshore venture out the Gate and then around the Farallon Islands.

*His Majesty presented a picture to St. Francis Yacht Club after the visit. It survived the Clubhouse's devastating fire shortly after, but not without significant marks of smoke, water and other damages.*

Crown Prince Harald and his crew came to San Francisco well before the races and stayed for 28 days. They needed the time to trim and adjust the *Fram X* that had been shipped over from Norway, and to try to get used to the special conditions in the Bay and outside the Golden Gate. The Pacific and San Francisco Bay have some sailing characteristics that are different from many of the famous old yachting courses in Europe.

# Royal Visits

The team sailing the *Fram X* stayed at Norway House in Pacific Heights, only a short distance away from the yacht harbor and the St. Francis Yacht Club, which was the organizer of the 1988 World Championship in the one-ton class. The Norwegian Government Seamen's Services had refurbished the rooms of Norway House just for the occasion. Apart from the last days of the long stay when some of the crew members were joined by their spouses, the *Fram X* team had Norway House all to themselves. In those last hectic days almost twenty persons were attended to at Norway House.

The team managed to stay away away from the media most of the time. The newspapers followed the America's Cup in San Diego at the time of the Crown Prince's visit. Yachting America was more concerned about their own sailboat's possibilities against the large and strong challenger from New Zealand. The newspapers also reported that Lillehammer, Norway, had gotten the 1994 Winter Olympic Games.

The Norwegian community got a really good opportunity to see and talk to their Crown Prince. Well ahead of the competition there was a Sunday church service and a reception at the Seamen's Church. President of the Board Ole Kalve, Pastor John Arne Lund and shipowner Christian Blom met the Crown Prince, who unveiled a bust of his Grandfather King Haakon VII in the reception room. In a short address the Crown Prince expressed happiness at being present, and also conveyed the most hearty wishes from His Majesty the King to the Norwegian colony and the Church.

His Royal Highness was honored by the City of San Francisco at the Legion of Honor where Mr. and Mrs. Mayor Art Agnos greeted him. Crown Prince Harald stated that he was looking forward to the races, and mentioned that his father had always greatly enjoyed the challenge of the Bay. "Before I left, he expressly asked me to convey his best greetings to the City," said the Crown Prince. He also mentioned the many Norwegian-Americans in the Bay Area and their involvement in shipping and high-tech industries. "We have not forgotten that during the five years of occupation of Norway from 1940, several Norwegian ships had San Francisco as their home port, and many of the seamen who manned these ships have chosen the West Coast as their final port for retirement as war veterans," said Crown

*Crown Prince Harald, today's King Harald V of Norway, at the Norwegian Seamen's Church in August 1988. The pastor is John Arne Lund.*

Prince Harald. He signed off by saluting the mayor and the citizens of San Francisco. Later a reception was held at the Westin St. Francis Hotel, hosted by Consul General Per Borgen.

Two days later the Fish Club invited the Crown Prince and his crew to a western barbecue dinner. It started with cocktails at the home of Joan and Iver Lyche and continued at the Burlingame Country Club in Hillsborough with the Lyches as hosts. The Crown Prince and his team enjoyed themselves in the country-like settings of the estate together with members of the Fish Club and their ladies, about a hundred persons. An entertainment group from the Bohemian Club played and sang American western songs.

The following day a concert dedicated to Norwegian music was given in Herbst Theater, followed by a reception in the adjacent Green Room. The Norwegian-American TV entertainer Erik Bye was master of ceremonies. The event was arranged by the Consulate General and the Fish Club.

The start of the first race was disastrous for *Fram X*, as another boat turned around and gave no space for *Fram X*. The Crown Prince avoided collision but started last, well after all the others. But they did excellent sailing and advanced all the way into the leading group, ending fifth.

The long offshore race of 260 nautical miles was a crucial one and counted double. At the start of this race the Crown Prince and his crew gave a stunning demonstration in *Fram X*. People on Golden Gate Bridge clearly understood why the *Fram X* was the reigning champion. Masterful maneuvering close to shore and brilliant tactics left the opponents behind as the team slipped past the others, shot under the bridge and out into the Pacific as the first of 28 boats.

The sailing conditions outside in the Pacific were perilous with calms, variable winds and fog. *Fram X* lost hours to many of the competitors on the way out because of the lack of wind. But when they finally started sailing again *Fram X* improved. The New Zealander that won the first race took the lead. *Fram X* advanced well, passed twelve competitors the first night and two American boats the next night. *Fram X* needed 76 hours to finish, almost 24 hours more than expected. *Propaganda* achieved its second win, eight hours ahead of *Sagacious* with *Fram X* third.

Competition varied during the following days. The *Propaganda* was the faster but the *Fram X* fought hard and kept second. After the last race, where *Fram X* came in eighth, the boat ended third, beaten only by *Propaganda* and *Bravura* from the United States. *Fram X* managed to keep the other 25 boats behind. Crown Prince Harald handed the grand cup for the one-ton class over to the New Zealand skipper in respect for a great sailing competitor.

People interested in yachting knew that when His Royal Highness Crown Prince Harald succeeded King Olav V to the throne in January of 1991 to become King Harald V of Norway, his participation in yacht racing would decline.

In October of 1995 King Harald of Norway came to the United States on a formal visit with Queen Sonja. It was a grand tour basically arranged in the same manner as former royal visits. Their Majesties arrived in New York on October 7, where they were greeted by Ambassador Kjeld Vibe and Mrs. Beate Vibe. Their Highnesses then went on to Washington DC and Virginia, later traveling through the Midwest to the West Coast.

King Harald and Queen Sonja arrived at Oakland Airport Friday, October 20 from Fargo, North Dakota, and were greeted by Consul General Hans Ola Urstad and Mrs. Tone Urstad. Their Majesties departed in a motorcade for Napa Valley and a private week-end as guests of Mr. Thomas Perkins. On Sunday evening, the Royal Party arrived in San Francisco to stay at the Fairmont Hotel. They dined at Alioto's, or "headed straight for Fisherman's Wharf" according to the *Chronicle*'s Herb Caen. The Pulitzer Price winner also informed San Franciscans that "The King speaks softly and carries no cash..."

The following morning Their Majesties visited the galleries of the San Francisco Museum of Modern Art, admiring the paintings of Matisse

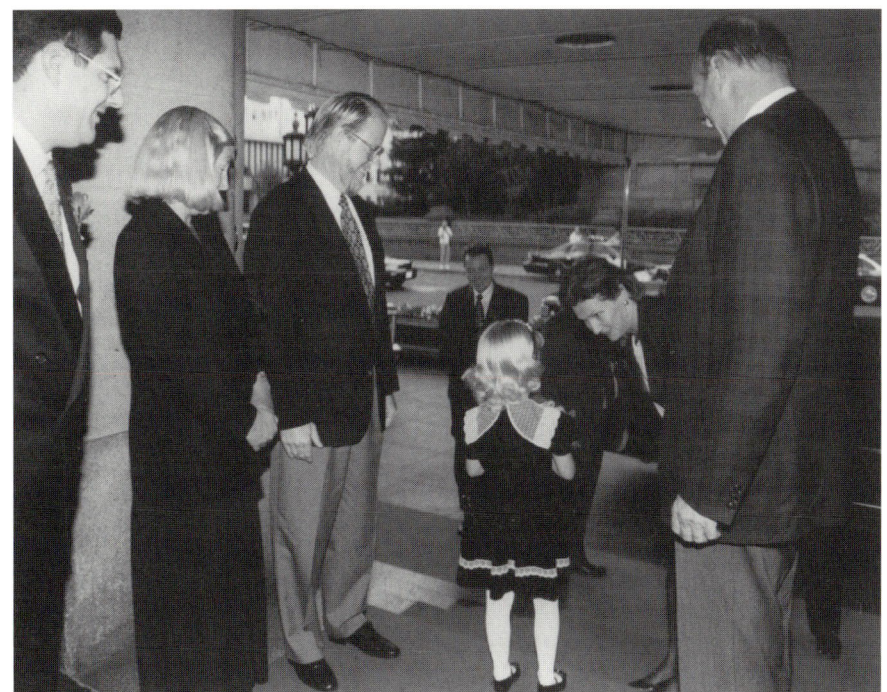

*Welcome to San Francisco. The King and Queen arrive at the Fairmont Hotel to be greeted by Consul General Hans Ola Urstad and his wife Tone to the left. Far left, Mark Huntley, director of the hotel. Photo by courtesy Frederic Hansen/Fairmont Hotel.*

Chairman of the Church Board, and Pastor Dagfinn Kvale at the Norwegian Seamen's Church had the honor of a visit by King Harald and Queen Sonja. Most of the local congregation as well as seamen were able to meet and shake hands with their King and Queen at the Church.

Before the banquet at the Fairmont Hotel the same evening, Mr. and Mrs. Iver Lyche gave a reception for Their Majesties at the Pacific Union Club, where the King and Queen were introduced to local dignitaries and people who have been particularly active in promoting Norwegian interests in the San Francisco Bay Area. The black tie banquet was a fund-raising event for the Norwegian-American Cultural Foundation with Mr. Tom Perkins as host and author Danielle Steel as hostess. Mr. Carl F. Blom proposed the toast for Their Majesties, and His Majesty King Harald for President Bill Clinton. The host and His Majesty gave short speeches.

and other celebrated works of art. The Royal Party continued to Silicon Graphics, a hi-tech company in Silicon Valley, where the King and the Queen were given an introduction to visual three-dimensional computer graphics and various demonstrations of virtual reality systems and other advanced computer technologies.

By noon Their Majesties had proceeded to Stanford University. President Gerhard Casper hosted a luncheon and introduced Professor James G. March of SCANCOR, a Stanford based organization with close ties to Norwegian research institutions. After admiring the Stanford Memorial Church, King Harald and Queen Sonja conversed with Norwegian students and their families at Stanford. Later the same day Mr. Ole Kalve,

The following morning His Majesty "cut the ribbon" at the Ashby BART station in Berkeley

*The all-electric PIVCO car was presented to BART officials by Their Majesties. This new and advanced development bears high hopes for lreducing pollution. Photo Kathleen H. Knudsen by courtesy Western Viking.*

# SHIPPING AND CULTURE

"DRESSED FOR A KING
*Norway's King Harald V was greeted by a girl in traditional Norwegian dress at Stanford University yesterday. The stop was made during a visit by the king and queen to the Bay Area."
Text and photo as presented by the Associated Press.
Printed by The San Diego Union-Tribune: Tuesday, October 24, 1995, A-3.*

for the PIVCO Station Cars, which were doing their first public run from the station to the offices of the software company Sybase in Emeryville. This Norwegian car is an all-electrical automobile which will help to fulfill future goals for a decline in pollution from cars. The el-car program is approved by California legislators. Following the inauguration ceremony at Sybase, the media was allowed to inspect, film and test-drive the electric car, while Their Majesties were given an introduction to the company and told of new technologies and the information superhighway. The King and Queen left for San Francisco Airport after lunch. The last three days on the West Coast were spent in Seattle.

The Royal Party returned to the East Coast for the last part of the packed schedule which included historic Williamsburg, Virginia, closing the long tour with a visit to the White House as guests of President Clinton and Hillary Rodham Clinton. Their Majesties stayed at the White House for the night. For His Majesty King

Harald it must have brought back memories from when he as a little boy. He first stayed at the White House during World War II. There can't be many people, not even in America, who can say with King Harald of Norway, "I stayed at the White House more than fifty years ago and again today."

Their Majesties King Harald and Queen Sonja returned home from Washington DC to Norway on October 31 after 25 exciting days visiting a large number of Norwegian-American communities in the United States.

For the Fish Club the 1995 visit of King Harald and Queen Sonja was an exciting event, even if the Club itself played a lesser part this time than during previous visits. Their Majesties' stay in the San Francisco Bay Area was given a distinct cant towards modern technology. It demonstrates that San Francisco, as always, manages to lead. Going back to the days of gold and the Bonanza, or the hey-days of ocean shipping, San Francisco was a leader, and the Norwegians came along pretty well, the Norwegian flag flying on big ships going through the Golden Gate every day of the year. Today's world embraces hi-tech and education. However, the old Club knows that the spirit of pioneering prevails in San Francisco and that the same Bay Area also is a good place for tourism, recreation, sightseeing and sports, with lots of friendly people. For the best in business as in culture, the rest of the world has to come to San Francisco.

*His Majesty King Harald and Her Majesty Queen Sonja together with Pastor Dagfinn Kvale at the Norwegian Seamen's Church in San Francisco, October 1995. Photo Ken Oprann.*

# Epilogue

This book has highlighted major events the Fish Club has been involved in over the years, events that have been of importance to the relationship between Norway and California on a cultural level during our century. Traditional thinking may lead to the belief that official support for the promotion of cultural exchange, developed over the last few years, will dissolve the Fish Club.

Many of the activities this Club has promoted have now been taken over by formal bodies like the Consulate. It is likely that more government participation in culture could trigger new activities and broaden engagement along the traditional fundraising lines; government participation may not only inspire, but also increase awareness and assist in the creative, preparatory stages of projects. There is always the need for a local consultant like the Fish Club with a good command of all the details and facts when propositions, decisions or actions are made.

There are many more cultural tasks to take on than any official body can handle. All experience shows that the state is slow in adopting new cultural philosophy. Usually it is devoted individuals and smaller groups that blaze the trail where thousands follow, and then finally, the legislature. To see the government adopt former "property" of the Fish Club is the greatest honor the Club can receive. It is the final proof that what they fought for and achieved was the right thing to do.

Everything is changing. The important thing is to find cultural sectors where things need to get started or where little has been accomplished. The important thing for the new members of the Fish Club is to stay awake, get engaged and be willing, as always, to do work for the benefit of all, including generations to come. That is what promoting culture is about. It is the ability to pull together for a good and worthy course, preferably in the old spirit, not to boast too much about it. Causes will increase in number as society grows. That alone gives prosperous predictions for the Fish Club. If new generations continue with the basic ideas of the previous ones, the Club will continue to contribute. The need to do cultural work never dies. It is always present.

# Notes and Sources

CHAPTER I:
THE FISH CLUB STORY

Books, Archieves, Files:
Ralph Enger, *The History of the Norwegian Club of San Francisco*, San Francisco 1947.
The Fish Club archives and files.

Personal communication:
Christian Blom, Per Borgen, Else Berit Eikeland, C.O.Jørgensen, Magne Lein, Dag Mork Ulnes, Per C. Prøitz, Olaf Solli, Sigvor Hamre Thornton, Turid Vizcarra.

CHAPTER II:
THE CLUB, JACK'S AND THE CITY

Books:
Michael R. Corbett, *Splendid Survivors*, California Living Books, San Francisco 1979.
G. Hansen and E. Condon, *Denial of Disaster*, San Francisco 1990.
J. Killeen, *Best Restaurants San Francisco Bay Area*, San Francisco 1986.
Doris Muscatine, *A Cook's Tour of San Francisco*, New York 1963.
Unterman & Sesser, *Restaurants of San Francisco*, Chronicle Books 1986.

Publications:
Kevin Starr, "In the Grand Style," *San Francisco Magazine*, August, 1980, p.11.

Newspapers:
*San Francisco Chronicle*, "Letters to the Editor", Raol H. Blanquie, 10-7,1965,40.
*San Francisco Examiner Extra*, 4-20,1906.

Archives, Files:
The Museum of the City of San Francisco.
Department of City Planning, Inventory, 1976. (Landmark #146, 240/14, 615 Sacramento). This material on Jack's was provided by Jean Kortum.
The Fish Club files.
The History Room, San Francisco Public Library.
The Presidio Army Museum.

Personal communication:
Christian Blom, Jose Campos, Richard Hansen, Ole Kalve, Dagfinn Kvale, Magne Lein, Birger Mathisen, Per C. Prøitz, Jack Redinger, Walter Taylor, Dominique Versailles.

CHAPTER III:
PANAMA PACIFIC
INTERNATIONAL EXPOSITION

Books:
Ira E. Bennett, *History of the Panama Canal*, Washington DC 1915.
Ralph Enger, *The History of the Norwegian Club of San Francisco*, San Francisco 1947.
Ewald & Clute, *San Francisco Invites the World*, San Francisco Chronicle 1991.
Sverre Norborg, *Norge i Vesterled*, Oslo 1974.
*Ships of the US Navy*, "USS Jason", C-12, p.507.
Frank Morten Todd, *The Story of the Exposition*, Vol.1-5, Putman New York 1921.

Publications:
The National Maritime Museum, San Francisco, *Sea Letter, No.29, 1979, p.6-7*.

Newspapers:
*San Francisco Chronicle*: 12-19, 1914, 3/3; 4-12, 1915, 1/1; 5-8,1915, 1/1-8; 5-9, 1915; 5-10, 1915; 6-2, 1915, 1/1; 6-3, 1915, 5/1-8+last page; 6-4, 1915, 4/1-8; 6-5, 1915, 6/6; 6-6, 1915, 26.
*San Francisco Examiner*: 4-12,1915,1/3; 4-16,1915,11/1.

Archives, Files:
National Gallery of Norway, Library, Oslo.
Norsk Hydro A/S, Oslo.
Munchmuseet, Library, Oslo.

CHAPTER IV:
GOLDEN GATE INTERNATIONAL EXPOSITION

Books:
Ralph Enger, *The History of the Norwegian Club . . .*, San Francisco 1947.
Jack James & Earle Weller, *Treasure Island, The Magic City 1939-40*, San Francisco 1941.
Eugen Neuhaus, *The Art of Treasure Island*, UC Berkeley 1939.
Richard Reinhardt, *Treasure Island, San Francisco's Exposition Year*, San Francisco 1973.

Publications:
Auburn Ski Club, *A Half Century of California Skiing*, p.12-13.
*Canadian Ski Yearbook 1939-40*, Montreal, p.114.
Golden Gate International Exposition, Official Guide Book 1939, rev.ed.
Golden Gate International Exposition, Official Guide Book 1940.
P. R. Poulsson, *Report and History of the Fair of 1940*, GK/SF, Riksarkivet, Oslo.
*PG&E Progress*, Vol.xvi, #3, San Francisco, February 1939.

Newspapers:
*Aftenposten*, Oslo, 18.2.39, "Eventyrøen med Eventyrbyen."
*NorgesHandels &SøfartsTidende*, Oslo, 25.3.39, "Skihytta vår i SF gjør stor lykke."
*The Call-Bulletin*, 12.23,38.
*Oakland Tribune*, August 12, 1938, "Nansen's speech."
*San Francisco Chronicle*, 8.5,38; 2.17,39; 3.5,39.
*San Francisco Chronicle*, Sporting Green: 2.18 - 23, 39.
*San Francisco Examiner*, 2.28,39; 5.27,40.

Archives, Files:
Riksarkivet: Archives of Norwegian Consulate General of San Francisco 1915-65.
Treasure Island Museum, Building One, Exhibition & Magazines.
Treasure Island Museum Library.
Western Aero Space Museum, North Field, Oakland.

Personal communication:
Christian Blom, Mary L. Gentry, Bill Kooiman, Edward von der Porten, Lloyd B. Ryland, Jakob Vaage.


CHAPTER V:
NORWAY HOUSE, SEAMEN'S HOME

Books:
Walton Bean, *Boss Ruef's San Francisco*, UC Press 1952.
James D. Hart, *A Companion to California*, Los Angeles 1987.
Stan Hugill, *Sailortown*, London/New York 1967.
Harold Huycke, *To Santa Rosalia, Futher and Back*.
Fred Klebingat, Memories of the Audiffred Building . . . , SF 1983.
Trygve Lie, *Syv år for freden*, Tiden Oslo,1954.
McNairn & MacMullen, *Ships of the Redwood Coast*, Stanford 1945.
Olmsted & Watkins, *Here Today*, Chronicle Books SF, 1968.

Felix Riesenberg Jr, *Golden Gate . . .* , New York/London 1940.
Lately Thomas, *A Debonair Scoundrel*, New York 1962.
David Thomson, *Europe Since Napoleon*, London 1957, Penguin 1966.
J.N.Tønnessen, *Den moderne hvalfangsts historie IV: Den pelagiske fangsten 1937-1969*, Sandefjord 1970.

Publications:
Alfred Abrahamsen, *Norges Hus*, 1950.
Norway House Inc, *Årsberetning 1990*.

Newspapers:
*San Francisco Call Bulletin*, 4.11, 4.20, 1945.
*San Francisco Chronicle*, 3.14, 4.20, 1945.
*San Francisco Examiner*, 2.21, 4.20, 4.25, 1945.

Archives, Files:
Riksarkivet, Oslo: Generalkonsulatet i San Francisco, pakke 36,37,55,183, tilleggspakke. 4.
History Room, San Francisco Public Library.
The Fish Club files.
San Francisco War Memorial and Performing Arts Center.
Jean Kortum did property research with Municipal Offices and provided documents and information on the early history of Norway House.

Personal communication:
Patricia Akre, Hans Berge, Christian Blom, Gladys Hansen, Rolf Jamvold, Ole Kalve, Per Kirkhorn, Jean Kortum, Karl Kortum, Oskar Moe, Trygve Morkemo, Dag Mork Ulnes, John Pedersen.


CHAPTER VI:
THE NORWEGIAN SEAMEN'S CHURCH

Publications:
Den Norske Sjømannsmisjon, *Årbok og Kretsberetning*, 1949-52.
Den Norske Sjømannsmisjon, *Bud og Hilsen* 1951, 1952-55, 1970-72, 1973-75, 1979-81, 1982-84, 1985-88, 1989-90, 1992 (Bergen).
*Fra Kirkebakken*, Norwegian Seamen's Church, San Francisco.
A.Falstad (ed.), *Den norske sjømannskirke San Pedro 50 år* (1991).
S. Roinestad, *A Hundred Years with Norwegians in the East Bay*, Typed compendium, Oakland/San Francisco 1970.

Archives, Files:
Kallsbok for San Francisco Stasjon, Norwegian Seamen's Mission, San Francisco
Research in Official Archives, Dept. of Public Works, San Francisco was done by Jean Kortum.

Personal communication:
Captains of Fosen Trafikklag A/S, Christian Blom, Turid and Jon Albert Ihlebæk, Ole Kalve, Dagfinn Kvale, Karen Erika and Birger Mathisen, Ellen Schoenlank.

CHAPTER VII:
SQUAW VALLEY WINTER OLYMPICS 1960

Books:
Knut Johannesen, *Fra Kampen til Squaw Valley*, Oslo 1960
Knut Johannesen, *På'n Igjen*, Oslo 1964
Håkon Brusveen, *3-2-1-Gå*, Oslo 1965.

Periodicals:
*Aktuell*, Oslo: No.10, February 27, 1960; no.11, March 1, 1960.
*Billed Journalen*, Oslo: No.8, February 17, 1960; no.9, February 24, 1960; no.10, March 2, 1960: Extra issue; March 5, 1960.
*Billedbladet NÅ:* Oslo: No.9, February 27, 1960; no.10, March 5, 1960.

Archives, Files:
Fish Club files on The Norwegian California Olympics Committee, San Francisco.
Fish Club files on the Squaw Valley Olympics and the Los Angeles Olympics.

Personal communication:
Author's own memories and conversations with Rolf Tangvik. Telephone interviews with some participating athletes, with FIS judge Jakob Vaage, with Per Jorsett, and interviews with members of the Norwegian California Olympic Committee.

CHAPTER VIII:
*GJØA*, THE SHIP IN THE PARK

Books:
Roald Amundsen, *Nordvestpassagen, Beretningen om Gjøa-ekspedisjonen 1903-07*, Kristiania, Aschehoug 1907.
Roald Amundsen, *Oppdagelsesreiser, Vol. I, Nordvestpassasjen*, Oslo 1928.
John R. Bockstoce, *Whales, Ice and Men . . .* , Seattle 1986.
Roland Huntford, *The Amundsen Photographs*, New York 1987.
Hans Nerhus, *Gjøa Vår verdenskjente minneskute*, Oslo 1980.

Publications:
John W. Allan, "Gjøa's Fantastic Voyage," *American Boating,* Oct. 1971.
William A Baker, "The Gjøa," *American Neptune* Vol.12#1, 1/1952.
George E. Boulter, "First to sail the Northwest Passage," *Ships and the Sea* Vol.7#1, Summer 1957.
Thomas P. Brown, "Amundsen and the *Gjøa*," *The Time Card* 1950.
Ralph Enger, "An account of the . . . ," *San Francisco Life*, 15:7-10, 5/1947
Francis P. Filice, "Biography of the Gjøa," *Pacific Discovery*, 5/6,1962.
*The Illustrated London News,* September 7, 1929, p.424.
Erik Krag, "The famous sloop Gjøa," *Pacific Marine Review,* 4/1949.
Lindy Lindquist, "Through the Northwest Passage Under Sail," *Motor Boating and Sailing,* November 1973, p. 51-53, 112-116.
John Lyman, "The *Gjøa*," *Log Chips*, July 1952, Vol.3#1.
*National Geographic Magazine,* January 1906, "A Modern Viking."
Margaret Graham Nelson, "A Ship on Ice," *The Skipper, Yachting, the Sea and Ships,* Vol.220#11, November 1960.
John Ross, "Det ligger et skip i Frisco by," *Veritas* #69, 5/1972.
San Francisco Chamber of Commerce, Bay Region, "The Gallant *Gjøa*," *Business,* December 1, 1961.

Newspapers:
*San Francisco Chronicle:* 4-11, 1906, 11/2; 10-20, 1906, 3/1; 10-22, 1906, 3/2; 12-10, 1908-9/4; 6-10, 1909, 11/7; 6-17, 1909, 18/2; 7-6, 1909, 18/1; 8-8, 1909, 5/1; 5-29, 1911, 5/2; 7-17, 1911, 12/4; 2-20, 1921, 41/2; 9-6, 1927, 3/2; 11-11, 1928, A12/2; 9-18, 1932, 7/1; 4-19, 1933, 8/4; 5-31, 1934; 7-1, 1934, 8/2; 6-12, 1934, C6/5; 1-21, 1939, 1/4; 4-16, 1939, 11/3; 4-27, 1939, 10/1; 4-28, 1939, 20/1; 4-29, 1939, 14/1; 5-5, 1939, 5/6 + 16/1; 5-7, 1939, 15(c); 5-9, 1939, 28/5; 5-10, 1939, 12/1; 6-7, 1939, 23/3; 12-25, 1939, 7/2; 1-23, 1940, 23/6; 1-24, 1940, 13/2; 7-3, 1940, 26/1; 4-11, 1942, 10/6; 4-22, 1942, 14/3; 3-11, 1946, 12/3; 5-17, 1946, 15/2; 7-11, 1947, 13/4; 7-14, 1947, 14/1; 11-10, 1948, 16/5; 11-18, 1948, 2/2; 3-9, 1949, 3/8; 3-20, 1949, 25/5; 4-6, 1949, 6/1; 4-16, 1949, 6/1; 5-11, 1949, 8/3; 5-15, 1949, 13/7; 7-19, 1957; 7-21, 1957, 20/1; 7-12, 1959, 1, 10; 11-, 1959; 2-7, 1960; 9-8, 1969, 6; 5-17, 1970; 7-24, 1971; 7-30, 1971; 3-30, 1972.
*San Francisco Examiner:* 4-15, 1917, 46/2; 5-19, 1926, 3/8; 3-9, 1949, 18+19; 5-15, 1949; 2-2, 1960; 10-7, 1968, 64; 9-4, 1969, 18; 3-27, 1970; 5-17, 1970; 5-18, 1970; 7-24, 1971, 1, 5; 7-27, 1971; 7-28, 1971; 7-29, 1971; 7-30, 1971; 4-20, 1972, 26; 2-2, 1973, 53.
*San Francisco Call Bulletin:* 5-12, 1939; 5-20, 1949.
*San Francisco News* (Letter & Wasp): 1-31, 1939; 12-15,

1939, 7; 1-26, 1940.
*Oakland Tribune:* 2-21, 1937, Knave, 1-B,4/1; 11-12, 1939, Knave,sec. C,4.
*Sacramento Bee:* 5-7, 1972, P-6/6. Palo Alto Times: 9-4, 1969.
*Daily Commercial News:* 4-17, 1939; 5-10, 1939; 5-19, 1939; 5-16, 1949.
*Weekly Commercial News:* 4-27, 1939. West Bay Sunday: 11-11, 1984, 8.
*Nordisk Tidende:* 3-9, 1939; 8-31, 1939. Scandinavian Times: 11-5, 1971.
*Washington-Posten:* 3-10, 1939; 3-31, 19 39; 4-21, 1939; 5-4, 1939; 9-15, 1939.
*Norges Handels og Sjøfartstidende:* 1-16, 1939; 3-13, 1939; 5-13, 1939; 8-15, 1939.

Archives, Files:
Fish Club files.
Files of the Gjoa Foundation.
Karl Kortum's research and interviews with Erik Krag, San Francisco Maritime NHP Library scrapbooks, archives, pictures.
The Museum of the City of San Francisco, archives.
The Norwegian State Archives (RNCG/SF), Oslo.
Norwegian Maritime Museum Library, archives, Oslo.
Sjøhistoriska Museet (SSHM), Stockholm.
Bureau of Architecture, Department of Public Works, City and County of San Francisco: Specifications for Repairs and Preservation, Ship GJØA: - 1939, - 1948, - 1961.
Ship model of *Gjøa*, (print/photoes): Model Shipways, Bogota,N.J.,1950.

Personal communications:
Christian Blom, Ben Brynildsen, Kristian Djupevåg, Ole Kalve, Bård Kolltveit, Karl Kortum.


CHAPTER IX:
THE WINDJAMMER

Books:
Olaf T. Engvig, *Skoleskipene*, Gyldendal, Oslo 1981.
Olaf T. Engvig, *Skoleskipet Christian Radich 1937-1987*, -Festskrift til 50-års Jubileet, i Oslo Konserthus, Oslo 1987

Archives, Files:
The Fish Club files; drafts, letters, itineraries, programs, notes.

Personal communication:
Captain, officers, crew and cadets of the Christian Radich 1979 - 1980, voyage from Oslo to San Francisco to Oslo. Hans Berge, Christian Blom, Ole Kalve, Bjørn Kvisgaard, Hakon Lunde, Iver Lyche, Per C. Prøitz, Øivind Schau, Lisbeth Smestad.


CHAPTER X:
ROYAL VISITS

Books:
*H. M. King Olav in USA,* Adresseavisens forlag, Trondheim 1975.
*International Who's Who, 1993-94,* London 1993.
Lord Feversham, *Great Yachts,* New York 1970.
*Märtha, Norges Kronprinsesse 1929-54,* Gyldendal Oslo 1955.
Jens Schive & Hans Olav, *Med Kronprinsparet - for Norge,* Oslo 1939.

Newspapers:
*Aftenposten,* Oslo: 9-9+10+12+14+16, 1988.
*Los Angeles Times:* 4-29, 1968; 1-18+19, 1985.
*Minneapolis Tribune:* 4-5, 1968.
*Oakland Tribune:* 4-22, 1968.
*San Francisco Chronicle:* 12-24+29, 1940; 8-3, 1952; 9-23, 1960 (UPI, Oslo, 9-10, 1960); 12-27, 1963, 18; 1-1, 1994, 5; 1-5, 1964; 1-15, 1964 (2ent.); 1-17, 1964 (3ent.); 5-2, 1968.
*San Francisco Examiner:* 5-18+20, 1939; 12-3+24+28, 1940; 12-20, 1941; 8-4,1942; 5-1, 1968.
*Seattle Post - Intelligencer:* 5-2+3, 1968.

Archives, Files:
The Fish Club files; drafts, letters, itineraries, programs and notes.
The Royal Palace Library, Oslo.
Riksarkivet, Oslo.
J.Porter Shaw, National Maritime Museum Library, San Francisco.
Treasure Island Navy Museum Library, San Francisco.
PR 1199, US Maritime Commission, Washington DC, 4-8, 1942.
Office of the Mayor of San Francisco, History of City Hall, 1.92, 1752a.
St. Francis Yacht Club, San Francisco.
C.B.Koester: "A Midshipman's Memoir," *Le Marine du Nord,* Journal of the Canadian Nautical Research Society: Vol.III, no.4, 10.1993.

Personal communication:
Christian Blom, Ronald N. Craig, Magne Hagen, Karl Kortum, Iver Lyche, Norman Ronneberg, San Francisco City Hall Officials. Members of the Royal Norwegian Consulate General in San Francisco.

# Index

## A

A. F. Klaveness Co. 18, 157
Aas, Roald 96, *103*
Aberdeen 142
*Abraham Lincoln* M/S 78
Abrahamsen, Alfred 16, 18, 20, 64, 67, 120
Acapulco 136, 145
Africa 75, 138
Africa's Cape 82
*Aftenposten* 21
Agnos, Mr. and Mrs Art 171
Alameda 60
Alaska 24, 115, 119, 165, 167
Alaska Packers Co. 36, 47
Alaska Packers Yard 47
Alcatraz Island 65, 77, 101, 166
*Alcides* 4-m bark 63, *64*
Alioto's (Restaurant) 172
Alioto, Joseph L. 21, 22, 32, 81, 125, 127, 162-167
Alma-Ata 96
Alphena 144
*Altmark* M/T 156
America 19, 37, 38, 43, 81, 91, 101, 103, 143, 150-153, 155-157, 159, 163, 164, 167, 174
America's Cup 171
Amundsen Gulf 115, 125
Amundsen, Roald 58, 72, 101, 110, *111*, -116, 119, 120, 123, 124, 128-132, 152
Anaheim 169, 170
Anders, William A. 21
Andersen, Hjalmar 97, 104
Andersen, Reidar 56
Andreassen, Jacob 20
Andreassen, Per 127, 128
Angel Island 165
Annapolis 45
Antwerp 63
Apollo 8 Expedition 21
*Apollo* HMS 160

Apple Computer 170
Aquatic Park 77, 118, 124, 130, 164
Arctic (Sea) 110, 111, 113, 130
Argentina 143
Arizona 24, 151
Ashby BART station 173
Atlantic 113, 128, 143, 145, 159
Auburn 56
Auburn Ski Club 55, 56, 57
Audiffred Building 67
*Augusta* bark 80
Azores 143

## B

Baffin, William 110
Baghdad 45
Balboa Park 47
*Balboa* M/S 43
Balchen, Bernt 80
*Balclutha*, ship 77, 126
Balliol 151
Bals, Herbert 137
Baltic fleet 17
Bank of America 167
Bank of Norway 21
Baptist Seamen's Mission 85
Barbados 136
Barbary Coast 63, 130
Barcelona 39
Barrows, Stanley 155
Barton Hill 76
Battle of the Atlantic 158
Beaufort Sea 114, 115
Beechey Island 113
*Bella Edvards* 42
Bendixsen, Hans 114
Berg, Astri 151
Berg, Dr. 151
Berg, Elisabeth (Lissi) 151
Berge, Hans 70, 137, 167
Bergen 18, 127, 130
Bering Strait 115

Berkely 154, 173
Berlin, Ivring 57
Bermuda 143
Berwick, Andrew 80
Bethesda, Maryland 157, 168
Bethlehem Steel 80
Beverly Hills 101, 102
Beverly Hilton 102
Bilbao 23
Billabong Shipping Co 127
Birkeland 44
Bislet 104
Bjelland 43
Bjoldstad, A. 47
Bjølstad, Consul 118
Blanquir, Edward F. 28
*Blitz-Krieg* 19
Bloksberg 151
Blom, Carl F. 173
Blom, Christian L. 18-22, *20*, 21, 24, 25, 33, 77, 80, 86, 90, 91, 99, 100, 103, 107, 120, 125-127, 137, 151, 153, 160, 161, 164-167, 171
Blom, Lissi (Elizabeth) 99, 100,
*Blücher* heavy cruiser 19, 156
Board of Supervisors, SF 126
Bocklin 39
Bohemian Club 172
Bombay 22, 63
Bommen, Vincent 167
Bonanza 28, 175
Bonita Cove 116
Bonnard, Pierre 101
Boothia Peninsula 113
Børde, Bjarne 22
Borgen, Per 23, 172
Borgersen, Arne 137
Boston 23, 145, 147
Boston Pops Orchestra 143
Boulder Dam 152
Bowley, A. J. 154
*Bravura* sailboat 172
Brazil 23

*Breidablik* 4-m bark 138
Brenden, Hallgeir 95, *103*
Brink, Christian 21
Bristol 39
Brofoss, Erik 21
Brun, Lyder 99
Brundage, Avery 94
Brusveen, Haakon 94, 95, 96, 100, 101, *103*, 103
Bruun, Lyder 20
Bruusgaard & Kiøsterud 18
Buchanan, Tora Bratt 80
Bull, Brynjulf 126
Burbank Airport 101
Bureau of Architecture, SF 124
Burlingame 85
Burlingame Country Club 23, 165, 166, 167, 172
*By-1-bud* 25
*Bybud* 18
Bye, Erik 172
Bygdøy 130
Bygdøynes 125, 129, 130
Byrd, Richard E. 80

# C

*C. A. Thayer* schooner 114
Cabot, John 110
Cabot, Sebastian 110
Caen, Herb 32, 172
California 15, 20, 21, 22, 24, 26, 39, 44, 50, 56, 58, 63, 76, 78, 93, 94, 97, 101, 104, 120, 135, 145, 151, 153, 154, 169, 170, 174
California Hall 58, 153
California Market 16
California Pacific Title & Trust Co 66
Californian Alps 89
Campos, Jose 33
Canada 56, 102, 159
Cape Cod 157
Cape Horn 35, 44, 64, 110, 112, 138
Cape Horners 63
Cape Kennedy 162
Cape of Good Hope 110
Cape Race 145
Capitol 163
"Carlsen, Alexander" 158, 159

Carquines Strait 77
Cash, Johnny 139
Casper, Gerhard 173
Center for Intergrated Systems, Stanford 170
*Charles Hanson* schooner *114*, 115
Chevalier, Maurice 32
Chicago 144, 167
*Chicago* USS 116
Chile 44
China 110
Chinatown 101, 152
Chinese Theater *135*, 143
Christensen, Lars Jr. 64
Christensen, Lars Sr. 19, 64, *65*, 65, 67
*Christian Radich* ship 23, 26, 135-150
Christiania 47, 142
*Christiania* sail-training bark 142
Christiania Schoolship Association 142
*Chronicle, San Francisco* 32, 38, 45, 55, 56, 117, 158, 168, 172
Church of Norway Abroad 86
Churchill, Winston S. 20, 158
Cinderella 169
Cinemiracle 136
Cisco 56
City Attorney, San Francisco 127
City Hall, San Francisco 162, *163*, 163, 164
*City of Flint* S/S 156
Clausen, A. W. 167
Clausen, Tom 21
Cleveland 144
Cliff House 116
Clinton, Bill 173, 174
Clinton, Hillary Rodham 174
Coast Guard Treasure Island 77
Coast Seamen's Union 63
Colma 127
Colombia Theater Orchestra 65
Colorado 24
Columbus, Christopher 78, 110, 167
Cook, James 58, 110
Coos Bay 128
*Cordonazo* S/Y 165, *165*, 166
*Corinthian V* sailboat 155
Cortina 90, 94, 97
Coubler, Hans 33

Crabtree, Lotta 46
*Creole* schooner 145, 146
Crissy Field 155
Crocker estate 165
Crosby, Bing 32, 57, 99
Crown Prince Harald 72, 81, *82*, 168, 169, 170, *171*, 171, 172
Crown Prince Olav 58, *68*, 68, 72, 121, 151, *152*-156, 158, *159*, 159, 160, 164, 167, 169
Crown Princess Märtha 58, *68*, 68, 72, 121, 151, *152*-156, *157*, 157, 159, 160, 168
Curtis, Pilsbury and 121
Cushing, Alexander C. 89, 94
Cypress Point Country Club 167

# D

Dalrymple Rock 113
Daly City 127
*Danmark* ship 145, 146
Darre-Hisch, Hans Jørgen 21
Daughters of Norway 48
Davos 96
Del Monte Lodge 167
*Den norske sjømannsmisjon* 86
Deneen, J. A. 65
Detroit 144
*Devonshire* HMS 158, 160
Disko Island 113, 115
Disney, Walt 94, 99, 101
Disneyland 101
Disneyland Hotel 101
Ditlev-Simonsen 20
*Dixie Clipper* seaplane 158
Djupevåg family 130
Domaine Chandon at Yountville 169
Dominique (Versailles) 33
Drammen 138
Du Pont 55
Dumbarton Oaks 68
Dutch Windmill 132

# E

*Eagle* USCG bark 114, 145, 146
East Boston 140, 145
East Coast 135, 174

East Germany 23
Edinburgh 23
Edison, Thomas A. 46
Egypt 82
Eidsvoll 102, 153
Eikeland, Else Berit *33*
"Einarsen, Peter" 158
Eisenhower, D. 56
El Tovar Hotel 152
Ellsworth, Lincoln 119
Elmar, Otto F. 69, 70
Emeryville 173
Engen, Alf 56
Engen, Hans 168
England 110, 151, 158
Erikson, Leif 47, 167
Europe 38, 56, 75, 84, 91, 104, 110, 142, 143, 146, 156, 168
*Eva Mudocci* 42
Evang, Karl
*Examiner, San Francisco* 54, 162, 158, 159
Exploratorium 46
Exposition Preservation Board 46
Eyde, Sam 44

# F

Færder 143
Fairmont Hotel 58, 68, 151, 152, 164, 172, 173
Fairy Land Olympics 100
Far East 110
Farallon Islands 170,
Fargo 164, 172
Fariello, Lois E. 107
Feragen, Jens 20, 21, 77, 99
Ferry Building 75, 77
Fiedler, Arthur 143
Finmark 99
First World War 107
Fish Club 15-26, 27-33, 35, 37, 47, 51, 54, 64, 65, 70, 72, 76, 84-86, 89-93, 95, 98, 99, 103, 104, 107, 120, 123, 125, 127, 128, 132, 136-138, 145, 150, 160, 161, 164, 165, 170, 172, 175
Fisherman's Wharf 77, 138, 164, 172
Fjeld-Hansen, Jan 138, 139, 146
Ford, Henry 46
Fort Mason 65, 77, 154

*Fram* house 125
*Fram X* sailboat 170, 171, 172
*Fram* expedition vessel 119, 129
Framnæs Mek Værksted 129
Franklin Strait 113
Franklin, Sir John 110
Fred Olsen Line 16, 18, 78, 112
Fredrikstad 85, 107
Frigg oilfield 147
*Frisk* 84
*Frivakt* 71
Frobisher Bay 110
Frobisher, Martin 110
Funchal 142
Furuseth, Andrew (Anders) 63, 66, 67, 68

# G

Gade, F. Herman 16, 37, 38, 47
Galbe, Jørgen 20, 22, 122
Garland, Judy 57
Gatun 45
Geiranger 84
Genoa 39
Geographic North Pole 119
Geographic South Pole 119
Germany 158, 170
Ghirardelli Square 164
Gjoa Committee, Fish Club's 125, 128
Gjoa Foundation 24, 72, 120-128, 153, 164
Gjoa Haven 113, 130
Gjøa Committee, Oslo 125, 127, 130
*Gjøa* sloop 23, 24, 25, 48, 58, 101, 109-133, 152-154, 164
Gjøahavn 113, 114
Goethals, G. W. 46
"Golden Fish" *3*, 18
Golden Gate 44, 48, 51, 116, 126, 136, 137, 138, 139, 166, 170, 175
Golden Gate Bridge *49*, 50, 77, 101, 138, 155, 169, 170, 172,
Golden Gate Exposition 49-61, 64
Golden Gate Park 58, 101, 116, 119, 123, 125-128, 130, 152, 163, 164
*Golden Gate* revenue cutter 116
Goodall, T. A. 139
*Gorch Fock* bark 145, 146, 147

Gracey, J. S. 137
Graham, C. G. 120
Grand Canyon 152
Gravem, Nicolas 16, 18, 20
Great Britain 38, 83, 142, 159, 160
Great Highway 127
Great Nordic War 17
Green Room 172
Greenland 110, 113, 115
Greenwood, J. O. 77
Grieg, Edvard 47, 143
Gris, Juan 101
Grisjin, Evgeni 96
Grønningen, Harald 95, *103*, 103
*Guayas* ship 145, 146
Gulf Current 146
Gunneng, Arne 21

# H

Hagerup, Nils 112
Haight Ashbury 72, 164
Hakulinen 95, 96, 103
Halse, Peder L. 36
Hamar 97
Hambro, Carl Joachim 51, 156, 158
Hamburg 143
Handy, W. C. 57
Hankø 151, 155
Hansen, Godfred *111*, 112, 114
Hansen, Helmer *111*, 112
Hansteen, Christopher 111
Hardanger 109, 130
Hart, Ralph Warner 77
Haugesund 56, 156
Hawaii 24, 58
Heiss, Carol 94, 98
Helly Hansen 144
Hemmingway, Ernest 32
Henie Onstad Center 101
Henie, Sonja 54, *101*, 101
Henrik Ibsen Lodge 48
Henry, Ken 93
Herbst Theater 69, 172
*Heroes of Telemark* 98
Herschel Island 115
Hexberg, C. 120

Heyerdahl-Hansen, Jens 16, 18, 36, 60
Higgins, H. R. 120
Hillsborough 165, 172
Hilton farm 102
Hilton, Augustus (Gus) 102
Hilton, Conrad 102
Hitler, Adolf 19, 156
Hobat Building 20
Høeg, Per 24, *25*, 99, 107, 127, 137
Holck, Ole Elias 81, 167
Holland 96
Hollywood 99, 101, 135, 136, 143, 154
Holmboe, Thorolf 39
Holmenkollen Ski Arena 104, 167
Holyday on Ice 101
Homestead Act 164
Hope, Bob 57
Hotel Meridien, Newport Beach 170
Houston 162
Hudson, Henry 110
Hull, Cordell 21
Huntington Hotel 169
Huntley, Mark *173*
Hyde Park, New York 157
Hyde Street Pier 77

# I

Iceland 22
Idaho 24
Ihlebæk, Jon Albert 81, 82, *84*, 85
Illinois 152
India 75, 110
Innsbruck 102, 104
International Olympic Committee (IOC) 89, 90, 94, 102
International Sports Committee 71
Inuit 114, 115
Iowa 152
Isachsen, director 118
Israel 82
*Italia* airship 119
Italy 90, 102, 119

# J

J. L. Stuart Corporation 122
Jack's Restaurant 16, 20, 21, 23, *27*, 27-33, 84, 90, 127, 137
Jackman 110
Jacobsen, Alf A. 67, 69
Jamvold, Rolf 85
Japan 110
Jarlsberg cheese 144
*Jason* USS *38*, 39
Jenkins, David 98
Jensen, Aslak 20, 76, 77, 78, 86
Jensen, Laura 99, 100
*Jeremiah O'Brien* S/S 21, 132
Jernberg, Sixten 95
Jerving, Mr. 167
Johannesen, Hans Christian 110
Johannesen, Knut 89, 93, 96, *97*, *101*, *103*, 104
Johannessen, F. 69, 70
Johnson, Consul 17
Johnson, Mrs. Lyndon B. 161
Johnson, Lyndon B. 161
Jordan, Frank C., Secretary 78, 120
Jørgensen, Carl Oddvar 22, 168
Jøssingfjord 156

# K

Kaastad 97
Kalve, Ole 25, 86, 107, 127, *128*, 137, 167, 173
Kampen 89
Kandahl, Torolv 21
Kansas 152
Kara Sea 110
Kavli cheese 144
Kaye, Danny 99
Kazakhstan 96
Kennedy, John F. 32, 168
Kiel 142, 170
Kildal, Reidar 17
King and Queen 23
King Edward VII 160
King Haakon 18, 47, *69*, 78, 81, 151, 156, 158, *159*, 159, 160, 171
King Harald 72, 168, 172, 173, 174, 175, *175*
King Karl's Land 110
King Olav 18, 23, 25, 72, 80, 81, 125, 160, *161*, 161, *162*, 162, *163*, 163, 164, 165, 166, 167, 168, *170*, 171, 172
King Point 115
King William Island 113, 130
Kingman 152
Kings Bay 119
Kiønig, Arne 80
Klaveness, A. F. 157
Klaveness, Dag 80
Klaveness, Fredrik 80
Klee, Paul 101
Klyce, H. A. 77
Knudsen, Jacob Frode 81, 137
Knudsen, James 137
Knudsen, Trygve 167
Knutsen, Tormod 98, 102, *103*
Koren, Finn 22, 126, 127, *128*
Kortum, Karl 124, 125, 127, 128, 129, 164
Kositsjkin, Victor 97
Koth, Halfdan 156
Koth, Paul 21
Krag, Erik 24, 120, 123, 127
Kristiansand 145, 147
Kristiansund 36
Krogh, Christian 39
Kuppern 97, 98
Kvale, Dagfinn 80, 81, 84, 85, 173, *175*
Kvisgaard, Bjørn 144, 145

# L

Labor Day, Norwegian 80
*Lady Gray* ship/bark 142
Lake Tahoe 59, 89, 93, 95, 99, 104
*Landkjenning* 47
Lange, Halvard 78
Lange, Olaf 39
Larsen, L. A. 47
Las Palmas 143
*Latham* airplane 119, 120
Laundal, Øyvind 79
Laurvig, J. Nilsen 39
Lawrence, Andrea Mead 93
League of Nations 51
Léger, Fernand 101
Legion of Honor 164, 171
Legion of Merit 164
Lend-Lease 21
Lensvik 103
Libæk, Sven Erik 143

Liberty Bell 45
Lie, Anton 80
Lie, Trygve H. 69
Lillehammer 171
Lindesnes 147
Lindstrøm, Adolf Henrik *111*, 112, 113
Lisboa 142, 143
Little Norway 21
London 64, 80, 110, 136, 158
Long Beach 139
Long Island 102
Los Angeles 22, 23, 26, 91, 93, 99, 101, 107, 136, 137, 139, 151, 152, 162, 166, 167, 170
Lund, Anton *111*, 112, 113
Lund, John Arne 81, *171*, 171
Lund, Kjell 99
Lunde, Hakon 145
Lurie, Louis 32
*Lusitania* S/S 45
Luther College Band 47
Lyche, Iver 21-23, 91, 93, 99, 103, 107, 137, 165, 167, 172, 173
Lyche, Joan 172, 173

# M

Mackay, Gilbert 167
Mackenzie River 115
Madagascar 75
Madeira Islands 143
*Madonna* 40, *41*
Magellan 57, 110
Magic City *50*, 51, 55, 56, 60
Malmestrøm, Torsten 84
Malterud, Olaf 21
*Manhattan* S/T 125, 126
Mansfield, Jayne 99
Mäntyranta 96
March, James G. 173
Mare Island Navy Yard 116
Marin County 65, 169
Marin Headlands 77, 139
Marina 46, 46, 65, 77, 164
Marina Shore 155
Marseilles 39
Marstrand 17
Martinez 168, 169
Maryland 157, 168

Masstor Systems 170
Mathisen, Birger 76, 78, 80, 85
Mathisen, Karen Erika 77
Matisse, Henri 101, 172
*Maud* expedition vessel 119
Maud, Queen of Norway 114
Maybeck, Bernard 39
McKenna, James 115
McKinney Creek 93, 103, 104
Medal of St. Olav 159
Medal of War, H M Kings 68, 69
Merchant's Exchange Building 112
Meyer, Jeffery W. 107, 137
Meyer, Wilson 80
Michigan 152
Midwest 164, 172
Milwaukee 144
Minneapolis 23, 164
Minnesota 152, 164
Miró, Joan 101
Mission Dolores 152
Missouri 152
*Missouri* USS 45
Mohn, Christian 21
Mollén, Arne B. 107
Mondavi at Rutherford 169
Monique, Jaques (Jack) 28
Monroe, Marilyn 99
Monteray 165, 167
Montevideo 143
Montreal 102, 144
Moore, Charles C. 46, 48
*Mor Norge* 85
Morgan Stanley & Co 22, 107
Morgedal 93
Morgenstierne, Wilhelm von Munthe af 16, 21, 68, 80, 156, 158
Morkemo, Trygve 25, *33*, 167
Moscow 194
Mountain View School, Martinez 168
Muir Woods 101, 138
Mull, Gary 165
Muller, Harald 18, 120
Munch, Edvard 39, *41*, *42*, 101
Murmansk 67
Muscatine, Doris 32
Muscory 110
Museum of History, Oslo 114

Museum of Modern Art, SF 172
Myrvold, Peter 18, 67

# N

Nansen, Fridtjof 111, 124, 129
Napa Valley 169, 172,
Narvik 19, 158
*Nasjonal Samling* 156
National Gallery of Norway 38
NATO 169
Navy Museum, Treasure Island 56
NBC-TV 124
Nevada 24, 94
New Jersey 46
New Mexico 24
New York 18, 38, *43*, 64, 91, 102, 118, 142-144, 152, 156, 158, 161, 172
New York Stock Exchange 22
New Zealand 19, 59, 60, 171, 172
Newport Beach 170
Nicolaysen, Astri 151
Nicolaysen, Emil 151
Nilsen, Svend 21
Nilsson, Ivar 96
Nixon, Richard M. 94
Nobel Pics Price 18
Nobile, Umberto 119, 120
Nome 115, 116
Nordheim, Sondre 93
*Nordmanns-Forbundet* 16, 46, 47
*Norge* Royal Yacht 160
*Norge* airship 119
Norges Idrettsforbund (NIF) 90
Norheim, Sondre 55
Normandy 19, 21, 69
Normanna Glee Club 123
*Norna VI* sailboat 155
*Norsk kirke i utlandet* 86
*Norsk Sjømannsmisjon* 84
North America 110, 111
North Beach 72
North Dakota 164, 172
North East Passage 119
North Magnetic Pole 111, 113, 114

North Point 77
North Pole 93, 119
North Sea 113, 143, 145, 147
Northwest Passage 109, 110, 111, *112,* 113, 114, 115, 116, 125
NORTRA 23
Nortraship 18, 19, 64, 69, 158
Norway 22-25, 35, 36, 38, 43, 46, 51, 52, 58, 60, 63, 64, 83, 85, 86, 97-102, 107, 110, 111, 119, 121, 123-126, 129, 130, 136, 139, 142, 143-145, 153, 155, 156, 158-161, 164, 165, 167, 169, 170-172, 175
Norway Day 46
Norway House 19, 23, 25, 28, 63-73, *66,* 128, 137, 138, 159, 167, 171
Norway Lodge *59,* 60
Norway Place 23
Norway Relief Inc. 19
Norway's Ski Lodge *54,* 55, 58, 59
*Norway* S/S 82
Norwegian America Line 18
Norwegian American Chamber of Commerce 139
Norwegian American Cultural Foundation 173
Norwegian American Trade Mission 169
Norwegian Athletes Association 90, 91
Norwegian Calefornia Olympic Committee (NCOC) 91, 99
Norwegian Club 15, 16, *17,* 46, 51, 16, 120, 128
Norwegian Consulate Gen. SF 16, 17, 20-24, 33, 46, 60, 70, 90, 91, 120, 122, 126, 127, 136-139, 144, 156, 160, 161-167, 168
Norwegian Embassy Washington DC 118, 136, 139, 156
Norwegian Evangelical Lutheran Church 48
Norwegian Evangelical Lutheran Singers 48
Norwegian Export and Trade Council 136, 144, 145
Norwegian Food 139
Norwegian Government 35, 36, 123, 136, 161
Norwegian Government

Seamen's Service 70-72, 82, 171
Norwegian International Ship Register 81
Norwegian Lutheran Church 76
Norwegian Maritime Directorate 70, 71
Norwegian Maritime Muesum 118, 125-127, 130
Norwegian Ministry of Foreign Affairs 136, 167
Norwegian Olympic Committee 90, 107
Norwegian Pacific Singers 48
Norwegian Relief 60
Norwegian Rescue Service 43
Norwegian Seamen's Church 19, 25, 75-87, 91, 100, 107, 137, 138, 164, 167, 171, 173
Norwegian Seamen's Mission 75-87
Norwegian Seamen's Union 64, 76
Norwegian Shipowners Association 52
Norwegian Singing Society 123, 153
Norwegian Ski Lodge 153
Norwegian-American Sesquicentennial Jubilee 164
Notodden 43
Nut Tree 100
Nygaard, Enok 137
Nygaardsvold, K 68

## O

O'Brien, Parry 93
Oakland 77, 154
Oakland Airport 172
Oakland Bay Bridge 49, 50, 51, 77, 101
Oakland Hotel 51
Oakland Singing Society 58
Occident 51, 58
Ocean Beach 101, 116, 117, 123, 131, 132, 152, 164
*Ohio* USS 45
Oksøy Fyr 147
Old Guard 161
Olsen, Fritz 16, 112

Olsen, Klaus 16
Olsen, Thorbjørn 85
Olympic Village 91, 98
Onstad, Niels 101
Operation Sail 143
Order of Maritime Merit 164
Order of St. Olav 18
Order of the Golden Fish 17
Oregon 24, 47, 128, 155
Orient 51, 58
Orre, Knut 22
Oscar 135
Oscarsborg Fortress 156
Oseberg 43
Osebergship 131, 132
Oslo 18, 23, 26, 89, 90, 93, 101, 102, 104, 107, 125, 126, 137, 139, 143, 145, 147, 150, 156, 162, 169
Oslofjord 113, 130, 156
*Oslofjord* S/S 152
Ostende 143
Overseas Shipping Co 20, 24, 107, 127, 137
Oxford 18, 151

## P

Pabst, Gudrun 60
Pacific (Ocean) 15, 18, 58, 61, 63, 77, 110, 145, 153, 170, 172
Pacific Coast 47, 115,
Pacific Coast Singers' Association 47, 48
Pacific Diesel Engine Co 36
Pacific Gas & Electric Co 127
Pacific Hights 22, 64, 171
Pacific Northwest 164
Pacific Union Club 164, 173
Page, C. R. 120
Palace of Fine Arts 37, *39,* 42, 46, 77, 129, 164
Palace of Fine Arts Annex 37
*Pamir* 4-m bark 143
*Pampanito* USS 132
Pan American Clipper 60
Panama 110
Panama Canal 35, 38, 43, 45, 46, 63, 84, 116, 128, 136, 145
Panama Pacific Exposition 15, 16,

27, 35-48
Panama Pacific Singing
 Association 48
Papoose Peak 93
Park Commission, SF (City) 116,
 118, 120-125, 127, 132
Parry, W. E. 110
Patagonia 110
Patterson, Thomas 21
Paulson, T. B. 16
Pearl Harbor 156
Pebble Beach 167
Pedersen, Einar 18, 20
Pedersen, John 70, 71, 137
Peel Sound 113
Pelton Water Wheel Co. 36
Pennsylvania 45
Perkins, Thomas 172, 173
Pesman, Jan 96
Pet 110
Petersen, E. 67, 120
Philadelphia 45
*Philante* yacht 160
Picasso, Pablo 101
Pillsbury and Curtis 121
Pillsbury, A. F. 120
Piraeus 39
PIVCO Station Car 173
Point Barrow 115
*Pol 3* patrolboat 156
Poland 156
Ponta Delgada 142
Pook's Hill 157
Porsgrunn porcelain 58
Portland, Oregon 155
Poulsen, Whyne 89
Poulsson P. R. *15,* 16, 17, 18, *20,*
 27, 32, 59, 60, 65, 120, 128, 138
Presbyterian Children's Hospital
 22
Presidio 77
Presidio Golf Club 22, 23, 26, 100
Prince Alexander 159
Prince Bertil 93
Prince Carl of Denmark 159, 160
Prince Harald 151, *157,* 157,
 *168,* 168, 169
Prince of Wales Strait 125
Princess Astrid 151, *157,* 168
Princess Märtha of Sweden 151

Princess Ragnhild 151, *157,* 168
*Princeton* USS 116
Prøitz, Per C. 23, 136, 137, 165, 167
*Propaganda* sailboat 172
Prudhoe Bay 167
Pulitzer Prize 172

## Q
Queen Maud 160
Queen Maud Gulf 114
Queen Sonja 172, *173,* 173, 174, *175,*
 175
Quisling, Vidkun 156

## R
Rafoss, Torvald 167
Recknagel, Helmut 97
Red Cross 59, 60
Red Mountain 56
Redinger, Emile 28
Redinger, Jack 28, *32*
Redinger, Michael 28
Redinger, Paul 28, *32*
Reno 92, 99
Restauration 167
*Restauration* sloop 81, 165
Rex Sole 15, 18, 19, 20-22, 25, 65,
 90, 99, 136, 161
Richmond 77
Ristvedt, Peder *111,* 112, 114
Rjukan 43
Robinson, Elmer 78, 123
Rockall 145
Rolph Jr, James 47
Rome 102
Roosevelt Family 157, 159
Roosevelt, Eleanor 157, 158
Roosevelt, Franklin D. 19, 51, 68, 73,
 157, 158, 159, 160,
Roosevelt, Theodore 46, 116
*Roseville* M/S 157
Ross Ice Shelf 119
Ross, John 110
Rosse, James 170
Rossi, mayor 120
Rotterdam 83, 130
Royal Escort 154
Royal Garden, Christiania 46
Royal Navy 160

Royal Viking Line 166
*Royal Viking Sky* cruiseship 81,
 165, 166
Ruef, Abe 65
Ruggles, Pricilla *161,* 168
Rusk, Dean 161
Russia 112
Russian Hill 76
Rutherford 169
Ruud, Rolf 137

## S
Sacramento 69, 78, 91, 100
*Saga* sailboat 155
*Sagacious* sailboat 172
Sail Training Association (STA)
 142, 143, 145, 150
Sailor's Union of the Pacific 68
Salbu, Erik 107, 170
Salvation Army 75
San Diego 47, 139, 145, 152, 171
San Francisco 15-25, 27-33, 35,
 36, 38, 39, 42-48, 50-52, 56,
 59-61, 63-70, 72, 75-86, 89-91,
 99, 101, 103, 107, 109, 114-120,
 124-132, 136-138, 145, 147,
 150-52, 154-157, 159-163,
 165-175
San Francisco International
 Airport 60, 61
San Francisco Maritime
 Museum 124, 127
San Francisco Shipping Service
 25
San Jose Airport 170
San Pedro 76, 78, 80, 152
San Quentin 65
Sandefjord 64, 139
Sarajevo 38
Sather Tower 154
Sausalito 77, 116, 169
SCANCOR 173
Scandinavian Airlines (SAS)
 93, 136, 139, 144, 145
Scandinavian Lutheran Church
 152
Scandinavian Lutheran Seamen's
 Mission 75, 76, 86
Scandinavian Navy 47, 67

Scandinavian Shipping Office 64, 69
Schau, Øivind 145
Schmitz, Eugene E. 65, 66
Schmitz, Julia 65, 72
Schou, Rolf 99
Schou, Rolf B. 20, 21, 24, 25, 122, 123, 127, *128*, 164
Schou, Rolf H. 25
Scotland 138
Scottish Rite Hall 48
Sculley, John 170
Seal Rock 164
Seattle 24, 164, 174
Second World War 92, 126
Secret Service 165
Seiersten, Torstein 96
Sesquicentennial Jubilee 164, 165, 166
Settlie, Erling 70
Sexe, Asbjørn 110
Sexe, Gjøa 110
Shanghai 63
Shannon, Warren 121, 154
Sheedy Trucking Co 127
Shetland 147, 160
Shuman, Agnew & Co 22
Sierra Nevada 55, 89, *90*, 92, 98, 104
Silicon Graphics 173
Silicon Valley 170, 173
*Sjømannsmisjonsforeningen Tabita* 75
*Sjømannsorganisasjonenes Velferdskomite* 67
Skaala, Knut Johannesson 109
Skagerrak 113
Smemo, Johannes 21, 80
Smestad, Lisbeth 137
Smith, Art *45*, 46
Smith, Christopher Furst 16
Snowshoe Thompson 55, 93
"Snowshoe Thomson" *92*
*Sogn og Fjordane Fylkesbilar* 84
Sohlberg, Harald 39, *40*
Solli, Olaf 23
Sommerfelt, Søren Christian 166
Sons of Norway 46, 48, 51
Sopwith, Sir T. O. M. 160
*Sørlandet* ship 142, 143, 144
South America 116

South Pole 58, 72, 80, 114
Southern Pacific Railway 155
Sovjet Union 96
Spain 23
*Sport of the Seven Seas* 71
Sprinz, Joe 58
Squaw Valley 21, 22, 26
Squaw Valley Club 89, 103
Squaw Valley Inn 104
Squaw Valley Olympics 80, 88-105, 124
St. Catherine's 151
St. Francis Hotel 116, 121, 154, 162
*St. Francis* sailboat 155
St. Francis Syndicate 165
*St. Francis VI* sailboat 165
St. Francis Yacht Club 77, 155, 164-167, 169-171
St. Lawrence Seaway 144
St. Moritz 90
St. Olaf 43
*St. Olaf* S/S 160
St. Olav's Church, San Pedro 78
*St. Roch* cutter 126
St. Thomas 136
Stadland 160
Stanford Memorial Church 173
Stanford Stadium 170
Stanford University 26, 107, 170, 173, 174
*Star Billabong* M/S 127, 128, 130
*Star of Empire* ship 142
Star Shipping Co 25, 127, 128, 130
*Statsraad Ericksen* sail training brig 142
*Statsraad Lehmkuhl* sail training bark 143, 144
*Stavangerfjord* S/S 156
Steckmest, Sigurd 17, 60, 67, 120, 152, 156
Steel, Danielle 173
*Stiklestad* M/T 69
Stockholm 156
Stoltenberg, Thorvald 21
Storen, A. C. 120
*Stortinget* 15, 19, 23, 35, 36, 51, 52, 154, 156
*Strider* sailboat 155
Strøm, Halfdan 39
Suez Canal 35, 82, 110

Sunde, Gerner *159*, 159
Svalbard 110, 119
Svanevik, Leif 67, 69
Svensgaard, A. 59
Sweden 112, 157, 170
Switzerland 89
Sybase 173, 174

## T

*Tabita* 25, 76, 80, 86
Tait, F. Dudley 77
Tall Ships Race 143, 145
Tandberg Data 169, 170
Tarzan 57
Telemark 93
Teller, Alaska 119
Teller, SF Park Commission 123
Tenerife 136
Thailand 23
Thaulow, Fritz 39
Thoma, Georg 97
Thor Dahl 64
Thornton, Sigvor Hamre 25, *85*
Thorsen, A. H. 76
Thorsen, Mrs. A. H. 86
*Thorsgaard* M/S 71
Thunder Bay 104
Tiburon 77
Titus, Warren 137
Torbay 142
Tordenskjold, Admiral 17
*Tordenskjolds Soldater* 17, 18, 37, 60
Tordenskjolds Soldiers 128
Toronto 144
Torp, Oscar 80
Tørvikbygd 130
Traders Vics 24
Trafalgar Room 24
*Traviata* M/S 163, 164
Treasure Island *50*, 51, 55, 56, 60, 61, 77, 152, 153
Tromsø 110, 119, 158
Trondheim 17, 36, 167
Trondheimsfjord 103
Truman, Harry S. 164
Twin Peaks 58, 152

# Index

## U

UC Berkely 52, 154
Ullensaker 36
Ulnes, Dag Mork 23
UN Labor Organization 71
Union Ice Co 56
Union Labor Party 65
Union Square 116
United Nations 21, 68, 69, 72, 75, 89, 160
United Nations Conference 68
United States 15, 19, 21, 25, 30, 35, 37, 56, 60, 63, 68, 83, 86, 89, 91-93, 95, 98, 110, 122, 135, 136, 144, 145, 151, 153, 154, 156-161, 164-170, 172, 175
Unitor Ships' Service 144
Urstad, Hans Ola 23, 24, 172, *173*
Urstad, Tone 172, *173*
US Coast Guard 137, 138, 139
US Custom 137
US Life Saving Service 116
US Marine Corps 47
US Navy 35, 38, 39, 58, 60, 124, 138, 139
US Ski Association 167
US Task Force 143
Utah 24

## V

"Vaffel-Olsen" 85
Valparaiso 63
*Vampire* 40, *41*
Vanderlinden, Alex 137
Varren, Mathias 56
Vasco da Gama 110
*Velferden* 84
*Velferdstjenesten for Handelsflåten* 70
Venice 38, 45
Versailles, Dominique 33
Veterans Auditorium 69
*Vi seiler* 142
Vibe, Beate 172
Vibe, Kjeld 172
Victoria Island 114
Vikane 151
Viking longboat 47
Vikings 55, 130
Vingrom 101
Virginia 161, 172, 174
Vogue 119
Voll, Nils 16

## W

Waaler, Per 128
Waldron, W. L. 66
*Wapama* S/S 24
Warenskiold, Axel 36, 47
Warren, Earl 56
Washington 24, 47
Washington DC 45, 68, 116, 156, 157, 159, 161, 163, 172, 175
Watson, Thomas J. 154
Webster, D. A. 120
Weismuller, Johnny 57
Werenskiold, Dagfin 80
Werenskiold, Erik 39
Werner, August 58, 153
Wessel, Peter 17
West Coast 136, 164, 168, 171, 172, 174
Westfal-Larsen 18, 20
Westin St. Francis Hotel 172
White House 157, 161, 174, 175
Whitehall Country School, Bethesda 168
Wiik, Gustav Juel *111*, 112, 115
Wilhelmsen, Tom 125
Williams 152
Williams, Ester 57
Williamsburg 174
Willoch, Kåre *161*
*Windjammer, The* 135, 136, 141, 143, 144
Wisconsin 152
*Wisconsin* USS 45, 116
Wisting, Oscar 119
World Affairs Council 164
World War I; 38, 48, 59, 156
World War II; 19, 24, 31, 59, 64, 68, 73, 75, 89, 92, 142, 146, 157, 164, 174
Worren, Torleif 81, 84
Wyoming 24

## X-Y-Z

*Yankee Clipper* seaplane 159
Yerba Buena Club 154
Yerba Buena Island 50
Yerba Buena Shoals 49, *50*, 51
Young People's Association of the Synod of the Norwegian Evangelical Lutheran Church of America 48
Young Scandinavian Club 72
Yountville 169
Yukon 115

## Æ - Ø - Å

Østby, Einar 96, *103*
Østlandets Skoleskip 136
Øxnevad, Einar 127, *128*
Ålgård, Ole 21